Endorsements

Praise from "Over 40s"

"This book offers an insightful explanation of the key technological differences between the US and China and their future innovative potential. Paul's introductory chapters provide a good background with his keen observation of history and numbers. Austin's personal story of his own struggle is fascinating and I believe there is much we can learn from it."

Tipsuda Thavaramara, Bangkok
President, Thai Fintech Association

"Outstanding analysis that focuses on the ideological and cultural differences between millennials of both superpowers, which will be pivotal to the geopolitical dynamics in the future, especially in technological and digital realms."

Chia Hock Lai, Singapore
President, Singapore Fintech Association

"Paul looks at how technology is shaping our world through two defining lenses. The first is the generational shift in the adoption of technology and the second is the geo-political machinations between China and the US. How this plays out will define the world we live in!"

Rob Jesudason, Hong Kong
CIO, Serendipity Capital
Former President of Block.one

"No person can tie the sociological, political, financial and technical issues at hand better than Paul. He once again tells of revolutionary and evolutionary changes that can only be ignored at one's peril. If you don't think that Paul is accurate in his assessments, then reread this book 18 months from now."

Frank Wang, Hong Kong
Former Co-CEO of OCBC Wing Hang Bank

"Rapid advances in financial technology are causing us to re-think how to deliver financial services in a modern, digital way with multiple services across a common data architecture. Paul is not only one of the foremost students of this phenomena but has also contextualized these lessons to become a sought-after commentator on how these changes are affecting modern finance. Paul's perspective as an American living in Asia adds another dimension that makes this book a must-read."

Peter Early, New York
Partner, Business Development, Exos

"To get a clear picture of today's winner in the tech space, this book is a must-read. It succinctly clarifies the differences in the current state of affairs in technology, social affairs and economic conditions between China and the US. It brings great case studies that will spark much needed conversation."

Barbara Thole, Hong Kong
Founder, The Executive Forum

"The authors strike at the heart of the issue of why America is falling behind in the technological and economic race. Fascinating read and insight on some of the factors and drivers for the increasing disparity between these two rising superpowers."

Kenneth Ng, Bangkok
Founder, NT Asset

Praise from Millennials

"American millennials need a clear understanding of the domestic and international landscape to effectively take on the mantle of leadership and carry our society's values into the future. Paul and Austin offer a clear-eyed, compassionate, and unflinching perspective that belongs in the center of American discourse."

Abraham Sorock, Beijing
Outgoing Curator, Global Shapers Beijing II Hub

"This book is a story of American decline and China's entrance into the world of hegemons. Millennials across the US have been generationally doomed by the opioid crisis, classroom gun violence, onerous student debt, toxic bipartisanship, and impending climate catastrophe. As Schulte artfully argues, without serious political action, these problems will not soon end. The result is a chronic anxiety among millennials which psychiatrists and doctors are happy to treat with even more opioids, benzos or SSRI's."

Roman Shemakov, Philadelphia
Henry Luce Foundation Fellow

"This treatise on an IoT-driven world by Austin Groves and Paul Schulte flips the conversation on the US–China technological race, unveiling the overlooked socio-cultural and demographic assets accelerating the latter's tech progress way ahead of its peers. This book is a timely and provocative read for decision makers on winning amidst the rapid pace of technological change and the globally decisive race between two superpowers."

Tan Yinglan, Singapore
Founding Managing Partner, Insignia Ventures Partners

"Perhaps the most valuable aspect of Schulte and Groves' research is not just the emphasis they place on powerful novel technologies, but the way in which this technology is placed in conversation with larger cultural and policy challenges that stifle US progress in the international community. Millennials have experienced America in the midst of one of her greatest failures, and the need to remedy and rebuild this divisive generational rift is paramount for the success of her future."

Jason Kang, Cambridge, MA
Fellow, Narang Labs, Harvard University

"This book crackles with the familiar electricity of unspoken truths about China and its relationship with the US. Its many keen observations and insights surge forward at an irrepressible pace, as if mirroring the rapid change it is describing. It is a prophetic window into the future and a sound handbook for what to do when we get there."

Hu Maomao, Beijing
Partner, Eigen Capital

"This book encapsulates how society and culture of the last few decades have shaped the millennials, how that in return is shaping the future. The book specifies how China has raced ahead, and what the US can do to revitalize its innovation culture. Highly recommend the book for those who want to understand not only how the current geopolitical landscape is playing out, but also how they came to be."

Hussain M. Elius, Dhaka
CEO, Pathao

"A very tough subject to encapsulate, but the authors did a great job of condensing and framing it. US millennials are deeply concerned about their future, and the political infighting is hurting the US more than we think. Big changes need to be made for the US to keep up."

Diego Graterol, San Francisco
Account Executive, Samsara

"This book offers insight into today's most important issue: the tech race, and why the West is losing. Schulte's unique position at the intersection of tech, mental health, and where East meets West gives him an unparalleled understanding of why the West is losing the tech race, and what to do about it. As a Western millennial living in China, I witness the accuracy of Paul's thesis every day. My only hope is that all Western business and political leaders read this before it's too late."

Corentin Trebaol, Paris
CEO, Aconia Group

"An eye opener... With considerable detail and rigor, this book provides a comprehensive assessment of the two global geopolitical powers tussling for supremacy. Schulte makes a compelling narrative that analyzes the prevailing mainstream opinions of China's impressive economic rise. A wonderful book for a broad audience."

Galen Law, Hong Kong
Chairman, Velcron

"Paul is fantastic at taking in the myriad of events occurring simultaneously all over the world and processing it into a clear and cohesive picture of what is happening in the world, and where we are going. As we are moving toward a world of higher uncertainty, we should all take the time out of our busy days to stop, and reflect upon what is happening around us. Reading this book has provided not only an entertaining read, but also provided key insight into the fast-paced political, technological, and societal changes around the world."

Benedict Prinz, Hong Kong
Associate, Data Analytics, UBS

"Paul Schulte masterfully explains the systemic issues causing millennials to burn out before they can ever take off. With limited opportunities and unlimited obligations, millennials no longer believe in the American Dream and feel resentment toward a generation that never taught them how to succeed. Paul extracts the seven primary drivers from a colossal amount of terrifying and depressing sociological data and instils a sense of urgency in the reader to support the change that must be made going forward."

William Stuart, Atlanta
Sales Executive, Precision Medicine Group

Praise from Academia

"Finally! A book on the current affairs of China and the US that takes a multi-disciplinary approach: economics, policy, social science, technology, and philosophy. This is a must-read book for readers interested in a holistic view of the underlying differences between the US and China, the millennials and the old generation in the two countries. A cogent read with great insights on the four sub-cultures."

Virginia Cha, Singapore
Adjunct Professor, INSEAD and NUS Business School

"Few people can bridge the east and the west, the millennials and the older generations better than Paul Schulte. Well-written, brilliant and balanced, this book offers a timely insight into the frontiers of technology and the two leading countries: US and China in their quest for global leadership in the age of new technologies."

Ben Shenglin, Hangzhou
Professor & Dean, International Business School & Academy of Internet Finance, Zhejiang University

"Groves and Schulte weave together incisive cultural insight and analysis of the digital economies in China and the US. They set out the root causes of the anxiety-ridden and alienating millennial experience in the US ecosystem, and of the more hopeful and motivating one in China. In doing so, they map America's innovation deficit and short-sighted responses to Chinese competitiveness — as well as the challenging but pragmatic path to take before it's too late. A must-read for anyone concerned with the digital — as well as the inter-generational — divide."

Brian Ganson, Stellenbosch
Professor, Stellenbosch University
Director, Africa Center for Dispute Settlement

"This is another thought-provoking book by Paul Schulte since the last book on AI and Quantum Computing. With similar rigorous style, Paul and his co-author have researched deeply into the topic and uncovered facts that are changing society, technology and labor in both the US and China. This book discusses latent trends that will revolutionize the global economy. This is a book for anyone who wishes to understand the latest ideas and thoughts in finance and technology."

David Lee, Singapore
Professor, Singapore University of Social Sciences

"Few people are as up-to-date with global techno-economic developments and at the same time as thought-provoking as Mr. Schulte. The book is a clear articulation of challenges and opportunities millennials in the US and China face. The case studies will be great tools to reflect with students and executives alike on how to manage life and business as exponential change occurs in technologies."

Daniel Liebau, Singapore
Founder, Lightbulb Capital
Adjunct Faculty, Singapore Management University and Erasmus University

THE RACE FOR

5G

SUPREMACY

Why China Is Surging, Where Millennials
Struggle, & How America Can Prevail

THE RACE FOR

5G

SUPREMACY

Why China Is Surging, Where Millennials Struggle, & How America Can Prevail

Austin Groves
Gao Shan Enterprises, China

Paul Schulte
Schulte Research, Singapore

World Scientific

NEW JERSEY · LONDON · SINGAPORE · BEIJING · SHANGHAI · HONG KONG · TAIPEI · CHENNAI · TOKYO

Published by

World Scientific Publishing Co. Pte. Ltd.

5 Toh Tuck Link, Singapore 596224

USA office: 27 Warren Street, Suite 401-402, Hackensack, NJ 07601

UK office: 57 Shelton Street, Covent Garden, London WC2H 9HE

Library of Congress Control Number: 2020010785

British Library Cataloguing-in-Publication Data
A catalogue record for this book is available from the British Library.

THE RACE FOR 5G SUPREMACY
Why China Is Surging, Where Millennials Struggle, & How America Can Prevail

ISBN 978-981-121-870-5 (hardcover)
ISBN 978-981-122-271-9 (paperback)
ISBN 978-981-121-871-2 (ebook for institutions)
ISBN 978-981-121-872-9 (ebook for individuals)

For any available supplementary material, please visit
https://www.worldscientific.com/worldscibooks/10.1142/11780#t=suppl

Desk Editors: Aanand Jayaraman/Yulin Jiang

Typeset by Stallion Press
Email: enquiries@stallionpress.com

Dedication

About the Authors

Paul Schulte first went to China as an equity analyst with Credit Suisse in 1992. He has analyzed seven Five Year Plans and has conducted research on Chinese equities for over 25 years having worked with Barings, Lehman, Nomura, and China Construction Bank International in Hong Kong. He has also been teaching millennial graduate students on five continents since 1999. He has written three books on China's technological rise and has taught in China at Tsinghua, Fudan, and Zhejiang Universities. He also worked at the White House NSC, the House of Representatives, and the International Trade Commission. He was also an advisor to the Indonesian Minister of Finance in the 1980s.

Austin Groves grew up in a small city in upstate New York where alcoholism and addiction are rampant. Somehow by dumb luck and the support of a few relatives and friends, he created a career in technology which has allowed him to work in IoT projects with Accenture, Verizon, AT&T, and Coca-Cola (Coke). By the age of 27, he implemented IoT projects in over 40 countries. He ended up in a NYSE listed company in Shanghai which dealt directly with Alibaba and JD.com. He hired a large Chinese team and built an e-commerce business from scratch. His is an unlikely journey of a millennial traversing two worlds — the US and China.

Other Books by Paul Schulte

Finance

The Next Generation in Our Credit Driven Economy: The Advent of Financial Technology.
Wiley & Sons. (2015).

Handbook of Blockchain: Digital Finance & Inclusion: China Tech, Mobile Security and Distributed Ledger.
Elsevier. (2018).

AI and Quantum Computing in Finance & Insurance: Fortunes & Challenges for China and America. (With David Lee).
World Scientific. (2019).

Mental Health

Cravings for Deliverance: How William James, Father of American Psychology, Inspired 12 Step Programs.
Lantern Press. (2014).

Paths to Recovery for Gay & Bisexual Addicts: Healing Weary Hearts.
Rowman & Littlefield. (2015).

Acknowledgments

I am very grateful to some of the best thinkers in the world on financial, economic, and social trends in both the US and China. They fall on all points of the political spectrum and offer brutal honesty at the drop of a hat. They have kept me in line. They are as follows: Rob Citrone, Adam Levinson, Rob Jesudason, David Halpert, Eric Bushell, Amit Rajpal, Gary Ang, David Lee, GaoXiqing, Charles Liu, Frank Wang, David Courtney, Fred Feldkamp, Kyu Ho, Jim Stent, Daniel Tu, Simon Ogus, Madame Tipsuda Thavaramara, Jeremy Kranz, and Michael Brett.

Most of all, a special thanks to millennials who taught me to learn all over again and to reverse mentor. Watch these people for they will be running the show in 20 years: Jason Kang, Zhan Qing, Dean Sun, Terry Sun, Mao Mao Hu, Alecia Quah, Wayne Xu, Corentin Trebaol, Suraj Sajnani, Boris Burgess, Lawson Emanuel, Philipp Hultsch, Ivana Sun, Jean JY Low, David Toh, Mixo Das, William Stuart, James Naylor, Nicholas Ingram, Gorlen Zhou, Jason Zhao, Tony Verb, Cristina Ventura, John Lau, Matt Cheng, Robert Greene, Scott Reid, Jasper Swaak, John Mak, Jesse McWaters, Abraham Sorock, Benedict Prinz, and Roman Shemakov, who did the tough task of fact checking, bibliography and index. Special thanks to JY Phuang who put up with my Virgo perfectionism and did an excellent job editing the book. Brian Ganson from Stellenbosch University was terrific with much needed unknotting of knots. Thanks to Virginia Cha of INSEAD and NUS for the great feedback on the early drafts. Thanks to Jiang Yulin, publisher extraordinaire, and to Austin Groves, a true phoenix who has risen from the Poughkeepsie ashes.

— Paul Schulte

I am very grateful to those whose shoulders I could stand on: Sarah Sholes, Graham Groves, Karen Kao, William and Janice Barry, Stuart and Ruth Sholes, Steve Hallman, Nathan Viles, Dave and Mary Sholes, Alexander Elsby, Helen and Gerry Groves, Shawn Groves, Robert Taylor, Gloria Lin, Kelly Groves, Joey Hickox, Tom Cervoni, Jeffrey Sawyer, Boris Burgess, Suraj Sajnani, Ray Underwood, Ekton Castrejon, Durlabh Jain, Dennis Mehta, Paul Schulte, Frank Santamorena, Louie Lopez, Paul Nieminen, Matthew Belisle, Jerrilee and Paul Relyea, Eryn McAuliffe, Tyrone James, Colleen Groves, Brian Dittman, Liven Pillay, Caroline Bridges, Chris Kluever, William Tuttle, Fred Fu, Dave Gill Eric Olander, Yang Yu, Christopher Gessner Walter Gregg, Dale Lockwood, Danny McLellan, Thomas Fiet, Shah Bash, Nicholas Desloges, Steven Sholes, Andrew and Michelle Morollo, Kevin and Beth Barry, Holly Chang, Khanh Nguyen, Ric Murray, Sharon Sutka-Doughty, Brian Scott, and Bill Leber. And a special thanks to my Father, Jeff Groves, RIP.

— Austin Groves

"The world is spinning in two different directions. ...Isolation and fragmentation in the West stand in sharp contrast to the Silk Road since 2015. The story of... linking the Pacific through to the Mediterranean has been about consolidation, collaboration, defusing tensions, building alliances and providing the platform for long-term cooperation and collaboration. ...Improving relations boosts exchanges."

Peter Frankopan, *The New Silk Roads*, pp. 50–52

Contents

Introduction

This book describes the journey of an American millennial moving between two worlds — one young and digitized, the other older and, for lack of a better word, analog. One world is a digital world into which they were born and which they mastered by the time they were teens. This is the generation born into the world of the internet, coding, PayPal, online anything. They first entered a workforce in 2004 with the IPO of Google and the last of the millennials are entering now. It has been a frustrating 18 years for these people. They lived through the Columbine mass shooting and 230 other high school shootings. They entered the workforce right after the collapse of the Nasdaq and all its scandals, 9/11, and the Iraq war. They endured Hurricane Katrina and its aftermath in 2005. They stumbled through the Great Financial Crisis (GFC) and large scale unemployment from 2008 to 2011. They accumulated the largest buildup of student debt in American history. They have lived through the scourge of OxyContin and a declining life expectancy and 18 years of endless war.

In between Two Worlds: US Millennials vs. Anti-government Complacent Boomers: "OK Boomer"

These millennials are hyper aware of the digital world — branding, coding, hacking, posing, following, commenting, and collecting data — and yet feel that the older generation of workers in manufacturing, consumer products, consulting, banking, telecom, and other industries do not understand where they come from and what they have to offer. They feel that they are not taken seriously and do not feel that the older generation appreciates the urgency of change that is required to keep up with another world. There is a lack of awareness of the kinds of talent needed to get to the next level never mind the kinds of products needed to get to the next level. One example of this is the virtual absence of 5G products by ATT and Verizon until very recently. This is contrasted with Huawei which already rolled out 5G in 50 cities last November. Another example of this is the absence of any domestic international payments system or banking products from Apple, Amazon, or Facebook until very recently. This is in contrast to Alibaba and Tencent which command the heights in payments and e-commerce in more than 50 countries and counting.

Between Two Worlds: US Millennials vs. Emerging Market Millennials Helped by Government

This is also the story of an American millennial caught between two other worlds. One is in the US which they feel is too set in its ways and which is oblivious to what is happening in other countries full of millennials and governments which are aggressively welcoming and supporting the young in a digital revolution. This is the outside world of China, Japan, Korea, Indonesia, India Poland, and Brazil. They are full of poor millennials who are hungry for change and have governments which are ready, able, and willing to help in many ways. Governments all over gladly participate in supporting and subsidizing goods and services of all kinds to startups — with legal help, financial aid, tech support, and space. No government did this better than Mayor Johnson of London for several years. China and many other large emerging markets have hundreds of millions of millennials ready to take on the world and offer powerful incentives to help by funding universities, think tanks, state-owned utilities, and other entities to leapfrog the US. They force the innovators on the boards of the slow-moving utilities. We catalog these developments in this book.

These two worlds are colliding. American millennials refer to advice from their American elders with a snarky retort of: "OK, Boomer". And American millennials look to places like China — with *five times* more millennials than America — and see a government at the front end of the spear when it comes to building a new infrastructure. It has built out digital payments, e-commerce, digital currency, and 5G which means nothing less than the elimination of checks, cash, and credit cards. It's not that American millennials feel grossly underpaid. That is bad enough. But they see a government unable and unwilling to build out a desperately needed digital infrastructure which is as vital and foundational as the interstate highway system or the copper-based telecommunications system. They are chomping at the bit but observe two phenomenon: domestic inertia among older American leaders who currently see government as something to be done away with. At the same time, they see countries like China, Israel, Singapore, India, Indonesia, Sweden, Canada, and many others explicitly and aggressively helping create a needed digital infrastructure.

These American millennials see SVPs or MDs in the existing world of copper, physical space, pyramidal management structures, and overpaid C-Suites who have an obsession with stock buybacks and higher stock prices any way you can get it. These millennials perceive corporate leaders as having a general disregard for newness, innovation, or significant change. Is it any wonder they don't stick around? They see a booming stock market but a broken corporate system in America that is hampering a generation of young people full of boundless energy, new ideas, innate technological skills, and an inclusive culture of acceptance. They feel that most large US corporations are still very short-term focused on their next quarterly report.

American Millennials See Corporate Complacency and Government Which is Ignoring International Trends

These millennials see managers who are nearing retirement and often care more about their ego and their stock price than creating new products. Retained earnings — and plenty of borrowed money — are going into stock buybacks rather than R&D. This creates higher stock prices but perilously perpetuates the *status quo*. Payout ratios for dividends are 50–60%, so companies turn their businesses into annuities rather than plow money into R&D. This is unsettling for many reasons, the biggest one being that Americans are relying on these companies to bring the US into the world of smart cities, 5G, autonomous cars, AI, robotics, energy storage, quantum communications, and solutions to climate change while China has ALREADY implemented much of this.

A large part of the polarization occurring in the US, which by no means can explain all of it, is the growing inability or unwillingness of millennials to buy into — or be let into? — the Fortune 50 companies so that they can play a vital and dynamic role in a desperately needed digital transformation. This book is about why they are not allowed into — or, more importantly, are opting out of — this world. It is also about what happens to them when they enter the corporate world but are not looked after. It is about an epidemic of anxiety among millennials — a very definite mental health crisis — which is getting short shrift by cynical older adults who think these youngsters should just pull themselves up by their bootstraps.

Absence of Policy Response on the Federal Level to Deal with Root Causes of Millennial Anxiety

The problem is that the US is now more polarized than ever. If you follow the news in the US, you will undoubtedly see the current divide in the country — a deterioration of the working class, a toxic view of the government as a way to advance national policy, an inability to stop gun violence, a runaway opioid crisis, and a mismanaged trade/technology war with China.

This is an anxious generation which thrives on fluidity but which has many unidentified and under-appreciated issues which need to be addressed at a societal level in order to get the most out of the next generation of leaders. It is they who will bring the US to the next level. You will see the 8D's throughout this book which we conclude are the root causes of this millennial malaise and anxiety: student debt, discharge of firearms, drugs, divorce, disorders of anxiety, disharmony about climate change, discord over endless wars, and a distorted sense of self from social media.

Chinese Millennials Live in a World That's Very Different than the US: Full Digitization!

On the other hand, the Chinese government is all-in on blockchain, 5G, IoT, AI, electric public transport, and quantum technology by not only supporting the private sector but also making huge investments in education, and in some cases directly funding the build-out. All these are essentially being done while Washington is at a standstill over various social issues like abortion, impeachment, gun rights, or religious worship. Meanwhile, China is turning into a technological powerhouse while flying under the radar. The financial system in China, for the most part, no longer uses checks, cash, or credit cards. It is ALL digital. Insurance of any kind is an online affair. And most any civic activity — tickets, visas, fines, court, births, marriages — are all online.

For reasons which we will explain, Chinese millennials do not seem to be hemmed in by the systemic anxiety experienced by American millennials. It is illegal to own guns, so there are no school shootings. There are no foreign wars, so there are few millennial veterans with problematic issues of PTSD and drug addiction. Universities are subsidized, so young adults don't graduate with tens of thousands of dollars in debt. Chinese millennials are more likely to grow up with an intact nuclear family and even two sets of grandparents living nearby. Addiction rates for dangerous toxic drugs in China, while growing, are a fraction of that of the US and it is very difficult to get access to drugs. China did not have a GFC in 2008, so the population has higher confidence in the government and other institutions. This has allowed innovation in financial services to flourish, as there is less need to have regulators and prosecutors breathing down the necks of bankers and financial innovators. The indisputable facts are that rates of incarceration, suicide, divorce, murder, shootings, and crime are ALL dramatically lower in China than in the US. These are not a matter of dispute.

It's not all roses, though, as a single child family does put considerable pressure on young men and women to succeed. That creates its own forms of anxiety, depression, and dysfunctional family dynamics. There is great pressure to succeed academically and toe the line. The dreaded "Tiger Mom" is always hovering. And many millennials had two "tiger grandmas" as well who lived at home. This is a trifecta of tigers all saying one thing: "STUDY!" Many of them spent 80 hours a week in high school preparing for the all important national exam to enter top universities. This pressure cooker approach to education causes depression later in life, as these people reflect on an adolescence spent buried in books.

Divorce is on the rise. Alcoholism rates are on a par with international levels. OxyContin is only now being peddled to hospitals in China, and we see early signs of inadvertent addiction to painkillers which are prescribed after any surgery. (As with Americans 15 years ago, Chinese are now also being told that OxyContin is not addictive!). China is, however, clearly not in a downward spiral wracked by political infighting or paralysis on basic social issues. This has been an unprecedented time in human history, as more people have been brought out of poverty — more than 300 million — now have a living wage. More importantly, the migration of tens of millions of farmers to the cities to seek out a higher wage and independence is also unprecedented in human history. The overall result is a sharp fall in overall suicide levels, led by for young women. This is because they can leave the strict cultural trappings of farm life and have a more independent life in the city with the hope of making good money.

Chinese Technology Policy Now is Like the US Industrial Policy in the 1950s

In summary, there is one underlying powerful trend we want to advance. As people, we tend to complain. And the butt of the complaints usually goes toward government. Our core view is that it is simply naïve to think that the digital superhighway will build itself. Governments all over are helping to build out a vitally important digital infrastructure just as important as the buildout of the physical infrastructure after World War II. China is doing this in Spain's. But so did Boris Johnson when he was mayor of London. His help to build up Canary Wharf turned London into a fin tech capital. Singapore has done a great job in public private partnerships on quantum computing, biotechnology, fin tech, blockchain, and other sciences.

Let's not forget what the US very wisely did after World War II. It spent a fortune to rebuild Europe with the Marshall Plan. This also soaked up excess capacity, so it was a win–win for everyone. It created government-subsidized mass housing. It had a GI Bill which let everyone go to college for free. It created NATO and kept the peace through a tightly controlled alliance. It kept global dominance through the buildup of a massive navy. And it generated phenomenal amounts of credit for consumption.

In many ways, China has, since 1990, been doing what the US did during 1948–1975. At that time, a host of international scandals and failed coups sponsored by the US were revealed and Congress demanded a new template for leadership. Interestingly, in this 30 year stretch of development since 1990 has not had a single foreign war or been responsible for a violent overthrow of any government. Let's see if this track record can be maintained.

How a Millennial from New York Navigated His Way from Upstate New York to the Heart of Corporate Americana and then to Shanghai

In conclusion, this book navigates these massive historical tides discussed above — social, professional, governmental, and technological — in very practical ways. It lays out the journey of a millennial who lived through the death of his father at age of 11 from alcohol-related causes. Prior to making his way into the center of the IOT drama with Accenture, we are shown a journey of courage and tenacity to overcome his own problems caused by the (mostly genetic) disease of alcoholism. The journey moves into 2012 with a global approach to IOT at Coca-Cola. He then went to Accenture and did many IoT projects in more than 20 countries, including work with AT&T. After that, he was hired by Verizon to do projects both in the US and internationally. He spent time in Mexico working on projects involving US Telcos and has fascinating insight into what Huawei was doing in Mexico. Then he went to China into the deep end with a NYSE-listed e-commerce firm. Austin was working closely with many of the leading Chinese companies in the area of e-commerce and payments.

This is an American millennial with fluent Chinese who has come from (1) the top US consulting firm in internet of things; (2) the top US telecoms company, and (3) a Shanghai based payments company in the middle of the Alibaba ecosystem. However, at its roots, is a story of someone with all the cards stacked against him who triumphed by reaching out to boomers. He used what worked, left behind what did not and created a world on his own with other millennials. This is what most millennials end up doing to the great detriment of the Fortune 100.

Layout of the Book: Comparison of US and China, How US Corporates Compare to Chinese Corporates

This first part of the book reflects on the major differences between the US and China through the eyes of a millennial. We have noted these above briefly and will go into deeper detail. We break down the differences by social, technological, economic, and educational. We realize that surveys differ, but we either use international surveys with solid credibility or individual surveys in both countries with plenty of caveats. The conclusion we draw whew is that China has an industrial policy that is similar to what the US did in the 1950s which was close government coordination with the building of highways, the Marshall Plan, structured telecom oligopolies, banks which expanded internationally in line with corporates, close cooperation with military and clandestine services to promote corporate interests in other countries, particularly Latin America.

The second part of the book looks at the evolution of the battle for technological supremacy first from Austin's eyes of working directly with Accenture, Verizon, and AT&T. After that, he offers insights from his years in Shanghai while setting up a successful e-commerce company working directly with Alibaba, Tencent, and JD.com. The differences between the US and China are quite radical. This is a singular person traveling on a career journey who sees paralysis and inertia in the buildout of a new digital superhighway. When Austin went to China, he saw that not only was it built out but everyone was going full speed in all directions. He notes several differences: much more solid levels of confidence among Chinese, absence of guns, no crime, safe transportation, General cohesion, trust in the government, confidence in the financial system, little to no evidence of drug addiction in society, and fairly high educational achievement in average staff.

At the end of Part II, we offer a detailed step-by-step guide of how to growth hack the seemingly impenetrable Chinese e-commerce market. These come directly from Austin's experience of building a multi-million dollar business from scratch in Shanghai.

What America is Planning to Do to Catch Up or Leap Frog: American Capitalism with Socialist Characteristics

Part III looks at the serious challenges facing the US as it tries to jumpstart a national initiative to catch up with China in many areas, especially 5G, payments along the Silk Road, and e-commerce. Solutions are available, but the current anti-government ideological forces running hot and heavy in the US need to reverse course and embrace some kind of public–private partnership in both social ills and technological shortcomings if the US is to stay on top. We think this is happening now.

Our view is that the US will now start to do what China has been doing for many years — pick national champions, merge military and civilian technological programs, and subsidize programs that are now considered a "national security" priority. Only a public–private endeavor can build out the digital infrastructure to get to the next level. We strongly believe the US is going that path now, so it will need to backtrack on its demands that China stop government support for smart cities, 5G, AI, autonomous cars, power storage, etc. The US is starting primarily through the Pentagon. In fact, a bipartisan group in the Senate proposed a $1 billion support package to 5G companies through the Federal Communications Commission in order to give it a jump start. We highlight two reports that are key to the new thinking about public–private programs. One is a Congressional Research Service report suggesting seven key areas for civilian–military cooperation. Another is a commission chaired by Eric Schmidt which investigates public–private cooperation in technology.

18 Provocative Workshops to Bring Millennials and "Grownups" Together to Thrash Out the Issues and Have Fun

Lastly, we have added one important feature with the aim to arrive at practical, tangible ways that millennials and older adults can have a dialogue about many of the issues named above. We have 18 "workshops" for broad discussion for groups in educational institutions or corporate offices. These are specifically for the young and the inter-generational can come together and hash out issues to find common ground. Millennials need to learn to upwardly manage adults who are trying to learn new things. And adults need to find the humility to allow themselves to be mentored by younger people. Millennials can learn to balance current branding with new digital opportunities. Inter-generational adults can learn to become more inclusive and open their minds to change. If there is any hope of solving the many serious problems confronting civilization now — whether they are technological and social — public–private programs must begin. Government cannot be seen as the enemy. Millennials and inter-generational adults/ boomers MUST find common ground. US corporates must look outside and see what is happening in "third world" countries where countries with no "copper legacy" are leapfrogging America and creating brand new purely digital financial systems on phones, sometimes merely with solar power. The world desperately needs to deepen the dialogue NOW. A few of them are even designed to have fun and share personal struggles.

Part I

Comparing the US and China in Economic Progress and Millennial Mental Health

This part of the book looks at the causes of the rift between the US and China through the eyes of a millennial. Where did this great Silicon Curtain gradually descending from the Sea of Japan to the Indian Ocean get its start? How did China become such an existential threat to the US? Just how far is China ahead of the US? Is there a secret sauce to China's success? We think the common narrative that China gets ahead by "stealing" is fatuous. There are real powerful dynamics going on in China which have great momentum.

On the other hand, how much of a role do the social ills plaguing America have to do with inhibiting millennial productivity? Is this really an important issue, or do millennials just need to pull-up their britches and grow up? When we started to write this book, we thought that the US merely needs an Apollo program of AI, 5G, and financial technology to catch up with China. We thought a closer relationship between the Congress, Pentagon, and the private sector in major cities could wake up the sleeping giant. Our somewhat shocking realization was that there are very serious social ills that are holding back millennials. They are the future of the country and these social ills are as important to solve as government gridlock.

We catalog these issues or what we call the "8D" — an opioid epidemic of legal and illegal drugs, debt, national disunity, Middle East discord, mental disorders, divorce, and a social media that distorts the human person. We follow on with the discarded millennial veteran — which society wants to forget — and their high suicide rates which push up overall suicide rates. We look to the "out of control" gun culture and the trauma many millennials experienced as they rehearsed for mass shootings and went through high school wondering, "Am I next?". We note the problem with the use of jails as a dumping ground for mental illness, creating by far the highest incarceration rates globally. We reflect on the rage of so many American millennials who look at a divided government utterly unconcerned by climate change while state governments on both coasts do what they can to protect coastlines. We see the reality of 650,000 millennial veterans from the discord in the Middle East, many of whom have legitimate mental disorders like PTSD (as many as 20% of veterans) which lead to drug and alcohol abuse. We noticed the pressure social media asserts on people through Facebook and Instagram to be more fabulous at any cost no matter what the reality. This leads to a toxic distortion between the real self and the public self, especially when many millennials are living in homes with stagnant or falling incomes and who can no longer afford a luxurious lifestyle.

Lastly, we highlight the fact that most college grads leave university with $35,000–$40,000 in debt with hundreds of dollars in interest payments per month before they even start to pay for their lives. America needs two Apollo programs (which we will lay out in Part III) which address both the social and the technological issues.

China simply does not have many of the ills of America: no guns, no wars, and no OxyContin. There are no wars, so no returning veterans. Universities are cheap. Drugs are very difficult if not impossible to get. China is doubling down on environmental issues and this is a top three issue for the government. Families are more intact. Say what you want about a "one party" state, but the Five Year Plan is created by millions of people throughout society (from the bottom up) and it is geared to one thing: solve the problems you have laid out and you get promoted. Once it is agreed to, they stick to it. No matter how many military commissions

Xi Jinping has under his thumb, he can't change it. Social media in China does, of course, create anxiety and the "one-child policy" puts great pressure on the son or daughter to achieve. But the result is that China is climbing the ladder and is now in the top 10 best overall high school educational scores while the US has fallen to the low 20s.

As we discuss the overall differences between the two countries in Part I — again, through the eyes of a millennial — we will use the third person. We want to be as fair as possible to highlight the positives and negatives. As with all good narratives, the underdog (China) is given a little benefit of the doubt and the king of the jungle (The US) justifiably deserves greater scrutiny. That is the point of this section.

Chapter 1

Where Did It All Go Wrong with the US and China?

In analyzing the path to digital commerce for both the US and China, we do not want to criticize America or to praise China or anywhere else. Every country has its own social, economic, and educational problems. The US is still in a position to be a dominant player in the world for decades to come. But, the US needs to wake up to the fact that EVERY country in the world, especially China, is coming to eat America's lunch. They are doing this for one simple reason: to make a better life for themselves and their children as well as to take care of their parents in old age. India is also a juggernaut in this respect. Other cities like Jakarta, London, Singapore, Barcelona, Sydney, Dublin, Amsterdam, Berlin, and Seoul are on the cutting edge of technological development led largely by millennials. There are even "long shot" cities which are now coming alive with millennial vibrancy — Bucharest, Manila, Dhaka, Dubai, Nairobi, and Lagos. They will not stop.

Meanwhile, In America... Most American millennials received a good education and were kept safe in the 1980s and 1990s. They had clean, safe streets, and a consistently safe supply of food and water. They are fairly technologically adept. However, a new generation of millennials throughout the emerging markets — several hundred million — have also now been educated, kept safe, fed well, have clean water, no civil war, and are well-educated. They are now technically adept and hungry. They are guided by one simple goal; to make a better life for their families (both older and younger generations). They are humble, hungry, motivated, and want a bigger piece of a pie that is not getting any much larger. Many millennials and older people today in the US do not realize this. At best, they are not taking enough corrective actions to maintain "the lead". At worst, they have buried their heads in the stand for years and are now out to sabotage any country that wants to get in the lead.

This is all to say that in the fall of 2018, Washington appears to have woken up to the fact that China was pulling ahead in many areas of technology. We think the spark was the launch in China of a quantum communications satellite in the middle of 2017 which showed that China was ahead in the quantum space race. However, rather than taking a page from China's book and making similar investments or engaging in public–private partnerships — a new Apollo project if you like — the strategy has been to "Stop China at all costs". This is akin to the response of taxi drivers to Uber — try to stop them from evolving and expanding. Germany is being blackmailed to stop using Huawei because the US said to stop using its equipment or the US would slap tariffs on German cars. It tried to blackmail the UK by saying that it must stop using Huawei equipment or it would be deprived of the flow of US intelligence.

The policy response to China's technological lead is to act like taxi companies with Uber: stop what is inevitable at any cost.

At first, the US first blacklisted ZTE. Then it tried to blacklist Huawei domestically. Then it arm-twisted its allies (the "Five Eyes" countries of Canada, Australia, New Zealand, and UK) to stop using Huawei's equipment. It basically blacklisted many other companies as well as imposed other tariff and non-tariff barriers. It seems the US was more fixated on the intentional destabilization of China rather than actually competing. This is surprising, since isn't the US narrative all about self-reliance, innovation, and new frontiers rather than knee-capping and playing the victim? Is the US playing a schoolyard bully?

At the very least, the following chart shows that the US is trying to create a technological "silicon curtain" to prevent the vital technological centerpiece of China — Huawei and its affiliates — from buying any more technology from US companies as well as prevent them from expanding in foreign markets, and it is trying to prevent any NATO ally from buying any technology from Huawei. Huawei had even offered to sell Huawei 5G equipment — which the US currently does not make — with the course code freely available. The US refused.

This leaves Qualcomm, Verizon and AT&T to rapidly create an infrastructure for 5G from a standing start, something many think is unrealistic. This causes European allies great consternation because their competitiveness will be jeopardized since China and its alliances have already implemented 5G in November in 50 Chinese cities and will roll it out in more than 300 cities by the Fall of 2020. Huawei has an 80% market share in cell towers. Who can fill this market if the US unilaterally stops its allies from purchasing towers from the only company that sells them.

Why is the US doing this? All countries at all times look to destabilize their adversaries — distract them, cause them to panic, and force them to make unforced errors. Countries want to create impotent 'buffer states' to protect themselves from invasion. They steal technology whenever and wherever they can. Everybody steals technology. They throw countries off their game by creating false narratives and distract them from progress. They want to stay on top. The problem here is that the US portrays itself as a beacon of hope — the shining city on a hill — where the rule of law, fair play, hard work, and self-reliance can make anyone a millionaire regardless of race, family, religion, or social status. What the rest of the world sees is a powerful country acting like a school yard bully.

The deeper issue is that the US sees itself as a victim and is acting in a revanchist manner.

We think, however, there is a deeper issue here at play. It is what got Donald Trump elected. In his book *Identity*, Francis Fukuyama describes a phenomenon in the US over the past decade or so which is social deterioration in the middle class. This is most powerfully reflected in one data point. We see in the US an opioid and alcohol epidemic that has broken out in rural and working class communities. In 2016, this led to more than 60,000 deaths through overdose and is causing a drop in life expectancy in the US for the first time since World War I.

Why? Fukuyama says that many of these people have seen their real incomes fall for more than 10 years and have stopped being counted in employment statistics. Tens of millions are on permanent disability, on parole or have stopped working altogether. The result, he claims, is a perception of invisibility and lost dignity. Most of all, they feel resentful and they want someone to blame for their loss of dignity. They feel someone has 'cut in line'. China is that convenient scapegoat. How can we have not seen this coming given that some of the most popular shows on cable — Breaking Bad, Hung, Sopranos, Shameless — all celebrate the attempt at validation or redemption of invisible men and women through violent or illegal hell-raising, and lots of guns! (Fukuyama's poignant description of

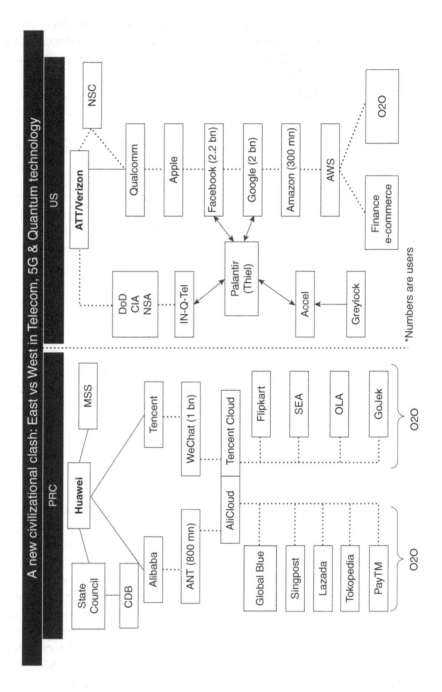

a people who are invisible and walk around with a lost identity also seems eminently applicable to the woes of Hong Kong!).

The American Middle Class: Feeling Poorer and Less Secure

The loss of this middle-class status is particularly frightening because these people had known prosperity and then lost it. Someone needs to be blamed for the loss of their prosperity and their security. So, they feel a need to point an accusatory finger to someone — to the elites, to Latino immigrants, to China. Whichever sticks. They have had a taste of the American dream and lost it. Now, they conclude as a group that someone has "cut in line" and stolen it. For Americans, the loss of real incomes is a loss of identity. This penetrating insight seems applicable in cities which are experiencing great upheaval and blame some "other" outsider who cut in line — London, Istanbul, Hong Kong, Beirut, and Barcelona. They see a foreign power — which is either imposing its will or its refugees or both — on cities which want to preserve their autonomy and way of life.

Why do Americans in particular feel they have lost their identity? Hard work in the American context confers identity. Their identity and dignity have been taken from them by "someone else". This someone else has "disrespected" their right to work. It can't be that the plutocratic elite — the greedy 1% who now have more wealth than ever — have taken their identity, for that is Un-American. Right? Furthermore, some in the religious community will claim that believers have been disrespected by non-believers. The betrayal by this foreign non-believer has led to the impoverishment of the middle class. So, this is a crime against God, too! See the following chart to show the way in which fast growth, low inflation, and high productivity allowed China's GDP measured in purchasing power parity to seemingly pass up the US between 2014 and 2016. (This essentially measures the "expensiveness" of, say, a haircut inside each economy by an actor inside that economy.) Essentially, the price of a haircut is becoming "more affordable" in China.

The view that godless foreigners are cutting in line and stealing the American Dream from under the noses of erstwhile middle-class folks — a view which would appear strange to some readers — has sticking power. It is convenient. It sounds credible. It passes the buck to the foreigner, i.e. a "godless" China or "rapists" in Mexico. There is no need to reflect on

United States vs China by GDP

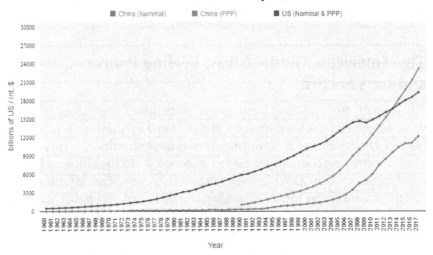

Source: IMF, World Bank, 2019.

either the creation of inequality by internal greed, corruption or the failure of the US government to offer adequate vital digital infrastructure to get to the next level. The chart above shows how, in purchasing power terms, China has surpassed the US. This grates on the "sole superpower" left on Earth.

The Eight Ds: Divorce, debt, drugs, discharge of weapons in schools, disorders, disagreement on climate change, discord from endless wars, and a distorted sense of self from social media weigh heavily on millennials.

The specific middle class examples — in particular Austin's journey as a millennial — laid out in this book feel that they have become invisible within their own society and see themselves as betrayed by outside forces. They are afraid and their backs are against the wall, with no one to help or support them. They feel particularly betrayed by the Democrats who were in the pay of the banks in the midst of the Great Financial Crisis (GFC). These people we describe in this book in the US — including some millennials — are navigating their way in a world where their parents feel they were betrayed by the system. Someone has to be blamed.

Here's the problem. More than one-third of these millennials come from single parent divorced families and most of these families have seen a deterioration in real incomes. These millennials are saddled with student debt. Hundreds of thousands of young veteran millennials wander American cities dealing with alcoholism and disorders like PTSD. There is an out of control culture of gun violence. So many millennials know of a school or a person close to them who was affected by a school shooting. There have been 230 shootings since the Columbine High School Massacre in April 20, 1999 — one per month for 20 years. More than 400 teenage high school students have been shot during this time.

In addition, they are highly likely to be affected by addiction with a family member. They live in a culture of terror attacks in Western cities starting with 9/11. They see "boomers" who are unconcerned by climate change and this understandably makes them very angry — great discord. They have been affected by a culture of resentment due to social media caused by a failure to have their inside and outside match.

This spills over into their social media where appearances of bountiful success must be maintained while many live in effective poverty. This magnifies the resentment of the "have nots" because they have been coaxed into showing a false side of themselves on Instagram or Facebook which bears no resemblance to reality. They become hypocrites and live in a secret poverty while portraying success — and knowing others are doing the same. They can feel like split personalities, hypocrites, fools. They ask themselves how they can buy into something so shallow, yet they carry on with appearances. This creates anger because these millennials resent the people who have created platforms which they feel force them to lie about who they are.

Millennial Obsession with Image on Social Media Reinforces Feelings of Hypocrisy

All of these dynamics create great anxiety. Millennials ask themselves: Who am I if I am not my social media presence? Why do I feel betrayed by adults who have broken the financial system, the political system, and the climate all at once and have no solutions? Why did I take on $75,000 in debt with no job that can allow me to have a good life AND pay my interest payments? Why has Congress done NOTHING to protect me during my high school and college years from gun violence? Why do millennials keep going off to wars that never end and come back addicted messes? There very clearly a distortion of who and what

I am when it comes to reconciling me own person from my social media presence.

In addition to this anxiety, the economic decline — or an inability to even get on the highway of economic success — is seen as part of a loss of social status and identity, especially when the Fortune 500 do so little to accommodate millennials in the workplace. Someone has to be held responsible, and resentment is a highly contagious emotion. It says "we are victims", and victims are only ever present at a crime scene. Someone must be to blame for the crime. A culprit must be found.

While China was Building out Its Infrastructure, the US was Fighting Endless Wars

The first millennials turned 18 in 1998. The year before was 1997 and this was the first year OxyContin went on the market and the beginning of a runaway opioid epidemic. The year after was 1999, the Columbine shooting, and the beginning of a schoolyard shooting epidemic. The year after that was 2000, then the NASDAQ peaked and began an 80% descent plagued by scandal and financial illegalities. It is, however, arguable that the year after that — the tragic events of 9/11 — largely defined this generation of millennials. The first millennials left college in May of 2001 with the narrative of a conquered USSR and a global, unquestioned, and beneficent Pax Americana that was benefiting all.

After 9/11, a new narrative emerged that not everyone in the outside world was in love with America — the shining light on the hill. That young fanatical Islamic men could capture planes and drive them into the heart of American symbols killing 3,000 people was a wake up call that all was clearly not well. The narrative of Pax Americana that the millennials swallowed with unquestioning loyalty was unraveling. Most were proud when all NATO allies came together to support the US in its hour of need. At the same time, many could not understand or fathom how so many in the world could cheer as the planes hit the World Trade Center. Something was very clearly wrong in the world and the narrative needed to be recast.

Dear Millennials: Welcome to Adulthood! Here's OxyContin, Columbine, 9/11 and the Iraq War

The years 2001–2003 were real turning point for millennials. This generational turning point is borne out in numbers that are very closely watched by the US government. For more than 20 years in the 1980s and 1990s, the incidence of alcohol and drug addiction among 7th–8th graders (aged 13–14) were falling. In 2002–2003, the numbers showed an alarming reversal. They spiked. For the first time in many years, the incidence of drinking and drug use began to move up. This has important implications for the entire system — police forces, jails, and courts. The US justice system watches these numbers very carefully in anticipation of how many prisons to build and what kind of infrastructure is required for the court system.

It was an ominous uptick and caused the system to get in gear to anticipate greater levels of criminality in later years caused by alcohol abuse and drug addiction. It is also interesting to note that the same time that the national numbers for 13–14 year olds getting involved in drugs and alcohol began to rise for the first time in decades, the national suicide rate stopped falling and instead began to rise. The trauma and confusion of 9/11 and the entry into the Iraq war — with tens of thousands of damaged veterans returning from active combat — all came to gather to cause a rise in national data on drug use and suicide. The age of mass incarceration began about this time.

At this same time, the war in the Middle East was spreading into other continents. This would grow beyond Afghanistan to what many thought was an illegal and unjust war in Iraq. When the Iraqi army was disbanded, its remnants would spread to many countries and morph into the many-headed hydra that is now ISIS. So, the war was taken to Syria, Pakistan, Turkey, and many parts of Africa. Young American soldiers barely out of their teens — hundreds of thousands — were being deployed to many violent countries on three continents with imprecise and dangerous mandates for which they were not trained. Many came home as 'millennial veterans' with PTSD and aggravated the rising drug abuse numbers which seem to have their roots caused by the residual shock and trauma caused by 9/11. (Let's not forget that an exhaustive study into why the US intelligence community missed the attacks on the US on 9/11 were due to dysfunctional relationships between CIA and FBI as well as a profound failure of imagination by the nation's intelligence community.)

The result of these endless wars in the Middle East is that many of these veterans returning from foreign wars started in 2003 had undiagnosed PTSD. This disorder is often accompanied by alcohol and drug abuse. According to the Congressional Research Service, the number of veterans that are disabled due to suffering from "wounds and injuries" is about 150,000. So, the issues with millennial veterans cause the opioid numbers to really pile up. The mental health apparatus was overwhelmed quickly. The only answer the US system had to the problem of drug addiction at the time was mass incarceration. What is more disturbing is not the number of drug addicts piling up. The real concern is that the drugs people are now taking in mainstream society are more pure and powerful and, therefore, more toxic and deadly. For instance, crystal meth can cause long-term brain damage and is very toxic. It only takes a small incremental dosage of fentanyl to cause instant death. OxyContin can trigger dependence after only a few doses. According to a *New York Times* article ("A New Scourge: Deaths Involving Meth Are Rising Fast"), since 2018, meth has caused more deaths in 14 of 35 states than fentanyl or OxyContin.

How potent is fentanyl?

Opioid strengths are measured relative to morphine, a powerful drug often prescribed for severe pain. Illicit narcotics are significantly stronger than the prescription painkiller as shown below in percentages relative to morphine.

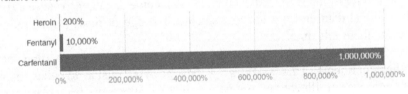

Source: CNN, Heroin — WHO; Fentanyl — DEA; Carfentanil — DEA.

Wars are also problematic because they are extremely expensive. As the military budgets rise overseas, domestic programs designed to help drug addicts at home are sacrificed, and law enforcement has to fill the gap and act as arrester, councilor, therapist, and detox center. It is simply not cut out for this. The numbers for the ongoing wars in Iraq, Syria, Afghanistan as well as other parts of the Middle East and Africa exploded in the prime of the millennials. From 2001 to 2013, the cost of the "endless wars" was estimated at $6 trillion. This is $75,000 for every household when long-term medical care and disability compensation was considered. The hundreds of thousands of millennial "wounded warriors" are very expensive to nurse back to health, not to mention the reduction in productivity and a falling contribution to growth. More needs to be done for them. (Frankopan, *The Silk Roads*, p. 481).

On top of a burgeoning drug addiction problem starting in 2003–2004, something else was happening at the same time in the US. Silicon Valley was digging itself out of a deep hole during a wild and corrupt speculative bubble that ended in an 80% collapse of the NASDAQ in 2001 as well as multiple arrests and prosecutions of tech bankers. This disillusionment was occurring in tandem with Silicon Valley starting a new revolution in the digital age as the internet was starting to embed itself into society. This was the beginning of the replacement of labor with technology. This was the beginning of the end of unskilled labor — something that was already ongoing but which would pick up pace. This was also the beginning of the trade agreements which would force the US workforce to compete head on with China, Canada, and Latin America but without their healthcare and safety net systems which served as a fallback during health emergencies. At this same time, a new company in China arose to take advantage of this new technology: Alibaba.

As we will explain later, this same time in China was a time of peace — zero wars. Few millennial wounded warriors. No long-term care for disabled veterans. No overseas adventures. What was happening was a boom in domestic infrastructure. China spent trillions and built fleets of electric buses and high speed trains, highways, hospitals, clinics, stadiums, arenas, parks, megacities. It moved 300 million people from the country to the cities. It pulled hundreds of millions out of poverty. It poured money into electric cars, payments, blockchain technology, quantum communications, e-commerce, online medical services, environmental cleanup, and many other technologies.

In summary, the millennial generation entered adulthood with the following:

(1) **The scars of 9/11:** Just as the first millennials turned 21, they saw on live TV the center of finance of the US as well as the Pentagon being attacked by terrorists from the Middle East — this was the first significant terrorism attack on US.

(2) **Endless wars:** As the first millennials turned 20, the inexplicable wars in the Middle East, notably Iraq, began which politicians could not justify and which caused hundreds of thousands of young veterans to return home without help for drug-related mental illness and PTSD.

(3) **Deluge of new info:** There was increased stress on the middle class from the rollout of the internet given the mountains of new information to digest, starting in 1998–1999, when the millennials were turning 18.

(4)   **Student debt:** The mountain of student debt for millennials averages about $600–800 per month in payments and the absolute amount is north of $1.2 trillion, most of which is owed by millennials.

(5)   **The emergence of millennials in Global Emerging Markets (GEMs):** Let's not forget that this was the same time that millions of poor, hungry millennials in emerging markets were willing to work 90 hours a week for nothing in order to make something of their lives. This created hyper competition from trade agreements with China, Latin America and Canada. In addition, when the USSR collapsed and China gave up on communism and created capitalism with socialist characteristics, 2 billion people joined capitalism and the global workforce. China woke up to private sector competition.

(6)   **Social media appearances:** Constant "in your face" pressure being was created by social media sites like Facebook and Instagram to show glamorous lifestyles which were betrayed by a declining lifestyle for millions.

(7)   **New hard drugs:** When the first millennials were 16, the Sackler family brought us OxyContin. The arrival of these new and highly toxic drugs like purer meth and OxyContin lead to high death rates from addiction. Crystal meth devastated gay communities all over the West.

(8)   **Financial scandals created by the parents of millennials:** A disillusionment about institutions set in caused by endless scams like Enron, the Nasdaq crash, the GFC, Madoff, Fannie Mae, GE, AIG, Catholic Church, Boy Scouts, on and on.

(9)   **School shootings:** Rising stress came from a spate of school shootings beginning with Columbine in 1999 and persistently continuing with more than 230 high school shootings since then. More than 400 students have been shot. This caused millennials to persistently ask, "Is my high school next?" Or worse, "Am I next?".

(10) **Apathy by inter-generational adults and boomers over climate change:** New evidence of systemic and potentially irreversible damage from climate change is enraging millennials who see their parents apathetic about a phenomenon which could leave many cities under water by the time millennials are 45.

These millennials have lived through major equity market collapses, a string of financial scandals, terrorist attacks, endless wars, a dramatic rise in drug addiction, and the GFC in 2008 — the effects of which are STILL being felt today.

No wonder they do not trust institutions.

No wonder they want to do things among themselves rather than work in a firm.

No wonder they don't want to own assets.

No wonder they live at home.

No wonder the addiction rates are up significantly.

No wonder about 30% of them say that anxiety affects their work productivity.

No wonder they don't trust older people.

No wonder they have helicopter parents — their fawning is an effect, not a cause.

In conclusion, in towns where Austin came from — and hundreds of others from the Appalachian belt to the Southwest — there is a problem of lost identity. The result is a desire to escape from a reality that many find unacceptable. Many logically turn to alcohol and drugs. The problem is that the recent proliferation of highly toxic drugs like crystal meth and

Life Expectancy of US vs. China (1990–2017)

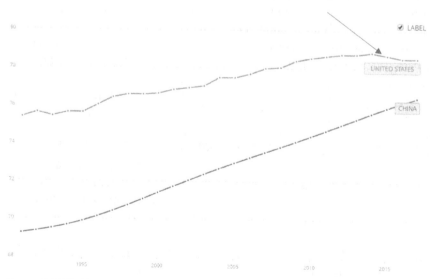

Source: IMF, World Bank, 2019.

OxyContin means that accidental overdoses are alarmingly common. In addition, the use of a firearm is a highly effective way to commit suicide. Half of all suicides in the US are with a gun. So, the combination of highly toxic drugs and the proliferation of firearms — in the midst of an identity crisis of the American work ethic — means that the life expectancy of Americans is falling for the first time since the Spanish Flu epidemic of 1918. The following chart shows that life expectancy for Americans is falling for the fourth year in a row while the life expectancy of Chinese continue to rise. We all need to explore why this is so. That is the theme of the coming chapters as seen through the lens of Austin's journey from suburban Pennsylvania to Shanghai.

What was China Doing in This Same Time?

Meanwhile, China had been moving from strength to strength. China had no foreign wars from 2000 to 2018 — zero. So there were no returning millennial veterans with mental disorders prone to violence or aggression. One commentator put it well: "The US spent $4 trillion on wars in the Middle East. China spent $4 trillion on its own infrastructure". Due to strict laws, there are no guns or drugs. As a result, the Chinese economy went from being the sixth largest economy globally in 2006 to the second largest economy globally in 2018. As we point out in the text earlier, no foreign wars meant no returning veterans with widespread mental health issues. The system had a good handle on crime — there was little or none. Guns are outlawed. There is an almost fanatical approach to education. There was a sense of mission in a middle class which came from nothing and was extremely poor only 15 years before.

This recent burst of growth in China has also occurred at a time of great global disruption caused by a flood of technological innovation, especially the iPhone. This disruption favors the country with a more primitive economy which has "greenfield" technology. It penalizes entrenched older economies which, over 50 years, built out a complex physical and legal infrastructure which is difficult to dismantle. The proliferation of billions of iPhones starting in 2011–2013 occurred just at the time when China had recapitalized its banking systems and gathered the courage and confidence to begin experimenting with financial innovation with little legacy infrastructure to hold it back. Jack Ma, the founder of Alibaba, was also in the process of raising large amounts of money for the burgeoning online shopping sites TMall and Tao Bao. This was a case of right place, right time, and right circumstances. In addition to the explosion in e-commerce and cellular payments, China was undergoing a productivity boom. As seen in the following chart, productivity growth (inflation free growth due to innovation and other factors) in China was running at 8–9% for 20 years while productivity growth was slowing to 2.5% for many years. The cumulative effect offers much higher growth rates with lower inflation. Hence, the increase in GDP was measured by purchasing power parity.

United States vs. China by GDP Growth

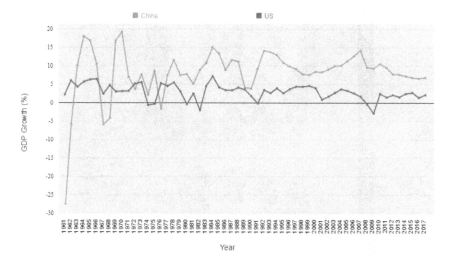

Note: Average annual productivity growth for China from 1992 to 2017 was 8%; the US was 2.5%.

Source: IMF, World Bank, 2019.

From 2012 to 2018, while the US was litigating the GFC and Europe was mired in Mediterranean corporate insolvency, China used the cellphone to create a new financial architecture for 1 billion people. China did this in large part because it was unencumbered by a financial crisis and had no legacy, physical, legal, and lobbying apparatus. The US was dealing with: (1) a 50-year old legacy financial system made from paper checks and rusting copper; (2) mountains of toxic derivatives; (3) district attorneys who were on the warpath for bank malfeasance; and (4) a housing market in free fall.

China was able to invent a new banking system from scratch without entrenched lobbyists, copper-based telecom companies, confusing

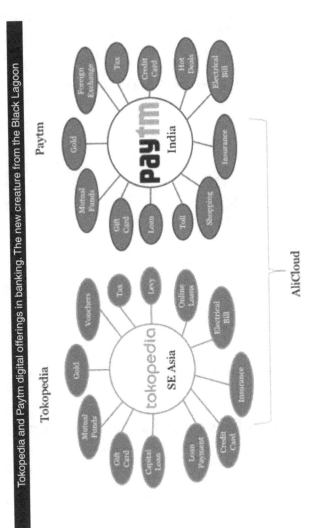

Tokopedia and Paytm digital offerings in banking. The new creature from the Black Lagoon

state regulators, and top heavy internet companies who were chasing Hollywood dreams. It cleverly linked these financial services directly to people's lifestyles. In this way, Alibaba and Tencent were able to not only offer financial services alongside lifestyle services, but also to link them together on one platform. Online purchases could be linked to savings, investments, insurance, tickets, utilities, fines, entertainment, travel, and even education. Alibaba became a "one stop shop" for almost all parts of life. It became a super-app. Nothing in the US remotely resembles this.

Tencent's Wechat was becoming a ubiquitous chat facility for 1 billion people. In addition, Alibaba went on a stealth acquisition binge (while Tencent expanded to 49 countries) making large item purchases like PayTM, Lazada, Tokopedia and acquisitions in Europe, Thailand, Philippines, Bangladesh, Korea, and Japan. In geography, reach, product offerings and customers, no financial institution globally has the reach of Alibaba. Furthermore, no financial institution EVER was able to combine more services for banking activity and lifestyle activity to more people in more countries. As far as the "space race" for financial services in GEMs and frontier markets was concerned (where billions of up and coming tech savvy millennials were lapping up these services), it was game, set and match. US banks, consulting firms, financial services companies, brokers, and insurance companies were caught flat-footed.

Of course, there are great pockets of immense innovation and productivity in America. But these pockets are increasingly found on both coasts — Los Angeles, San Francisco, Seattle, and Portland on the West Coast, and New York City, Boston, DC, Raleigh/Durham and Atlanta on the Eastern Seaboard. Cities in the middle of the US which are innovations hubs include Austin, Denver, Chicago, Minneapolis, and a few others. These are university centers and are making great technological strides in healthcare, bio pharmaceuticals, finance, insurtech, e-commerce, agriculture, entertainment, lifestyle, music, climate change, among others. The question is whether there is enough of a critical mass of zip codes to bring the entire country in a new direction.

Chapter 2

US vs. China by the Numbers

In this chapter, we want to lay out the main issues which we think have a profound effect on millennials as both social and economic actors. As we said in "Introduction", all countries have their problems and all societies deal with ills. It is the human condition. However, after we did an exhaustive search on many societal issues which put pressure on millennials, we conclude that the situation in the US contributes significantly to millennial angst or anxiety in ways that Chinese millennials simply do not. We lay out 10 markers and at the end we offer a Workshop on what needs to happen to remedy these ills. One of the powerful conclusions we have arrived at is that the Apollo program that American society needs to create in order to pull ahead of China is NOT technological but social. The core issues of drug addiction via opioids, millennial veteran mental illness, and gun violence (especially in schools) — and mass incarceration as a way to deal with these ills — all need a new approach. On all these fronts, these issues hold back American society and create intense anxiety on millennials which inhibit their ability to focus, concentrate, and thrive. These ills are profound and affect the ability of people to maintain resilience in the face of obstacles or failure. The Apollo project America needs is a social one. The technological one will follow quickly.

Millennial Angst: How Many are There and Why are American Millennials so Anxious?

The chart in Section 1.1 shows that there are 80 million millennials in the US, about 24% of the population. This is in contrast to 400 million millennials in China, a much higher 29% of the population. So, China has five times more millennials than the US and four times more than Europe — and a much higher proportion than both. In addition, if we compare this against the overall workforce, American millennials make up about half the workforce given that there are 160 million workers, the same as China. Chinese millennials alone are more than two times the entire US workforce.

A few other data points are instructive here. One quarter of the world's population are millennials. Gen X represents 20% and Boomers represent 17%. There are 102 million millennials in Europe, or about 20% while boomers represent a much larger proportion, or 34%. This likely is caused by low birth rates among boomers and Gen X in Europe. This legacy problem of low birth rates is most acute in Spain, which has the lowest representation of millennials in Europe, only 18%.

Millennials: How many?

Number of millennials (in millions)

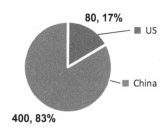

80, 17%
■ US

■ China

400, 83%

Source: HSBC, https://www.business.hsbc.com/navigator/made-for-china/six-things-you-may-not-know-about-chinese-millennials.

Anxiety (US): Where is the anxiety coming from?

The following chart shows that the data reflects the narrative above. The 10 reasons laid out above appear to cause the high levels of anxiety (essentially debt, divorce, drugs, guns, and social media pressure) among millennials. It does not seem to be about intellectual ability or self-confidence about capacity to perform skills. It is an accumulation of unhealthy, stress-inducing situations which millennials see as toxic and unacceptable but which so many inter-generational adults see as matter of fact and should be accepted as unsolvable problems. This makes millennials question their grasp on reality. There are many issues which millennials find unacceptable but which older people see as "facts of life" and cause fierce debate. These are gun control, mass incarceration for drug-related offences, climate change, ease of prescribing painkillers, systemic corruption in banks, the perceived failure of the institution of marriage, among others.

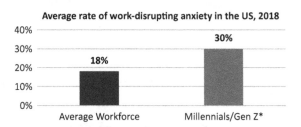

Note: *Millennials/Gen Z represent workers aged 18–34.

Source: *Quartz*, SurveyMonkey Alliance, December 2018, https://www.talentinnovation.org/_private/assets/DisabilitiesInclusion_PressRelease.pdft.

Anxiety (*US vs. China, 2018*)

If we examine those who report "often or always debilitating" levels of anxiety in the workplace in the US, the numbers start at 18% and can rise to 30% in many studies. The level as discovered by the Chinese Academy of Sciences in a survey of 33,000 people in 17 provinces is at 5%. These levels are much lower. Presumably, these same people do not fear hand-guns, school shootings, and do not have access to dangerous drugs. The family would appear to be more intact and young adults are not saddled with tens of thousands of dollars in debt. The levels of homicide, crime and overdose are all dramatically lower as we will see. We want to be very clear here that the ways in which the two surveys have been conducted are different and, therefore, not exactly apples to apples. Also, these surveys on both sides are "self-reporting". So, people may not always tell the truth as there is shame involved in admitting mental illness in both cultures. The point here is that there is a marked difference even when we take these issues into consideration.

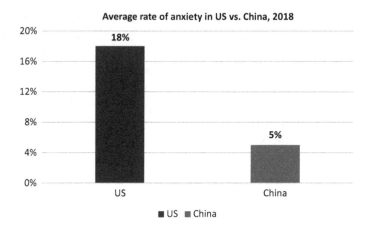

Source: *Quartz*, SurveyMonkey Alliance, December 2018, https://www.talentinnovation.org/_private/assets/DisabilitiesInclusion_PressRelease.pdf.

We want to note here that several scholars who have reviewed the book prior to publication did note that China may only now — in 2020 — be starting to experience a general feeling of malaise as: (1) an economic slowdown hits people's pocketbooks; (2) sagging property prices make people feel less wealthy; (3) and reduction in subsidies for industry and social welfare are curt back as the government tightens its belt. China's per capita passed up the important $10,000 level which suggests it managed to go over the hump of the middle class trap often experienced at $7,000–9,000. This means that its GDP is measured at $14.3 trillion. But the stock market has offered poor returns. Property prices are stagnant. GDP growth is the lowest in 25 years. This can lead to middle class problems like increasing alcohol abuse, drug abuse, obesity, or domestic violence. As odd this writing, these numbers are not yet showing up.

Mental disorders in China

Interestingly, while anxiety in millennials in the US is substantially above the levels of anxiety noted by older Americans, levels of depression and anxiety among Chinese millennials is actually below that of Chinese adults. Depression is a feature of Chinese society, but it seems to be concentrated in the older population of those over 65 and is dominated by women. Also of interest is the extent to which levels of happiness rise (and depression falls) as people (especially women) leave villages and move to the cities. It seems that the cities offer a kind of independence and self-reliance to create a new future away from the restrictions of village life. The important takeaway here is that there is a marked improvement in mental wellbeing as people escape the economic, cultural, and social restrictions of farm life and move into cities in China. As we pointed out earlier, the important takeaway in China is the dramatic drop in suicide among females as they migrate from farms to cities. The interesting contrast in the US is that people are *leaving* the labor cities and returning to smaller cities as major cities are simply too expensive for young workers!

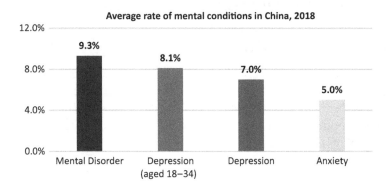

Source: Chinese Academy of Sciences, *Lancet*.

Mental disorders (US) are linked to physical sickness

One of the main reasons that younger people can spiral downward and allow unaddressed mental issues to spill over into alcohol abuse or depression is that they are more likely to think there are not enough treatment options. 1 in 5 are not seeking treatment either because they have not diagnosed their issues or do not realize that there is a way out. Again, there is a greater acceptance in discussing and tackling mental illness on a public level in the US compared to China, but China is catching up. This is likely due to the reality that mental illness invariably has physical manifestations, notably in the incidence of obesity, Type II diabetes, and absenteeism. China is seeing more of this as well. However, there is a growing problem of obesity and Type II diabetes among US millennials.

Major depression diagnoses are increasing faster in Millennials and teens than in any other age groups

63% TEENS

47% MILLENNIALS

1 IN 5 MILLENNIALS ARE NOT SEEKING TREATMENT

Note: Adults represent white collar workers aged 21–65.

Source: *Quartz*, SurveyMonkey Alliance, December 2018, https://www.talentinnovation.org/_private/assets/DisabilitiesInclusion_PressRelease.pdf.

Mental disorders and diet

Most Americans with major depression also have one or more serious chronic health conditions. Millennials have the fastest rate of growth for Type II diabetes. High levels of anxiety and depression spill over into poor sleep, bad nutrition, fast food, lack of quiet time, and inattention to "volunteerism" which seems to revivify the spirit.

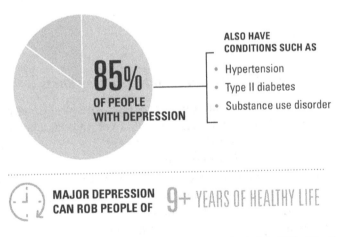

85% OF PEOPLE WITH DEPRESSION

ALSO HAVE CONDITIONS SUCH AS

- Hypertension
- Type II diabetes
- Substance use disorder

MAJOR DEPRESSION CAN ROB PEOPLE OF 9+ YEARS OF HEALTHY LIFE

Source: Blue Cross Blue Shield, the Health of America, March 04, 2019, https://www.bcbs.com/the-health-of-america/articles/two-million-commercially-insured-americans-diagnosed-major-depression-not-seeking-treatment;https://www.talentinnovation.org/_private/assets/Disabilities Inclusion_PressRelease.pdf.

Workshop 1: Mental Health

Issue: Should mental health become a common workplace issue?

1. Ellen Meara, a professor at Dartmouth's Institute for Health Policy and Clinical Practice, says that economics, stress, and a deterioration in the family are all a cause of anxiety among millennials. "There is no single smoking gun". Millennials feel worse about themselves and their futures. This is leading to self-destructive behaviors which cause a deterioration in self-care about health.

2. Nadine Burke Harris, the Surgeon General of California, is a Pioneer of Adverse Childhood Experience tests (ACE). Her Ted Talk has 2.5 million hits. She claims anxiety is a kind of millennial epidemic and this untreated trauma (much of these potential issues are discussed in Chapter 1) causes adverse adult outcomes. She is a champion of a public debate on this issue. Her pragmatic solutions for adults are easy: (A) how can we sleep better; (B) how can we eat better; (C) how can we meditate better; (D) how can we use therapy better; (E) how can we achieve better mindfulness?

3. Aaron Harvey, the Founder of Made of Millions Foundation, quotes the WHO which says that depression and anxiety cost the global economy $1 trillion. He makes the case for an urgent workplace conversation that is safe for employees and addresses an epidemic of anxiety in the workplace among millennials. He has created a guide to mental health in the workplace and started #dearManager social media campaign to address the issue of mental health that causes billions of dollars in lost productivity.

Discussion: Some Psychologists say that bringing up mental health in the office creates issues of privacy, legal exposure, and discrimination. Should the impetus come from the employee? Is there lingering stigma to see an in-house therapist? Ten out of ten of the world's best tennis players have coaches. Why shouldn't a company's leaders? At the very least, shouldn't Dr. Burke Harris's five areas be given a public airing at **voluntary** lunches?

The Four Horsemen: Civilian Suicide, Veteran Mental Illness, Guns, and Mass Incarceration

Suicide: Civilian suicides rate per 100,000, 2019 (major countries)

China has made great strides in reducing the suicide rate. This rate has collapsed from more than 20 per 100,000 to 9 per 100,000. In fact, this phenomenon of dramatically reduced suicide rates has been a significant factor in the increase in people on earth. At the same time, the suicide rate of Americans has risen about 20% from 12 to 15. In the past few years, most studies point to the death rate from dangerously potent drugs like OxyContin, fentanyl, and crystal methamphetamine as the cause of the suicide rate. The fact that handguns are a highly effective way to kill one's self means that the proliferation of guns in American society guarantees successful attempts at suicide.

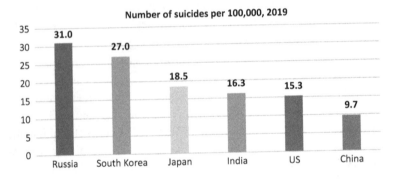

Source: World Population Review.

US Veteran Suicides, 2017: The peak troop deployment in Iraq was almost 200,000. These troops were rotated out every 12 months. So, it is not surprising that the CRS estimates that there about 150,000 "walking wounded" mostly millennial vets in the US. The issue of veterans returning from the "endless wars" in the Middle East, Central Asia, and Africa plays a significant role in the overall suicide rates. The suicide rate of millennial veterans (and there are hundreds of thousands of them after

12 month deployments in constant wars since 2002) is 45 per 100,000. If we compare this to the chart presented previously, it is three times higher than the overall US average, and it is the highest group of all veterans. The number of those who have committed suicide is on the upswing and has averaged 6,100 per year. This is 20 per day — almost one every hour! There are about 500,000 combat veterans that have served in Iraq since 2003.

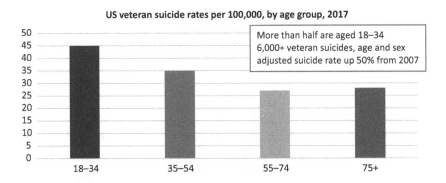

US veteran suicide rates per 100,000, by age group, 2017

> More than half are aged 18–34
> 6,000+ veteran suicides, age and sex
> adjusted suicide rate up 50% from 2007

Source: US Department of Veteran Affairs, 2019, https://www.mentalhealth.va.gov/suicideprevention/data.asp.

To show how problematic the dilemma of "endless wars" can become, we put the issue of millennial veteran suicides in the context of global suicide rates in the following chart. If we compare millennial veterans as a group to various countries, the rate of suicide per 100,000 is 30% higher than Russia, and *this serious mental health problem of suicide among veterans shows a rate which is three times higher than the general population*. Suicide has caused the deaths of far more veterans than combat since the Middle East wars started in 2001. The following chart bears repeating. It shows suicide rates of millennial veterans against world averages. It highlights a serious health crisis among veterans as these US veterans have suicide rates which are *three times* higher than the US average.

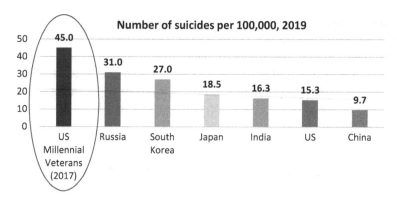

Source: US Department of Veteran Affairs, *World Population Review*, 2019.

The data point in the following table also shows that millennial veterans face higher unemployment rates than the population. They face unemployment levels which are more than three times higher than the adult population. In contrast, China has not had an external military conflict since 1989, so basically has no returning veterans from international conflicts. The frequency of military interventions globally for the US has real and palpable consequences for hundreds of thousands of millennials who return to normal life. They face PTSD, drug addiction, aggressive behavior, and consequent incarceration, high unemployment, and marital problems. It's vital for a country to have precise war aims, win wars quickly and return soldiers to inactive reserve. The phenomenon of endless wars is not just spilling blood and treasure. It also has serious consequences for those who return to society with trauma — physical and mental. JP Morgan does good stuff in this area with explicit programs to hire veterans.

- **326,000** unemployed veterans in 2018
- Unemployment rate for veterans aged 21–24: **14.9%** (2015)

Sources: JP Morgan Chase: https://www.jpmorganchase.com/corporate/news/stories/gen-odierno. htm, CNBC: https://www.cnbc.com/2019/07/25/how-veterans-can-successfully-transition-into-the-civilian-workforce.html, US Department of Labor: https://www.dol.gov/agencies/vets/latest-numbers.

Firearms

The ownership of firearms in the US is the ultimate third rail. No one wants to touch it. Millennials located in cities overwhelmingly are against the wide proliferation of weapons while older people, especially in the South, overwhelmingly see it as a right to own as many weapons as they can buy. The result is a society which has the highest gun ownership rates in the world. How much higher? The prevalence of guns in American society is more than two times higher than Yemen, which is enduring a full-scale civil war. The US has 120 firearms per 100,000 people. This equates to more than 300,000,000 guns — one gun for every man, woman, and child. This leads to a high homicide rate. But it also leads to a significant number of accidental deaths, and as we saw earlier, 50% of suicides are done with a gun. In contrast, China's gun ownership is 3.6 per 100 people, one of the lowest globally. So, there are no mass shootings or school shootings because there are no guns to shoot. China is dealing with a rash of terrorist incidents mostly by separatist Muslim groups which involve machetes or knives. These tend not to be lethal and cause serious injury. Guns are lethal and cause mass casualties. Knives don't.

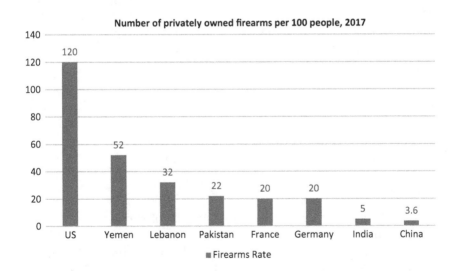

Number of privately owned firearms per 100 people, 2017

Source: *World Population Review*, Worldometer, 2019.

The following table shows the problem with gun ownership. In the US, there are as many guys as there are men, women, and children — with 50 million guns left over. China is at the bottom of the list globally at 3.9. There are two commonalities of countries with the most guns. One is a group of countries involved in recent civil war or regional war. These include Yemen, Montenegro, Serbia, Cyprus, Lebanon, Pakistan, and Bosnia. The others are countries with a big outback and involve hunting and Defense against wildlife near people's homes — Canada, Finland, Norway, and Sweden. It is interesting to see how these countries can avoid mass shootings.

Top 25 countries by firearms/GDP per capita ratio, 2017

#	Country	Firearms Rate	Total Firearm	Population 2019	GDP per Capita
1	United States	120.5	393,347,000	329,064,917	$59,939
2	Yemen	52.8	14,859,000	29,161,922	$1,123
3	Montenegro	39.1	245,000	627,987	$7,720
4	Serbia	39.1	2,719,000	8,772,235	$4,642
5	Canada	34.7	12,708,000	37,411,047	$44,841
6	Uruguay	34.7	1,198,000	3,461,734	$16,341
7	Cyprus	34	285,000	1,198,575	$18,695
8	Finland	32.4	1,793,000	5,532,156	$45,778
9	Lebanon	31.9	1,927,000	6,855,713	$7,857
10	Iceland	31.7	106,000	339,031	$73,233
11	Bosnia and Herzegovina	31.2	1,185,000	3,301	$5,387
12	Austria	30	2,577,000	8,955,102	$47,261
13	Macedonia	29.8	621,000	2,083,459	$5,418
14	Norway	28.8	1,537,000	5,378,857	$75,428
15	Malta	28.3	119,000	440,372	$28,585
16	Switzerland	27.6	2,332,000	8,591,365	$80,296
17	New Zealand	26.3	1,212,000	4,783,063	$43,415
18	Sweden	23.1	2,296,000	10,036,379	$54,075
19	Pakistan	22.3	43,917,000	216,565,318	$1,467
20	Portugal	21.3	2,186,000	10,226,187	$21,316
21	France	19.6	12,732,000	65,129,728	$39,827
22	Germany	19.6	15,822,000	83,517,045	$44,680
23	Iraq	19.6	7,588,000	39,309,783	$5,114
24	Luxembourg	18.9	110,000	615,729	$105,280
25	Bahamas	18.8	74,000	389,482	$31,858

Note: Firearms rate is number of privately owned firearms per 100 population.

Source: World Population Review, Worldometers (GDP per capita).

In 2019 alone, there were at least 45 school shootings in the first 48 weeks of the year out of which 32 were at K-12 schools. (*CNN*: In 46 weeks this year, there have been 45 school shootings", November 20, 2019). The number one location for shootings was in Texas. This was followed by Georgia, Alabama, Louisiana, and Tennessee. There were 26 gun deaths, including three suicides. According to everytown-research.org, the thousands of students who witness these scenes of violence are more likely to abuse drugs and alcohol, suffer from depression, anxiety, and post-traumatic stress disorder. They are more likely to have difficulties in school or engage in criminal activity. The website also tracked shootings on university campuses in 2019. *There were 30 shootings at universities in 2019 where are a gun was discharged on campus. The epidemic of gun violence is also prevalent on college campus life.*

Incarceration: Mental health crisis in jails

When we compare the incarceration rate globally, America comes out on top with 737 Americans out of 100,000 are in jail at any one time, and because jails are so full, sentences are often shorter. As a result, there are millions of people who on parole or probation wandering around looking to (1) make a living; (2) get cleaned up from drugs and alcohol; (3) stay out of jail. There are more than 2 million people in jails now and more than 5 million who are on parole or probation. The numbers are stunning. Around 50% of Americans know someone in jail. Between 1980 and 2010, the number of prisoners has grown five-fold. On top of the 2.3 million people in jails, there are more than 5 million on parole or probation and this is a revolving number. Other numbers that are worthy of reflection about the use of the US penal system as a cure all for drug addiction and mental health issues are as follows:

1. One of 37 adults in the US, almost 3%, is in some form of penal supervision.
2. The number of people who have been on parole since 2000 exceeds 10 million.
3. 40% of those who were arrested and jailed were on parole at the time.
4. Most of these come from the same 50 or so zip codes.
5. One in 12 African Americans is under some form of penal supervision.
6. 8.5% of African Americans are in the penal system!

7. The US makes up 5% of the world's population but has 21% of its prisoners.
8. African Americans are incarcerated at five times the rate of whites.
9. Prisons are magnets for infectious disease: 22% have TB, Hep B, HIV, or STDs.
10. Prisons are a $180 billion business (2017), almost equal to spending on veterans.

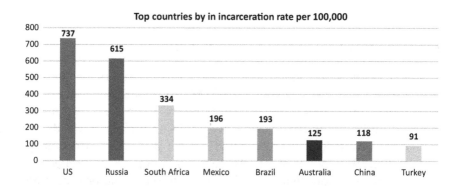

Top countries by in incarceration rate per 100,000

Note: Incarceration rate is the number of people jailed per 100,000 population.

Source: *World Population Review*, Worldometer, 2018.

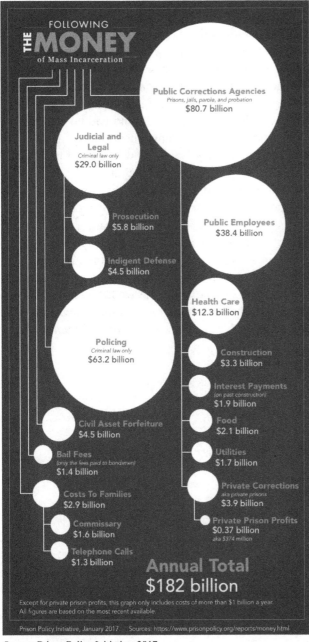

FOLLOWING
≡MONEY
of Mass Incarceration

Public Corrections Agencies
Prisons, jails, parole, and probation
$80.7 billion

Judicial and Legal
Criminal law only
$29.0 billion

Prosecution
$5.8 billion

Public Employees
$38.4 billion

Indigent Defense
$4.5 billion

Health Care
$12.3 billion

Policing
Criminal law only
$63.2 billion

Construction
$3.3 billion

Interest Payments
(on past construction)
$1.9 billion

Civil Asset Forfeiture
$4.5 billion

Food
$2.1 billion

Bail Fees
(only the fees paid to bondsmen)
$1.4 billion

Utilities
$1.7 billion

Costs To Families
$2.9 billion

Private Corrections
aka private prisons
$3.9 billion

Commissary
$1.6 billion

Private Prison Profits
$0.37 billion
aka $374 million

Telephone Calls
$1.3 billion

Annual Total
$182 billion

Except for private prison profits, this graph only includes costs of more than $1 billion a year. All figures are based on the most recent available.

Prison Policy Initiative, January 2017   Sources: https://www.prisonpolicy.org/reports/money.html

Source: Prison Policy Initiative, 2017.

The upshot of this massive incarceration industry as a solution for society's ills — most of which revolve around drug and alcohol addiction — is a massive bill which extends far beyond actual incarceration.

The chart on the left shows how much money is spent throughout the "jail industry".

It's a very hard juggernaut to stop as there are so many entrenched interests. The corrections business itself — jails, prisons, and transportation — is $81 billion.

The judicial processing is $29 billion.

Criminal policing is $63 billion.

The health care bill for these two million prisoners is $12 billion.

The other costs are construction, food, utilities, phone, bail, and defense.

Drugs

One of the great insights the authors gained from writing this book together is that we now know that the serious problems with drug addiction and alcoholism in our families are a feature — not a bug — of the American landscape. Much of Austin's story is a classic American morality tale. His Father had a long illness aggravated by alcoholism. His family was left with expensive health care bills. He was left fatherless at 11 and had no responsible adult male guidance. No wonder he — and many others of his generation — feel into alcoholism and addiction. Luckily — and with a lot of hard work, luck, guidance, and a spiritual life — he escaped that fate.

Unfortunately, the following chart shows that the deaths per 100,000 for adult males due to addiction to OxyContin have tripled. The same trend is true for females, even though they started from a lower level. The numbers are still not leveling off in 2019. Furthermore, the prevalence of injection of heroin is causing pockets in alarmingly high HIV infections. The result has been a drop in the life expectancy of Americans for the fourth year in a row. This is the first time we have seen a drop in life expectancy in 100 years. The bottom line is that there are more than 60,000 opioid-related deaths each year. *This is one opioid-related death every 10 minutes.*

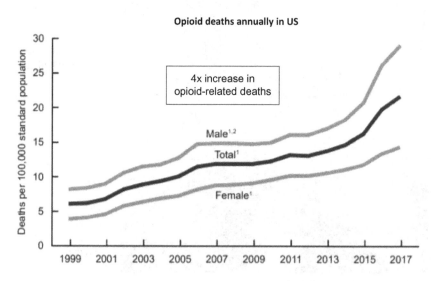

Source: Centers for Disease Prevention and Control (CDC), 2019, https://www.cdc.gov/nchs/data/databriefs/db329-h.pdf.

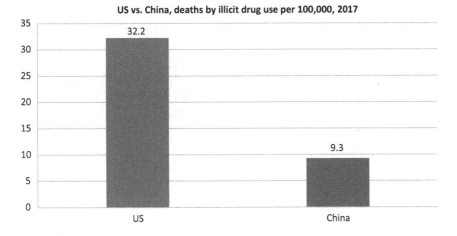

US vs. China, deaths by illicit drug use per 100,000, 2017

Source: Our world in data, https://ourworldindata.org/drug-use.

The above chart shows the big difference between China and the US in this regard. China has very strict drug laws which makes it very difficult to acquire drugs. The result of these strict laws is that hard drugs are very difficult to get hold of. Consequently, the rate of death by way of opiates in China is 72% lower. It is one of the lower rates globally. However, there are new data points emerging in China of Oxycontin dependence. In fact, starting in 2018, more than half of opioid painkillers were sold outside of the US. The euphemism is "medical drug abuse". Mundipharma is a Chinese pharma company owned by the vilified Sackler family and sales-people visited hospitals to sell the drug for pain relief. There is a wide scale criminal investigation of this episode, but the cat seems to be out of the bag.

The severity of penalties for dealing drugs finds it roots in China's own tragic national addiction to opium in the 1800s. At that time, British merchants were trading tea from India for opium from Afghanistan. Much of this was done through Hong Kong. From 1820 to 1880, the amount of opium exported to China via British ships increased nine-fold to 7000 metric tons. Opium dens were everywhere and the tax on opium was a major source of revenue. China never again wishes to repeat this sad chapter in its colonial history.

In the past 15 years, China has come to dominate trade of manufactured goods.

One of the remarkable feats of China since its entry into the WTO in 1990 is that it became the factory of the world. In 1990, its global footprint in trade was negligible. By 2019, there was nowhere that Chinese goods were not dominant. The following map shows the countries where Chinese trade is larger than that of the US. The reality is that with the exception of Central America, Canada, France, Austria, and Zimbabwe, all other countries in the world have more trade now with China than with the US.

Trade war: China usurps the US as dominant exporter
US or China as larger supplier of goods

Sources: Financial Times, Pictet Asset Allocation and Macro Research; IMF Direction of Trade Statistics, graphics by Liz Faunce.

China in the Technological Lead on Many Fronts, Especially in Applications of Advanced Technology

R&D/Education — Total research and development funding, US vs. China

The Council on Foreign Relations recently released a video which articulates the "Sputnik" moment for the US. There is a sense that the US is

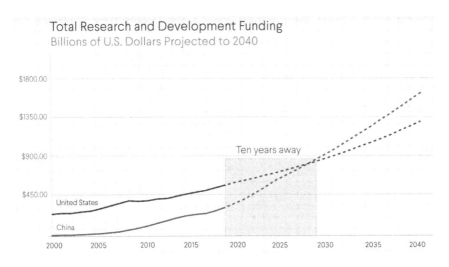

Total Research and Development Funding
Billions of U.S. Dollars Projected to 2040

Source: Council on Foreign Relations, *Keeping Our Edge*.

falling behind in many areas of technology, including 5G, advanced cellular tower technology, quantum communications, digital payments, e-commerce, autonomous cars, and digital currency coins, among other areas. It pointed out in a few poignant charts the justification for the fear. The following chart shows that in the next 3–4 years, China will outpace the US in R&D. There is much commingling between the private and public sector on this R&D, which is a serious sticking point in the trade negotiations. What is remarkable is that China was in somewhat of a standing start in 2005. Back then, there was very little going into R&D. That number exceeded $250 billion recently.

In the area of artificial intelligence, China is also showing great promise. The above chart shows that the market share of top 10% of AI papers which are quoted come from China. China dominance here was shown as it exceeded the US just this year. It is also the case that China had 70% of the world's patents for blockchain in 2017. Some dispute this number, but this is according to the International Patent Registration numbers. Furthermore, the proof is in the pudding, since the progress in blockchain by Alibaba, Tencent, and the PBOC are undeniable. The PBOC is the first central bank globally to launch a ledger-based coin. Tencent already has a blockchain-based system ready to replace its Currency system of payments.

R&D/Education — Market share of top 10% of AI papers, US vs. China

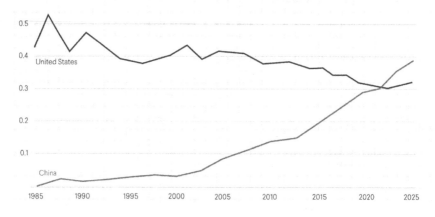

Market Share of Top 10% of Artificial Intelligence Papers

Source: Council on Foreign Relations, *Keeping Our Edge*.

In addition, many mainland Chinese who were studying or teaching in universities in the US are feeling a cold wind blowing through academia and are deciding to return to China to do research. There are very public stories of FBI agents visiting mainland students with student visas and asking about behavior and whereabouts. There are even stories becoming public of FBI agents interrogating Americans who have returned from fellowships at the prestigious Peking University. (Week in China, Americans at top Chinese university worried by FBI probes on return home, Aug 30, 2019 (WiC 464).)

That being said, there is a cold wind blowing inside China as well. As China stiffens its neck in response from what is perceived as an existential attack on its technological nerve center (Huawei), there are calls for corporates and academics to help row the boat faster. Some in academia in China also feel that academic freedoms are being subsumed to national imperatives. As the "state" tries to adjust to an America which has gone from friend to foe in a quick hurry, there are calls for both corporates and universities to do some form of national service and reduce public criticism.

Education trends: High school graduates

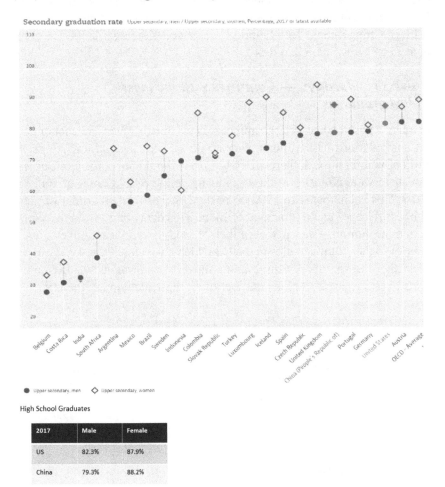

High School Graduates

2017	Male	Female
US	82.3%	87.9%
China	79.3%	88.2%

Source: Secondary Graduation Rate, OECD, 2017, https://data.oecd.org/students/secondary-graduation-rate.htm.

The above chart is a comparison between China and the US. They both rank highly on a global basis. However, China is now seeing high school rates for females exceeding the graduation rates of females in the US. The rate of graduation for boys is roughly similar at about 80%. In a recent OECD study, China ranked 6th behind Japan in math for high-school testing. China was 9th in science. The US did not get into the top 20. In a recent ranking from Program for International Student Assessment (PISA), China ranked 10th behind Canada and Korea while the US came in at 31st below Spain and Russia.

University education — Countries with the most STEM graduates

In many ways, the law of large numbers is in China's favor. The fact of having a population of 1.5 billion means if you are "one in a million", there are 1500 of you. In the US, there are only 370. It should not come as a surprise that there were almost 5 million graduates in the STEM areas of study in 2016. This is compared to 570,000 in the US. This is a 10x order of magnitude difference and double that of India. This data comes from the World Economic Forum. Even if the caliber of study in Chinese universities is inferior to that of universities in the US which have globally revered reputations, the sheer number of those in top universities inside China (assume it is 10%) still exceeds the total number of all those studying in the US.

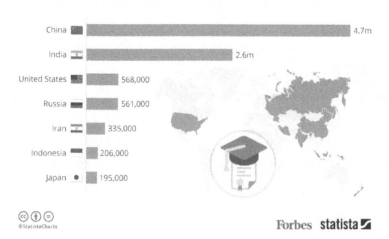

The Countries With The Most STEM Graduates
Recent graduates in Science, Technology, Engineering & Mathematics (2016)

China	4.7m
India	2.6m
United States	568,000
Russia	561,000
Iran	335,000
Indonesia	206,000
Japan	195,000

Forbes statista

Source: World Economic Forum, StatistaCharts, *Forbes*.

R&D/Education — Number of universities in US vs. China, 2019

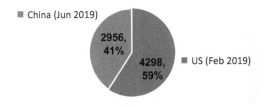

Sources: US Department of Education, https://www.usnews.com/education/best-colleges/articles/2019-02-15/how-many-universities-are-in-the-us-and-why-that-number-is-changing; Chinese Higher Education Preparatory website, https://www.dxsbb.com/news/38640.html.

China has pumped a great deal of money into its university system and now boasts almost 3,000 universities and over 20 million students enrolled. There are 14.6 million in the US. In fact, Xi'An in central China is the old imperial capital and one of the largest university towns in the world. It has in excess of 350,000 college and graduate students in more than 25 universities. So, China's universities by size and number are almost on a par with the US. There are almost as many universities in China as there are in the US.

US college grads owe more student debt than ever, and college costs are at all-time highs

College graduates owe $29,000 in student debt now — more than ever before

PUBLISHED THU, SEP 19 2019 2:06 PM EDT UPDATED THU, SEP 19 2019 3:34 PM EDT

Annie Nova @ANNIEREPORTER   Nate Rattner

KEY POINTS	The graduating class of 2018 owed $29,200 in student loans, up from $28,650 in 2017, according to The Institute for College Access & Success.
	Some states are harder hit than others by student debt. College graduates in Connecticut are $38,650 in the red, for example, compared with $19,750 in Utah.
	More students are relying on private loans to fund their education.

Source: Annie Nova and Nate Rattner, 2019.

R&D/Education — Student tuition fees (USD), US vs. China

Source: Mastersportal.

The above charts show one of the real burdens for millennials and the headline shows the problem. The debt levels for millennials finishing college stands at about $29,000. The monthly interest payments are, on average, $600–800 per month. So, by the time they start looking for work, they need to cover annual interest payments on student debt of about $8,500. In pretax terms, this is about $10,000 in revenue. This is about 20% of the average income of a college grad. If you assume that 35% of their income is spent in rent (in many metropolitan, it is more like 50%), this means that, on an after tax basis, they have $400 per week to spend on food, clothes, travel, and entertainment.

By contrast, Chinese universities are subsidized and cost a fraction of the price of a US university. There are exceptions and this varies. Peking University, considered among the best in China, is $17,000 per year. Tsinghua University, also considered among the best in China, is $7,500. Fudan University in Shanghai is $8,000. The MBA at Zhejiang University, considered one of the top tier universities in the country, is $5,000 per year. This is a small fraction of the price of an MBA in the US.

The following chart shows the real problem with US millennial debt. The main generator of degrees in the US is debt-funded higher education. This has gone from $580 billion on the eve of the GFC in 2007 to $1.4 trillion in 2018. This is a 135% increase in 12 years and has been a cause of highly inflated university fees as well as a boon to college towns like NYC, LA, Chicago, Boston, DC, Dallas, and San Francisco. (These 10 cities alone have almost 4 million students propping up the local economies with this debt load.) The result is that average outstanding debt since 2000 for a graduating student has gone from $14,000 to $29,000 today, as can be seen from above. If there is a recession in 2020 or 2021, there must be some sort of wide scale debt forgiveness program for college grads. Watch this space.

The price of education

Student debt has climbed nearly 85% in the past eight years, to $1.4 trillion, as college costs have soared. The federal government holds more than 90% of outstanding loans, according to industry data

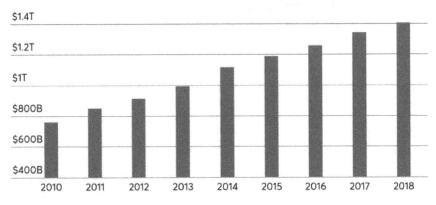

● Total student debt*

Source: Federal Reserve Bank of New York, 2019 (June 30 data).

Workshop 2: The Growing Mountain of Global Debt Concerns Millennials and Boomers Alike

Issue: Is the underlying cause of concern everywhere the overall levels of debt in both the US and China?

1. The evidence of a serious debt problem in China can be seen from the following chart. The first shows the overall level of debt in China. It shows the level of debt in China has reached an all-time high of 270% of GDP. The biggest growth has come from provincial governments and SOEs. These two sectors are now 140% of GDP. The plan here is to recapitalize the banks and clean out the bad debt. Then, there is a need

(Continued)

(Continued)

to transform many of these disparate companies into consolidated trusts (with consolidated debt) to create pricing power and economies of scale. (This was what the US did at the turn of the 20th century by creating companies like GE, American Tobacco, General Mills, etc.) Then the long-term debt is transformed into long-term paper and sold to insurance and pension companies — exactly what the US did in the early 1900s. That's the plan, anyways. It is sound. You extend maturities of debt, form credible ratings agencies, create inflation, and grow your way out of your problem. China has built out the country while avoiding wars and has no Medicare or social security liabilities which saddle the US.

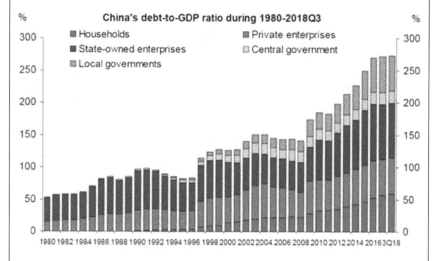

Source: Torsten Slok, Deutsche Bank Research, 2019.

2. The problem with the US is more complicated. See the following chart. In addition to the $1.4 trillion in student debt noted above, the US has added $6 trillion in federal debt since 2012. This debt is with central banks all over who buy this debt as they accumulate dollars from trade. In addition, the Federal Reserve holds a lot as do private banks. But there is a limit. There is something known as the Triffin Dilemma. The US as the reserve currency of the world — with the most open current account globally and the largest trading country globally — can theoretically print as much debt as it wants since. Until it can't. Triffin never said when this

(Continued)

dilemma kicks in. The only precedent we have is the UK. In 1900, the UK Pound was 70% of the world's reserves and the UK ruled supreme. Due to endless wars protecting what was, in retrospect, an inevitable loss of empire, it went broke from all these military adventures — arguably after WWI in 1919. It was forced to get a bailout from the IMF (ahem, the US) in the mid-1950s. It took a very long time for the British Triffin Dilemma to kick in (about 35 years), but it lost its reserve currency status and experienced a long period of stagnation into the 1980s.

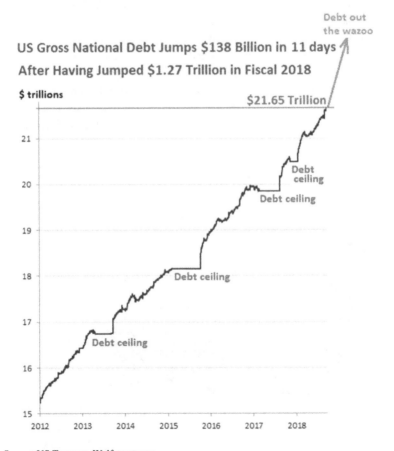

US Gross National Debt Jumps $138 Billion in 11 days After Having Jumped $1.27 Trillion in Fiscal 2018

Source: US Treasury, Wolfstreet.com.

(Continued)

(Continued)

3. The net result of the accumulation of debt in the US is arguably far more problematic than China. The total credit market debt/GDP is 381% of GDP (China's total credit/GDP is 270%). See the following chart. This absolute number is a whopping $55 Trillion vs. $24 Trillion for China. This does not include Social Security and Medicare liabilities due in the future, estimated to be $50 Trillion (for Social Security alone) as of 2017 for the next 50 years. (This is according to the 2018 Annual Report of the Federal Disability Insurance Trust Funds.) The middle line in the following chart shows the increase in debt ($54 trillion) relative to the bottom line (GDP of $15 trillion). So, the level of debt relative to the GDP to fund that debt is 4 times larger. The US is producing $1 of output for every $4 dollars of debt, not including federal obligations for retirement and medical care for an aging population ($50 trillion). One way to deal with all this debt is inflation. The other is default. So, inflation it is. Aging populations HATE inflation and will vote out politicians who allow inflation. So, the solution is to continue to federal-ize the debt, keep rates at zero, generate low growth, and say a prayer. Look at Japan!

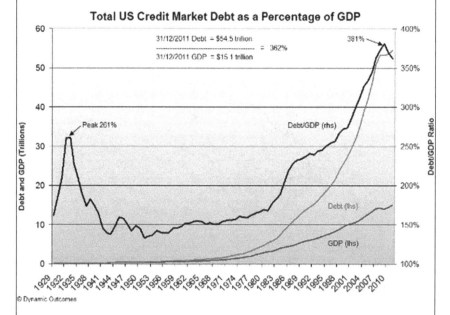

Total US Credit Market Debt as a Percentage of GDP

Source: Federal Reserve, Bureau of Economic Analysis, Census Bureau, Historical Statistics.

(*Continued*)

Discussion: Should we be that concerned about this mountain of debt? How has Japan been able to get its government debt to 200% of GDP? The federal debt to GDP of the US is about 95%. If this happens, growth must be kept low and inflation must be kept low. This is ideal for old people who own government debt since its value keeps going up. This is poison for millennials who want to borrow and need wage inflation. This will be a political hot potato. The alternative — a default — would bring a global depression. This must be worked out between millennials and boomers and is really the ultimate political problem in the future.

Evolution of E-commerce — Cellular Payments vs. Checks

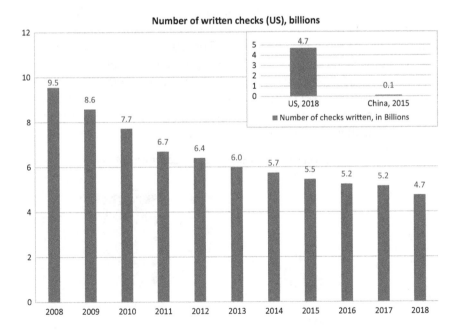

Source: Federal Reserve, https://www.federalreserve.gov/paymentsystems/check_commcheckcolannual. htm, SCMP.

Evolution of e-commerce — Retail e-commerce sales in 2020

One of the main reasons for the strategic panic attack that the US has had with regard to China is the reality that the PRC is far ahead in technology involving payments and e-commerce. This is true not just inside China but in most countries throughout the Silk Road, including SE Asia, South Asia, Central Asia, and Northeast Asia. Basically, Alibaba and Tencent cover more than 1.5 billion people across the Far East in just about any financial transaction they need. Meanwhile, the above chart shows The Central dependence that the US has on checks. While the number of checks written has been cut in half, the amount is still almost 5 billion per year. This is in stark contrast to China, where both cash and check have largely disappeared in favor of cellular or electronic transactions. The number of checks for the most recent year is about 100 million. This is 98% smaller than the US. While there are very sophisticated areas of the financial sector in the US, there are also very primitive areas which need a rapid overhaul. The writing of checks is one of them.

The point is made even harder by the following chart. China's estimated retail e-commerce sales will surpass $2.4 trillion in 2020 while the US should exceed $670 billion. In 2020, China's retail e-commerce sales will be four times larger than the US. The main reasons for this are, we think, regulatory in nature. After the GFC, there was great fear of regulators who were on the war path giving banks a total of $360 billion in fines. So, technology companies were not interested in playing in that area. When Trump came to power, the leash was put on the regulatory apparatus and tech companies waded into the deep end.

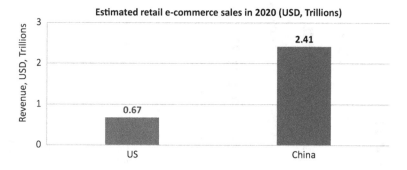

Estimated retail e-commerce sales in 2020 (USD, Trillions)

Source: eMarketer.

In addition, there was an awakening about how far ahead China was in all of the payments and e-commerce space. As a matter of national security, we believe the entire political apparatus in DC united and began a public discussion about how not to lose out on the Silk Road in this area. So, Amazon spent $5 billion in India. Facebook Libra was launched. Google and Apple accelerated their investments in this area. It is likely that The Best Bet (though a long shot) is that Facebook Libra will launch globally, despite loud objections from Congress.

Huawei: Dominating 5G

5G is vitally important because it allows (1) faster transmission of larger data streams; (2) better transmission of data in problematic conditions; (3) can support a wider array of sensors, wearables, and other devices. This will have powerful effects on many industries and will be a whole new level of disruption. Industries most affected are: Retail, Entertainment, Autos, Healthcare, and Manufacturing. What is driving all this? The four main technologies are: fiber optic cable, small cell deployment, and indoor fixed wireless technology. The fifth is important: high frequency spectrum. The higher the frequency, the faster the data. Impediments like Rainfall or trees can interrupt this. Also, satellites require line of sight to prevent disruption. 5G gets around many of these issues.

The charts in Sections 5.1 and 5.2 show the phenomenon that is Huawei. It has emerged as the predominant global player in 5G at a time when the US does not have a single major player in this area. Its total revenues have exceeded US$100 billion. It operates in more than 100 countries. It is the dominant player in Africa and Asia, and it has overtaken Apple in global market share. ATT and Verizon are trying to get up to speed but are at least 1–2 years behind Huawei.

Huawei's revenue have now surpassed Boeing and they are expected to be $120 billion in 2020. It now has 5G up and running inside China and five other countries. It should have its own 5G operating in 30 countries by the end of 2020. These countries are found along the Silk Road, Southeast Asia, and the Middle East.

Huawei has made great strides in cell phones in terms of variety, price, geography, and market share. It has a global market share of 31% in handsets, larger than either Ericsson or Nokia. On top of this, it has an **80% market share in 5G transmission towers**. In the smartphone area, its units shipped were 52 million at the end of 2018, passing up Apple's 46 million units. It is also a global leader in the cloud market.

So, the charts in Sections 5.1 and 5.2 show that Huawei is a serious threat to the global telecommunications network that, for decades, has been dominated by the US. Many people in the Pentagon and the government think that the potential loss of control over telecommunications is a serious national security threat. It is not surprising, then, that there is an effort to constrain Huawei's ambitions through an aggressive full court press with NATO allies. When the US put pressure on Germany's parliament to ban Huawei from Germany, the Chinese government countered with a threat to reduce access for German cars to the Chinese cars. If the US could make false "safety" claims about Huawei, why couldn't China make false "safety" claims about German cars in China? The conflict will continue for a long time.

Huawei revenue history

Source: Statista, https://www.statista.com/topics/2305/huawei/.

Huawei market share vs. competitors: Huawei passed up Apple in smartphones

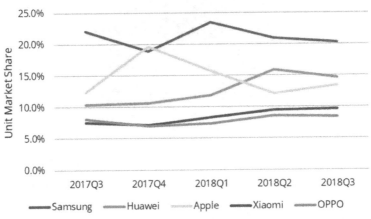

Worldwide Top 5 Smartphone Companies, 2018Q3 Unit Market Share

14.6% of market share – 52 million handsets shipped

Sources: IDC & Forbes. Available at https://www.forbes.com/sites/jeanbaptiste/2018/11/02/huawei-fortifies-2-spot-in-global-smartphone-market-beating-apple-again/#10b6cf3b1305.

Huawei infrastructure market share

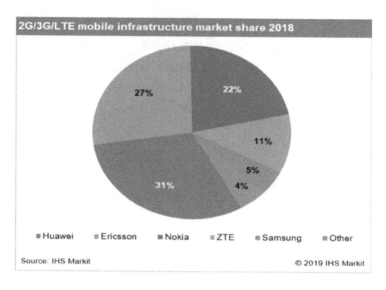

Source: Techblog, https://techblog.comsoc.org/category/global-mobile-infrastructure-market/.

Huawei market share vs. competitors

Company	3Q18 Shipment Volumes	3Q18 Market Share	3Q17 Shipment Volumes	3Q17 Market Share	3Q18/3Q17 Change
Samsung	72.2	20.3%	83.3	22.1%	-13.4%
Huawei	52.0	14.6%	39.1	10.4%	32.9%
Apple	46.9	13.2%	46.7	12.4%	0.5%
Xiaomi	34.3	9.7%	28.3	7.5%	21.2%
OPPO	29.9	8.4%	30.6	8.1%	-2.1%
Others	119.9	33.8%	149.8	39.6%	-19.9%
Total	355.2	100.0%	377.8	100.0%	-6.0%

Top 5 Smartphone Companies, Worldwide Shipments, Market Share, and Year-Over-Year Growth, Q2 2018 (shipments in millions of units)

Source: IDC Quarterly Mobile Phone Tracker, November 1, 2018

Source: IDC & *Forbes*, https://www.forbes.com/sites/jeanbaptiste/2018/11/02/huawei-fortifies-2-spot-in-global-smartphone-market-beating-apple-again/#10b6cf3b1305.

US vs. China in Home Ownership

For a country that Brand's itself as socialist, China weirdly has a very high private home ownership rate. In fact, it is one of the highest globally. Home ownership in China is running at 85%. Furthermore, only 11% of properties in China have a mortgage. In the US, home ownership slipped a few points from 68% to 66% due to the GFC. More people decided — or were forced — to rent instead. In addition, 30% of homes are paid off while 70% still have a mortgage. So, this explains better the very high savings rate of 50% in China vs. only 6–8% in the US.

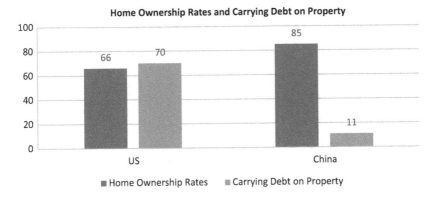

Source: World Bank, IMF, 2019.

Part II

A Millennial's Journey from Obedient Soldier to Disillusioned Renegade to Shanghai Entrepreneur

This part of the book is a personal story of the struggles of Austin, the millennial who has made his way in the world with inter-generational adults and boomers. It is a story of miscommunication on both parts and he admits that it is as instructive about what to do as what not to do. It is a story of a vast learning curve about how to tell IoT projects and other capital-intensive technology infrastructure to people with no experience in these technologies. It is a story about endless PowerPoint, frequent blow-ups, frightened older people who do not wish to (or can't) learn in the midst of massive technological upheaval. It is a story of not falling into drugs and alcohol, despite being surrounded by a culture of drugs and alcohol growing up.

It is about how millennials can upwardly manage older people and not let them fall into a trap of fear-based paralysis. It is a morality tale of being humble and remaining teachable. It is tales of being scrappy by taking advantage of every ridiculous or mean-spirited broadside attack by older managers and not taking them personally but instead turning them to one's own advantage. It is about coping with widespread alcoholism among adults in the family unit. Most of all, it is an educational journey about how internet of things is being applied in China in spectacular ways that are not even being imagined in the US. It is a wake up call for the US to get with the program or countries like China (and many others in emerging markets) will eat America's lunch. It is a call to change and not to play a racist blame game.

Because of this, most parts of this book will be told in the first person singular through Austin's own eyes and in his own voice. It is about how a millennial sees revered companies like Accenture, Verizon, Coca-Cola (Coke), and AT&T.

Chapter 3

While America was Fighting Wars, Chinese Tiger Moms were Drilling Their Millennials

Most retired people in China today grew up under the rule of Chairman Mao, who many still worship. Needless to say, while Mao unified the country after decades of civil war, this was a time of great despair and chaos in China. These people were dragged through the famine caused by the Great Leap Forward in the 1950s and the economic chaos (and lost educational opportunities) of the Cultural Revolution in the 1960s. Prior to this, China had spent the previous century being invaded, occupied, force-fed opium, and doing whatever necessary to try to be left alone. At one point in the early 20th century, China had 22 different sovereign court systems operating within its borders! These people have come from a history of invasion and very hard times. They are tough, gritty, and resilient. There is a saying about them: They learned to eat dirt!

The period from 1990 to present — a mere 30 years — was the first time in centuries China has had real political stability and could take a coherent and unified approach to growth, development, aid, farming, technology, and infrastructure. Importantly, it could do this from scratch — with no legacy copper wiring, entrenched lobbyists, and a maze of federal and local regulations and decades of corporate corruption. Arguably, it was the first time in 200 years for the country to really organize itself as a modern nation state. These people who survived the Cultural Revolution were in the driver's seat as the economy opened up, reformed, and innovated.

These now retired people — the Cultural Revolution generation — all had children who grew up and came into the workforce during the most incredible economic expansion the world has ever seen. Over 500 million people (almost 10% of the world's population) were lifted out of extreme poverty starting in the 1980s. In that time, Shanghai turned from a small fishing village to one of the largest cities in the world with an economy the size of Switzerland. Each year of their lives have been noticeably better than the previous year, and that has carried on ever since. This has created great confidence — nothing succeeds like success.

Where did this success in China come from as many Americans were in the splendid isolation of suburbia? Meanwhile, Tiger Mom *and* Tiger Grandma were growling away.

Discussion about the race between the US and China is, at its core, all about motivating, encouraging, and supporting young talent. A country is about creating the capacity for resilience among the young. At this moment in time, it appears that China — for now — is doing a better job of this than the US. The main reason is something we see in newspapers all over the US: a rampant problem with alcohol and drug addiction in America.

For Austin, living with a family in suburban Shanghai in 2013 was enlightening. The secret sauce of the millennial dynamos is simple. This generation has a Tiger Mom *and* a Tiger Grandma. These millennials are not spoiled. Quite the opposite. They are pushed in all directions to succeed and are often supported by two generations of mentors. What is the main aim when raising a child?

Throughout Chinese history, the path to upward mobility was within the government as mandarin was a "state-language", i.e. the savvy and cunning bureaucrat. The influence of Confucius caused many to believe that education held importance over all else. In order to gain access to this elite group and advance within the government, you had to take written tests (kaoshi). Unlike other countries who transitioned to market economies — and where you moved up through acquiring wealth in business — China did not make this market economy transition until very recently. Therefore, education and test scores have culturally remained the number one path to upward mobility.

These Baby Boomers who grew up under Chairman Mao's rule continued this tradition with a very strict focus on education for their children, especially engineering. While their children in the 70s and 80s were being lifted out of poverty and getting jobs at banks, etc., these grandparents then moved in with their children to help raise their one grandchild (due to one-child policy). They moved in because there was an insufficient social safety net for retirees. They needed to be supported by their children.

So, in the 1990s and 2000s, you have millions of families with three generations (grandparents, parents, and single child) all under one roof. The education in China is improving drastically and grandma and grandpa need to help raise the kid because mom and dad are always working. Guess what grandma and grandpa make the kid do??? STUDY!

Imagine growing up a single child with four grown people watching your every move, depending on you to support them when they are older. There is no safety net, Social Security, or even Roth IRA system in China. The unusual level of intellectual and emotional "care and feeding" of young people by two sets of adults may make for spoiled children. Then again, it could also make for young adults (who are constantly being pushed) with a solid center and powerful intellectual ability!

Workshop 1: Tiger Moms and the After Effects: Do They Create Star Performers or Neurotic Messes?

Issue: Tiger moms are everywhere. Should we just get over it? This can be a great icebreaker between millennials and inter-generational adults.

1. There's an old joke about tiger moms. The Jewish Tiger mom says to her son, "Eat your vegetables or I will kill you!" The Irish tiger mom says, "Eat your vegetables or I will kill myself!". Some children are dandelions who do well no matter what. Some are orchids who will wilt under severe pressure but bloom spectacularly with the right kind of detailed care, guidance, and love. Does an overstressed or abusive childhood — in Israel, Ireland or China — cause winners to emerge? Does the growling tiger mom quash these orchids and make them neurotic messes? Doesn't intense attention to achieve demonstrate its own type of love? Do we need more or fewer helicopter moms?

2. The Tiger mom is seen as against the liberal "anything goes" Kitty Mom. This is the mother who spares the rod and spoils the child. Little is achieved by screaming at children, they say. Forcing children to do what they hate (violin lessons at 7 years of age) will prevent them from naturally coming to love music. Is there a corresponding need for a "liberal" father who can offer some compassion and unconditional love? Does father's warmth compensate? Does a high value relationship outside the home (a teacher or mentor) offer a way out?

3. Does a strict and loving parent show love by imposing some sort of order? How can sons or daughters overcome the tiger's claw marks? Is a core connection of love enough even if it is surrounded by stern discipline? Isn't it a mix of love and discipline that matters? Some synthesis

---

(Continued)

of tiger and kitty? (Paul had an Irish Tiger Mom (Army veteran and teacher) and a (real) drill sergeant dad who was also in the Army.) Finding mentors outside the home is a way to cope, and reinterpreting the past — recreating memories — is important too.

Discussion: Everyone has a story about their tiger mom or a tiger dad. Do growling tigers turn sensitive children into orchids or messes? How can we change our interpretation of the past? Can we just take the good out of the past and change ourselves without blaming and being a victim? We all get better by talking about these issues. Group therapy is golden.

Chinese Millennials: Natural Dependence on the Group for Support
It's Not Communism — It's Confucianism

This book paints a somewhat benign portrait of Chinese millennials. They are in a different and early part of the evolution of nations (the take off stage which was probably similar to the Gilded Age in the US from 1890 to 1920) so they probably are better off than millennials in the United States. This is because as a society that has no legacy infrastructure and entrenched interests, there is great room for young people to invent, innovate, and create new products. There are some drawbacks as well.

The vast majority of the millennials Austin hired allowed him to have very positive experiences. He worked with incredible teams. People came to the office largely with a joyful, enthusiastic attitude. They cared for each other. They were generally interested in group success. However, it's not all rainbows and butterflies.

Growing up with the pressure of being the sole provider for your elders creates a great amount of anxiety. In addition to that, the one-child-policy created individuals smothered by parents and often two sets of grandparents with a strong emphasis on thing: studying. This can create one definite outcome: pressure. On the positive side, drugs are not at all in the picture. There are no guns. Crime is not even an issue in most cities. There are no wandering veterans as there are no foreign wars. Public transportation is ultra-modern. Infrastructure is truly 21st century.

But, these millennials did lack things like play dates and team sports. At times, people wonder if some Chinese millennials struggle to work together in team settings. To escape reality, many use the only resource they had while going from school to tutoring and then to their room at night to "do homework" — their cell phone. The teams were incredible but there is a great pastime of too many: playing video games.

However, in his years of dealing with Chinese, Austin noticed few negatives compared to the huge amount of positives. He hired 20 highly skilled e-commerce personnel in a matter of weeks at an all-in cost of under 300,000 RMB (US$43,000) a month, and they are incredibly grateful. Imagine trying to hire a team in Silicon Valley for that amount? By the time you factored in healthcare, salary, vacation time and bonuses, you could hire four or five Chinese millennials for that amount.

In the interview process for the company in Shanghai, Austin would give the candidates grueling job-related questions that they hadn't heard before to test their problem-solving skills under pressure. What he really wanted to see was how they could be different from the "standard practices" of the industry and find ways to bypass the typical roadblocks Chinese e-commerce companies put in place.

What Austin found was that one out of three candidates interviewed did this exceptionally well. He ended up putting together a great team. These were over 20 people from almost every different part of China, went to average Chinese universities in one of the larger Chinese cities. Most of their parents were farmers or owned small businesses but certainly knew nothing about technology or e-commerce. "But these 20 people knew more about direct marketing, customer service, and big data than the people I knew at Accenture making $200,000 a year."

In addition to the superior technical and functional knowledge of the industry within the team, they also worked very well together. Sometimes Austin would come across westerners who were under the impression that Chinese workers don't perform as well in team situations due to growing up without brothers and sisters and most of their early social interactions being with their grandparents. He can personally attest that his experience was the exact opposite. In fact, his team chemistry was the #1 contributing factor to their success.

The difference with his team was that everyone was willing to pitch in to help others as the company grew. There was a general level of compassion the teammates had for each other that is generally absent from many places in the world today. Every day, someone would bring in some kind of dessert or fruit for the whole team. The thing even Austin couldn't understand is they would make sure everyone on the team ate some before they even tried it. Many times, the team would eat their entire snack and the person who brought the food didn't seem to care. Taking care of their teammates was more important.

When they were very busy on Single's Day (November 11) and were bombarded with customer inquiries, Barbara, who was responsible for logistics, would without hesitation jump in and start responding to customer service inquiries to help out their customer service team. The woman responsible for customer service named Xiami would often stay up to midnight to answer customer questions to make sure a five-star rating is maintained on TMall.

One day, Austin stayed home sick and heard a knock on his door at 12 pm. Half of the team had used their lunch break to bring him hot soup and some Chinese medicine to feel better. It wasn't just because he was the boss either. They did the same for any of their teammates who were sick or had any kind of family or personal problem. These were flat out some of the most compassionate people he had ever met, and it was a pure joy to work with them every day. This in addition to superior technical capabilities were why they were able to succeed in by far the most competitive e-commerce environment on the planet.

Alcoholism and the Role It Plays in the American Family in the 21st Century

In contrast to the experience of many current Chinese millennials, too many American millennials grow up with families dealing with drug addiction and alcoholism, broken homes, and single parents. Austin recalls that, among his close friends in upstate New York, he can't really name one close friend he grew up with who wasn't directly impacted by alcoholism and addiction. Many of them were on the honor roll, or had a great talent early on for math, science, music, etc. At some point between 13 and 17, many lost their way and headed to the "normal" route, which is, in many cases, living paycheck to paycheck and dealing with alcoholism or drug addiction in the family unit.

The graduation rate at Austin's high school last year was 65%. He also notes that he never knew a Chinese person under 35 who hadn't graduated high school. In 16 states in the US, one in five people does not finish high school. Part of life in Austin's world of millennials is the reality that the one main cause of this failure to even finish high school is drug addiction and alcoholism in the context of broken families. How he escaped from it is nothing short of a miracle. He makes the case that this is not a bug but a feature of so many metropolitan areas in the so-called "Rust Belt" and the Appalachian region of the US.

Too many Americans came from a situation akin to that of the dreadful familial conditions of, J.D. Vance, the main character in the bestselling book *Hillbilly Elegy*. Austin's father died of cancer when he was 11 in which alcoholism played a definite role. He was raised by a single mother who somehow managed to raise two boys while starting her own business. Data across the US is starting to show that there is an argument to be made that this issue of alcoholism and drug addiction is a feature — and not a bug — of American life. It may be the case that this is the root of the difficult times we see for millennials in modern American society.

Is this a sign of American decline or a grassroots transition to a grittier, tougher population? You decide. Is this the world of a grittier, meaner generation looking for scapegoats? Is this transition from a high level of alcoholism and drug addiction to a more self-reliant and "pick yourself up by the bootstraps" nationalism a trend from which a stronger nation will arise? Will China lose momentum as the US is trying to orchestrate a nationalist recovery? Will China just wait around for the US to "rise again"? These are the questions we want to answer in this book. First, however, we want to try to get to the roots of much of the malaise of the United States.

Austin wanted to pretend everything was normal growing up. Far from it. At age 47, Austin's father had slipped into a coma and died from cancer when Austin was only 11. Treatment was expensive, and Austin's mom had a hard time making ends meet during his father's multi-year battle going in and out of different hospitals. Most of his family told him there was no defined reason for his death, until one day when he was 16. He was having a beer with his grandfather who told Austin the doctors told his grandfather that alcoholism had caused his father's disease to turn fatal at the end.

One of the earliest memories he had of his father was when he was 8 years old. He was on the way home from baseball practice and his father told him that he was going to die. For an 8-year-old, this wasn't exactly the thing you wanted to hear. His father had been sick most of his life and this gave him a different perspective than most. It also caused him to be very hard on Austin. When Austin was getting yelled at, he never took it as cruel and it did teach him independence at a young age. Unlike the way he saw Chinese people learning to fit into a group and put primacy on group decisions, his upbringing in New York was quite the opposite. The emphasis was on independence and self-reliance.

Workshop 2: The Undiagnosed Anxiety of the Millennials

Issue: Millennials as children of terror. Is this 9/11 generation tougher than we all think or has a string of unprecedented historical events created often debilitating anxiety for millennials?

1. Those born between 1980 and 2,000 grew up with the memory of the Twin Towers collapsing and 3,000 people dying. They have seen horrific terrorist incidents on TV in New York, London, Brussels, Paris, and many other cities. Furthermore, American millennials say that the problem of gun violence at schools is far worse and more traumatic for them. This creates a grittiness to the way they see life. It creates a complex bifurcation of mental toughness on the one hand yet remarkable cultural openness on the other. We forget the anxiety and stress caused by so many millennials who have heard about or seen shootings in 230 schools (yes! 420) since the Columbine mass shooting in 1999, the same year the first millennials turned 18.

2. Millennials have had greater access to education globally than at any time in history. They grew up in the height of Pax Americana, the collapse of Soviet communism, and a booming stock market. 9/11 and the GFC in 2008 brought all of this to a halt. While they were reeling from student debt and high unemployment, the creation of the iPhone and relentless social media comparisons caused great anxiety from constant comparisons to everyone else's best moments. The result is anxiety on the job front, huge financial obligation right after college, and then constant comparisons of those with more resources, fun, glamour, and travel opportunities.

3. The result is a large group of millennials which is anxious and unhappy. In addition, they are stuck with massive debt which averages $600–800 per month in payments. They are likely to come from a broken family.

(Continued)

(Continued)

They are very likely to know a parent or close relative with problems with addiction, and they are likely to know someone who is a returning veteran from Middle East wars with emotional difficulties. Their anxiety is high even as many of them have had the workplace advantage tipped in their favor since their life skills and knowledge of data science, entrepreneurialism, social media, and electronic interaction come more naturally. Older people are floundering in many of these skill sets (and should be far more anxious) yet millennials have shown far more manifestations of this anxiety. Study after study shows this to be the case. The numbers are in the high 20s or low 30s in terms of the percent whose work is disrupted "often" or "all the time" due to anxiety.

Discussion: This generation is, in general, much tougher than before. But the difficulties many have are often seen as being "flakey" when they are really symptomatic not of fear or irresponsibility but of anxiety. Hypercompetition for shrinking professional positions while social media creates impossible expectations on lifestyle is a wicked cocktail for an anxious generation. What is being done in the workforce to deal with widespread and often debilitating anxiety? This problem with anxiety is called an epidemic and can be a source of lost productivity. Programs in the office to deal with anxiety are very likely to result in rising productivity. These include access to individual therapy counseling, group therapy, insurance plans which cover psychological or psychiatric issues, public discussion on these issues, and institutional structures to deal with psychological issues. It's about time that the elephant in the living room is dealt with. (See the Ted Talk by Nadine Burke Harris, California's Surgeon General, on childhood trauma, and adult anxiety.)

The fact that his dad was dying of cancer caused him to emphasize self-reliance to Austin. He lived with a high degree of independence, perhaps too high. He knew there were at least two occasions where Child Services was notified by either his teachers or neighbors to complain about being Austin's absence from school or "hanging around town" unsupervised which was his father's way of preparing Austin for the inevitable. His adolescence was more Huckleberry Finn and less John Boy Walton.

His father had not finished college and worked part-time selling real estate, but mostly he spent time teaching Austin what he could do before his passing. After his dad died, there were 10 very bad years of despair for Austin. His family had no money due to the drag caused by health care costs and his mother was starting a new law practice. On the day of his dad's funeral, his grandfather said, "You're the man of the house now". He was 11. This is a scary thing without any real parental supervision. He was in a single parent home struggling to make ends meet and a mother trying to start a business while still managing to raise two boys the best she could.

To add to this, he had undiagnosed Attention Deficit Disorder (ADD) and had to read things 2–3 times to actually comprehend. From an early age, his brain was always going very fast — too fast. His mind was spinning fast and as school got harder and his depression got worse, he turned to the "wrong crowd" and drank heavily. His life slowly turned into a black hole, rarely showing up for school. He stopped caring to even call his mom. Most of the people around him, by that point, written off his chances of succeeding at anything. He was sent to several institutions for troubled youth.

Is it any wonder he developed a feeling that nobody believed in him and that everyone would be happy if he just avoided prison. Where did this come from? How does this slippery slope get going? Why are so many Americans in the grip of this terrible circumstance? Austin's experience was that once he was in "the system" as a troubled youth, the bar immediately got set very low. The institutions never encouraged anyone to go above and beyond. They never encouraged growth or challenged the imagination. It was a question of avoiding jail — not going toward something better.

In a country where the penal system is often the answer to drug addiction, is it any wonder that the suicide rate in the US has skyrocketed. Drug addicts with a disease (accepted as a disease of addiction by the American Psychological Association (APA) for more than 50 years) are removed from society and receive a permanent blemish on their record. They can't vote. They can't get good work. They often can't get into good relationships, and they are alienated from family. The result is an epidemic of suicide as seen in the following chart.

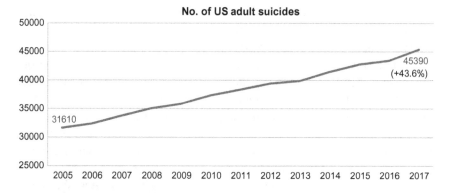

No. of US adult suicides

Source: US Department of Veteran Affairs, 2019, https://www.mentalhealth.va.gov/suicide_prevention/data.asp.

Breaking the Cycle of Decline and Addiction: Self-reliance is Ironically a Detriment

Austin had never felt so alone, but he needed to prove that he could make something of himself. His high school was a toxic environment characterized by apathy for anyone who was not a high achiever. Most of the teachers are stuck teaching an outdated curriculum offering no real-life skills. Hundreds of kids in the high school had parents in active addiction or working so much they weren't able to really pay attention to them. So, they cried out for help in all different kinds of ways. There are great teachers, but these great teachers are a bug and not a feature. Looking back on it now, it's easy to tell that these great teachers were being held back by a system that failed them. With a lack of funding or accountability (and standardized testing on outdated curriculums no longer useful in today's society), it's hard to imagine how any of them stayed motivated.

Austin left high school and decided to take his senior year at a local community college. He got two jobs to pay for school — one at a local pub as a bartender and one waiting tables. Every day for 2½ years, it was school from 9 am to 2 pm. The restaurant shift from 5 pm to 10 pm. Then, bartending from 10.30 pm until closing at 4 am. At 19 years of age, he was mopping the floor at 3.30 am and sneaking a Jack Daniels and Coke. It didn't help that he was probably drinking more than he served at these places. At 19, and in more emotional pain than he knew how to describe, the only way Austin knew how to avoid the pain was to avoid feeling anything, keep working — and drink. Dad was fond of the phrase "man up".

By some miracle, he did very well and got a scholarship to Drexel University where, again miraculously, he held a 3.94 GPA while drinking very heavily in the fraternity scene. Even after the scholarship, federal student loans and generous support from my mom he still didn't have enough money to attend Drexel. Luckily Austin's Uncle Bill and Aunt Janice still believed in him enough to lend me the rest of the money to attend school. The sadness and despair were getting worse by the day. The problem with trying to stop heavy drinking is that it seems to be a group exercise. Self-reliance doesn't seem to work because it is an intense concentration on the self. This is a problem because the base of addiction seems to be an obsession with the self. Some outside force is needed to "snap out of" the self-obsession. Reliance on others — not self-reliance — seems to be the key to getting better. Only a "community" approach can create a way out. So, a culture of rugged self-reliance to deal with a mass problem of addiction in American society will tend to backfire for the simple reason that addiction treatment seems to work when the person escapes him or herself and reaches out to others to help them heal. The problem he was facing as a problem drinker was a microcosm of the American addiction problem.

So, here's a 20-year-old skinny and broke young adult living alone in Philadelphia with years of untreated trauma from a father's early death. This was covered up by massive alcohol intake and fraternity hijinks at Drexel University. Austin set up his class schedule purposely for class only Monday through Thursday mornings because he knew he'd be useless from Friday to Sunday. Needless to say, Austin was determined to succeed, and he did well in his classes (miraculously ended studies at Drexel with a 3.94 GPA).

As we progress, let's review and connect the social to the technological. The future application, development, and innovation belongs to the millennials on both sides of the Pacific. There is a serious drag on American innovation caused as much by corporate indolence and an obsession with stock prices as there is with social ills which hold millennials back. China has, so far, neither of these. The main cause of the so-called "trade war" between the US and China is a deep fear that Chinese millennials (and young intergenerational adults) have taken the technological ball and have run much further and faster than the US. It is not about trade imbalances. It is about the lead China has in payments, e-commerce, IoT, 5G, and the mass rollout of other cutting edge technologies. Austin was at the center of the rollout of both of these in the past 10 years and is in a great position so compare why China took the lead and what the US can do to regain it. It is a question of whether ATT and Verizon can come alive and create a mass rollout of 5G like Huawei. Can any bank generate a mass rollout of payments and make checks a thing of the past? Can Facebook Libra take on Tencent in the international arena. That is what Part II is about. Can Amazon create change from an inventory delivery company to a "full service lifestyle bank" like Alibaba? He has serious reservations. Read on.

The Jump to Hong Kong: A Dying Breed of Old School Bankers

If you want to learn Chinese, there's only one thing to do: go to China. A scholarship was offered to me to attend Hong Kong University. The advice was: Off you go! This was September 2012 in Wanchai in a cheap hotel with two suitcases. Eating too much McDonald's, drinking in too many bars on Lockhart Rd, and ending up one night passed out on a bathroom floor. Imagine the feeling: destitute, empty, afraid. The same illness as dad — a diagnosis of alcoholism at 20 years of age. Stopping would force a deep look into the pain of the past. Keeping on drinking would guarantee an end to hopes and dreams. I was told by wise people that FEAR stood for Face Everything And Recover. So, I did, and it changed my life forever.

Jackie was a Chinese roommate in a tiny cramped room. It was cramped to say the least. The friendship with Jackie was important. Upon returning to the apartment, he would always say, "Hey, you come back!" I remember wanting to tell him, "Of course I come back". Later on, as more lessons started to pay off, it became clear that the phrase in Chinese "你回来了" is just another way for Chinese people to greet their loved ones when they return home. (It is equivalent to "how was your day?". In Chinese, they don't really ask "how are you"). This hit me really hard because the judgment toward one of the nicest people on the planet was uncalled for and out of proportion for the very simple reason that there was no direct English translation for what he wanted to communicate. From then on, Jackie became a great friend.

Along with slow improvement in Chinese, I had a summer internship at JP Morgan in the US and I had arranged a meeting through a contact. I had arranged meeting with a JPM banker in Hong Kong. This meeting was with a banker named Mark. Being determined to do whatever it took to learn Chinese and come out to do banking in Hong Kong, Mark offered some advice that was troubling and formed a lasting impression of how the American banks viewed China.

"Learn Chinese?" he laughed. "You don't really need to know Chinese to be a banker out here. What you need is experience and age". Mark was in his mid-40s at the time and the impression was clear: I NEVER want to end up like Mark.

Workshop 3: My Strategy of "Forgetting English" and Leaving Behind My American Mindset can Help to Better Understand and Cooperate with China

Issue: Learning the local language and its history is vital to understanding a country.

1. One of the fundamental things most westerners don't understand about China is the history and culture that led to where they are today. This is playing out in the trade negotiations and is a big reason the US isn't getting anywhere substantial. The Chinese have been invaded and pushed around for centuries. The Chinese felt especially ambushed by the ban on Huawei. Every day an entire 1.4 billion people work tirelessly to make sure this NEVER happens again. They will double down on technological advances to escape what they feel is a kind of "kneecapping" by the US.

2. Chinese peoples' lives are better than they've ever been. Most people don't care that they don't elect their leadership because they genuinely believe their leadership is doing the best thing for them. They don't care that they can't go on Facebook or WhatsApp because Tencent and Alibaba have built far superior super-apps that are integrated into everything you need for daily life. How did they achieve this? In ancient Chinese culture, apprentices would study a "master" for many years to learn a trade and eventually become a master themselves and make a good life for their family. The Chinese don't view what they do as copying; in their mind they are studying the US "The Master" and trying to learn so they can make a better life for their family.

(Continued)

(Continued)

3. Many Americans ask me, "Why do you hang out with Chinese people? They are so quiet and never do anything". But do these people speak a different language? Did you know that while their parents were growing up under Mao, people didn't speak to their neighbors because they were afraid of being reported to the government? Chinese people are some of the loudest, friendliest people I've ever met. Instead of inviting them to a bar, ask to go sing karaoke and see how social they really are. I have had great intellectual dialogue with a lot of people with great insight and perceptiveness.

Discussion: The Chinese language and Chinese history allow deep insights into the mindset and offers an objective look at the people. If we approach China or Chinese people in a judgmental way, they will immediately revert back to the "imperialist fear" mindset from the past centuries. You won't get anywhere. The current negotiations with Washington bear this out. A corollary of this is that companies who choose American leadership inside China (with no language or cultural background) is the #1 reason companies like Macy's have failed and lost billions of dollars.

The Jump to China: Learning Chinese and the Difference between Chinese Tiger Mom Family Values and American Self-reliance Gone Haywire

It was mid-February after Chinese New Year and the semester in Shanghai was beginning. While all the other students elected to live in the dorms and go clubbing at night, living with a local Shanghainese family made more sense. Grandma and dad were there at the airport and later introduced me to "mom" and "meimei" (younger sister). Every day consisted of a 6.30 am wake up call from grandma yelling upstairs while cooking breakfast. After breakfast was 4 hours of intensive Chinese classes with two teachers and four students. 2–4 pm was "one on one" lessons with Miss Song. Then dinner at 5.30 pm sharp followed by 3–4 hours of homework and studying. This was repeated every day for five long, but fun months filled with growth, pain, and frustration.

In Shanghai, the grandma is the boss of the house, and this was no different in this family. Dinner started at 5.30 pm sharp and it didn't matter who you were, if you were late, they started without you. By around 5.32 pm grandma was already yelling at meimei to "eat faster". Not exaggerating, she must have said it 10 times per meal. Kids were not allowed to talk or even look like they were having fun at the table. Every spare minute was dedicated to homework and studying.

My Chinese language skills improved very fast because the teacher did two things. She would make the students memorize the English meaning and how to say it. Secondly, she would tell a one sentence story about the origin of character so as not to forget. For example, she would divide up the word 时 (*shi*) — which means time — into two parts. One is 日 (*ri*) which means "day". The other is 寸 (*cun*) which means "piece". So, time simply meant "a piece of the day".

Obtaining Chinese fluency is one of the hardest things an English-speaking native can do. Asking why a character is this or that was not helpful. The teacher would only respond, "没有为什么!" ("There is no why!"). It took a while, but one learns that Chinese — and China in general — is a language and civilization that dates back 5,000 years. People growing up here are not taught to question "why". One just learns it how it is meant to be learned. The realization that there is no why — and that's just the way it is — is a good start to "forgetting English". Learning Chinese from a judgmental American mindset is a lost cause. There is an emotional mindset to learning Chinese.

Stopping the direct comparison from Chinese to English through direct translation is a must to the learning process. Immersion in the life and culture is a great help — learning all the animal parts in cooking. Even if your host mom makes wolf for dinner, allow her to save face and eat some — even it might be the worst thing you've ever tasted.

After many months in Shanghai, fluent Chinese was achieved as well as a transformation in thinking. Growing up in upstate New York in Pax Americana can make one think that the island that is the US is the best and there is no need to go anywhere else. Racially insensitive remarks or homophobic remarks were, regrettably, acceptable. But getting out in the world and being helped by the same people who were criticized or looked down upon by friends in upstate New York changes one's perspective. This is not to put down the US. But the air of superiority and condescension has caused America to look in other directions as China has built a completely separate — and soon to be totally self-sufficient and well-integrated — technology structure. This is what Chapter 4 is about.

Workshop 4: A Strategy Leaving Behind an American Judgmental Mindset can Help Any American or Westerner to Better Understand China

Issue: Many Westerners know, in general, China is that it was invaded and occupied from the early 1800s until its independence in 1949. The Chinese felt especially ambushed by the ban on Huawei and saw it as yet another imperialist "knee-capping". The current narrative is that China stole its way to the top of the 5G totem pole. What about its top position in payments, e-commerce, battery storage, electric bus fleets, autonomous cars, quantum communications, deep learning, and smart cities, among other areas. Was all this stolen?

1. There was a man called Joseph Needham from Cambridge University who, in the 1930s, traveled across China for 11 years cataloging all of its inventions over the past 2,500 years. Prior to its tragic demise into backwardness starting in the early 1800s, China had, over many centuries, invented or developed the ideas of paper money, gun powder, compass, movable print, blood circulation, blast furnace, forges, payload rockets, chain drive, waterwheels, wheelbarrow, crop rotation, iron plow, rice cultivation, cement, one, and on.

2. In ancient Chinese culture, apprentices would study a "master" for years to learn a trade and become a master themselves to make a good life for their family. The Chinese don't view what they do as copying; in their mind they are studying the US "Master" and trying to learn so they can make a better life. Everyone borrows from the smarter guy. In the 1880s to 1920s, the US "borrowed" technology from the UK and Europe such as the loom, sewing machine, airplane, locomotive, among others.

3. The Chinese don't care that they don't have American inventions Facebook or WhatsApp because Tencent and Alibaba have better super-apps for everything you need for life. Alibaba was invented from scratch. So was Tencent. So was JD.com. So was Baidu. So was PBOC's digital currency. Chinese people are some of the loudest, friendliest but also the most perceptive people you will meet. Invite them to a bar or go to a karaoke night. But, a night out with intellectual dialogue can go very far, indeed. Let's not forget! Simon Winchester's book on Thomas Needham (who was a scandalous womanizer) has an

(Continued)

Appendix in the back listing the inventions by China starting in 7,000 BC. The single spaced list is more than 20 pages long!

Discussion: If one approaches China or Chinese people in a judgmental or condescending way, they will tend to clam up. They remain respectful, but they will move on — and not forget. You just won't get anywhere. How can a respectful approach to discussion and negotiation be maintained in order to foster optimal outcomes? This seems so elemental but is so often overlooked.

Chapter 4

The Journey into IoT and the Cloud with Coca-Cola

Back in the US after some time in China, the 19-year-old skinny, broke, depressed drunk managed to escape the terrible epidemic of addiction which seems to have possessed America. Austin had turned into a sober college grad with a 3.9 GPA who was fluent in Chinese — and $50,000 in debt. The key to getting a job was persistently chasing any kind of loose lead. The alumni office is often a good place to start. For that is exactly how the job was landed. That is how the meeting with Steve from Shanghai happened, for he was an alumnus of Drexel University. He had worked for a software company started by a Chinese Drexel grad who we shall call Jonathan.

Steve was based in Shanghai and spoke Chinese all day. He wanted to hire a sales guy. The position involved traveling all over China and selling their software to enterprise clients in the US market. I honestly might have done it for free if I wasn't so broke at the time. Then Steve hooked me up with the head of the US — we'll call him Ben — who conveniently lived around 30 minutes from Philadelphia where I was living at the time.

Ben was shorter, 65 year old and Indian man and was incredibly intimidating. When going for the interview, there was no smile and he ignored me while I tried to shake his hand. His first question was, "What do you know about my company?" (For the purposes of this book, let's call the company Ace Software (AS)). I studied their website for a few days, so I knew a lot about the company. After a 45-minute interview with zero facial expressions from Ben, he emailed me a message in Chinese and told me to translate it. The translation was something like "door, head, car, tree..." We would consider it gibberish. Upon explaining this to Benjamin, he appeared to get angry and said: "My colleague in China wrote this, are you saying he's an idiot?" My face must have been bright red with panic but thank God I held my ground. It was a test to see if I would call a new colleague an idiot. I managed to ease out of the messy situation with grace.

After arguing for 10 minutes in a confusing manner, he then said, "I'm trying to decide what to pay you". Being totally unprepared for this question, I told him the average starting salary of a Drexel graduate is $53,000 per year. He laughed and backtracked to make me feel that — all of a sudden— he wasn't interested. After being rejected from so many jobs, I was so distraught that I pleaded with him to take me on. I felt pathetic but begged anyways. I knew this was the right opportunity and my ticket back into China. Finally we settled on $50,000. I vowed this would be the last time I ever begged for anything. When I asked him why he wanted me to translate the gibberish he replied, "I wanted to see if you had the courage to tell me it was nonsense". That was Benjamin in a nutshell.

In retrospect, there were all kinds of red flags which I did not catch. Why does someone interviewing a fresh graduate think it's ok to avoid a simple gesture of shaking hands? Why behave like an automaton during an interview — no politeness or smile? Why ask someone to translate incoherent garbage as a test to see if he would trash a colleague? Why feign total disinterest and laugh at someone during a negotiation? Is it a tacky gesture?

Soon after I was hired, I was sent to Shanghai to learn more about the company. It was time to meet my new colleague Steve. I imagined Steve as some McKinsey type — a young and upstanding citizen, laser focused on his career. That was far from reality. Getting out of the car near the office, I looked out and saw some scruffy American kid with glasses. I remembered he used to sell pot to one of my fraternity friends in college. Luckily he didn't seem to remember me.

Steve wasn't exactly an inspiring figure, but he knew a lot about software. The company developed sales applications for consumer goods firms who had sales reps going into retail stores and taking orders. When their reps went into retail stores, they could type in the order directly on their phone. It was 2013 and in China, this was considered relatively "cutting edge". At that same time in the US, companies were using applications that were far more advanced. This situation with China has changed drastically in the 7 years since this experience.

At the time, I did not know what software code was, or even what cloud computing meant. This was despite adding a major in Management Information Systems (MIS) at Drexel. The MIS major taught a lot of theory and gave exams, but I never actually learned about software code, engineering, or anything really to do with technology. Luckily Steve did! Because we became friends, he decided to overlook the fact that I was totally unprepared and unqualified to be selling software.

That week I had a crash course given by Steve on everything software. We had about 400 Chinese people in the office who at that point I could barely understand as technical terms are a whole different type of Chinese language. However, my language improved rapidly as did my technical knowledge. I knew I had to gather the humility to ask for help, be willing to learn and be friendly and grateful to those who could help me.

We really didn't have much going for us at the time in terms of technology, but Coke was our largest customer in China and somehow Jon — the head of the Shanghai office — also convinced them to become an investor. This makes the story much more interesting later on. Why? The web of cross-ownership causes people's judgment to get compromised and can bring about poor outcomes. It prevents people from cutting losses when it is apparent that the technology is not working.

Back in Philadelphia, Ben was not really good with numbers and budgets. When it came to sales, he was a bulldozer. He may not have been a big man, but he sure as hell had no fear. Ben didn't know much about the consumer-packaged goods (CPG) industry, so we started with the industry he was familiar with — packaging. Packaging companies sell to CPG's so I can see how he tried to make the connection. Essentially, we were getting nowhere fast. Ben knew we had to do something different. About a week later, he returned from a tech conference and said, "You have to check this out". Two other Indian guys in D.C. had a technology they were selling to hospitals to monitor refrigeration conditions for the cooling equipment used for sensitive drugs. They measured things like temperature and door openings. We didn't know it at the time, but these two guys were actually a few of the people in the world actually doing IoT in 2013 and getting paid for it.

Working on One of the First IoT Projects for Coke

Right away I saw what Ben did. This would be PERFECT for Coke. The next day, these two Indian guys from DC came to our little office in Langhorne, Pennsylvania for an introductory meeting. Ben asked me to check what kind of car they were driving which ended up being a new Audi A8, so we knew they weren't fooling around. (This was our due diligence!). We must have asked 100 questions about what was possible in terms of functionality.

Ben decided then to lessen the focus on the software being developed in Shanghai and focus more on the new hospital technology of his new friends from DC. He viewed them as something he could have more control over and they spoke the same language. I thought that the Shanghai folks wouldn't like this, but we weren't getting anywhere with their software in the current state. The current state was "unusable". Also, we knew that later on we could integrate the software of the Shanghai operation to add more value. It was a backup. The two Indians worked day and night to adapt a technology for medical coolers to the coolers holding Coke globally. Meanwhile, Benjamin and I told anyone who would listen about this new IoT application which gained interest very fast.

Our first meeting was with Coke's "app" director. Let's call him Chris. He will become much important later. Chris, like most Coke IT executives, probably had the best job in the world. His job was to fly around the world and provide feedback on the different apps used by different bottlers. At Coke, the bottlers are separate from the company who solely produces the formula and does global marketing. The bottlers are the ones who actually produce and deliver the bottles to the 7-Eleven stores and grocery stores around the world.

We met in D.C. on a Saturday morning. Jon flew in from Shanghai to see the technology in action. Chris had gotten the local bottler to deliver a real Coke cooler to the office which we tested day and night. When it came to the actual demo, the technology failed miserably (as with most demos). However, I setup the app to have certain automatic responses where we could hide some of the initial bugs. Chris was impressed and therefore the Jon from Shanghai was impressed. He begrudgingly agreed to introduce us to a few Coke bottlers in China. What I didn't realize was I was actually on my way to becoming likely one of the youngest sales executives for a major IoT solution dealing with CEOs of Fortune 500 companies at

22 years old. That's not the end of the story. As the saying goes: Sic Transit Gloriam Mundi — "All glory fades".

In 2013, there was no live solution on the planet that could tell the location of one of Coke's 15 million coolers while also providing temperature, door openings, and vibration in addition to an analyzed photo of the actual contents of the computer (purity and stock levels). In 2013, this was a huge deal because in some markets Coke lost 2–3% of these coolers annually. "Out of stock" and cooler "purity" were big issues. Coke wanted to guarantee that Coke was being sold in Coke coolers and that they were refrigerated consistently and always sold ice cold. The Indian team found a way to put a low power camera in the device and we trained an image recognition algorithm to detect non-Coke items. Purity refers to the percentage of items in the Coke cooler that are actually their products. Believe it or not, shop owners put everything from Pepsi to left over fried chicken from their lunch in these things. So, it was a multi-billion dollar problem for Coke.

We began a rollout in other countries. For over 6 months, I was facing daunting technical questions from CEOs and CIOs of the world's largest bottlers during the day, and at night, we had "all nighters" on the phone in Chinese with our technical team in Shanghai trying to integrate the two solutions. In this process, I not only became fluent in Chinese but also became an expert in IoT. I visited almost 15 countries in the first year, and couldn't get enough. Little did I know this would become a first-class education in one of the most important fields globally while perfecting the most important language. By 23, I had met with CEOs of Fortune 500 companies on three continents.

Coke in Mexico: How Not to Do IoT

The Monday after Chris's demo, I was on a plane to Mexico City to see the first bottler Chris introduced us to and he couldn't be happier. This was 2013 and it was the first country outside China I'd ever been for work. Coke Mexico CIO's name was Jose. He had a reputation for being a hardass who would squeeze every dime out of his vendors he could. He was a good businessman. Top executives from Microsoft and Salesforce couldn't even get him to agree to a discounted deal for standard services like Office 365 and cloud infrastructure. Needless to say, when we walked into their office in Monterrey, we were far from ready for what came next.

Jose loved our presentation, asked great questions, and couldn't wait to start a pilot. He even took us out for the best tacos in Monterrey. At dinner, Jose told us about how he had a bear in the backyard of his mansion in Monterrey that his kids saw yesterday before school. We traded raucous stories over dinner and had a great time. We called Ben after dinner and were sure we had a done deal. This was my first but not last naïve sales prediction.

We stayed up all night writing the pilot agreement, as we hadn't really sold the solution yet. At 10 am, we walked into the office feeling like a million pesos. However, we were very surprised to find nobody there. We called Jose several times, but nobody answered. Finally, around 11 am one of his developers came in and told us our price was way too high. We had a 3 pm flight and we already told Ben the deal was done. The entire cost of the pilot was around US$10,000. However, Jose suddenly decided he wanted it for free.

After a painful 2 hours of re-negotiating with Jose's team, we decided to leave out of principle. We both knew we had the only solution in the world that could do what we did for Coke coolers and were not stopping because Jose had wanted the whole pilot for free. When we got back to the office, Ben laughed as if he knew something we didn't. I began to learn a very important lesson in sales that nothing is finished until you get a signature.

We decided to employ a similar strategy I used on my brother when we were kids — ignore him. It got to the point where he was calling us but we always managed to wait 1–2 days to respond. Word got around to Microsoft that we were making inroads at Coke with an IoT solution. This was the point Azure was just starting out and was desperate to get an IoT solution on their cloud platform Azure. I came to learn later that most companies at this point were actually in the same situation as Microsoft and the first 3–4 years of the IoT revolution — 2012–2016 — was mainly just fluff and PowerPoint.

Microsoft invited Ben and I to Mobile World Congress in Barcelona in 2013 which is the #1 must-attend tech show globally for anyone in the IoT industry. Microsoft had the biggest booth in the whole place which cost ~$500,000. They even flew in a Coke cooler for me to do a demo. At the time, they were so desperate for a branded customer IoT solution they bought me a Coke outfit on eBay and made me wear it at the show. What the hell — I didn't care. I was 23 and they were putting me up at the W Hotel in Barcelona overlooking the Mediterranean.

By chance, our old friend Jose also happened to be at the conference, and I coincidentally hadn't responded to his email in over 5 days. He came by the booth and began to show renewed interest in the deal he abandoned. He asked me to meet with him after the show. We had a dinner planned with all the Microsoft executives responsible for the Coke account. They were key people as Coke was one of their largest customers. I agreed to meet him in the lobby of the hotel before dinner.

After 2 hours of walking through changes in the initial contract, we had a deal. I went to the front desk of the hotel to print out the contract and experienced one of the more defining moments in my career. Just as Benjamin and the Microsoft executives walked into the lobby of the W they saw Jose, the toughest CIO in our industry signing an IoT deal with me, a 23-year-old kid who didn't even know what software was a year ago. The timing couldn't have been better. This was the first ever real IoT deal for a Coke bottler any of us were aware of. We proceeded to go out to one of the most expensive restaurants in Barcelona for an all-expense paid Microsoft corporate dinner. I was a hero. The story is not over. The car crash is starting.

That night at dinner, the executive responsible for Microsoft Azure's China business and the whole team were stunned at what we just pulled off. This put us on the map as a serious player in the IoT space in consumer goods with a serious customer and serious backer. Microsoft followed by making us a key partner that would be showcased together around the world. There was a need to showcase a "real-world, in-use" IoT solutions on a major cloud platform. Microsoft flew me everywhere from Seattle to Shanghai to showcase this to major customers. I even got to meet Microsoft's CEO Satya Nadella.

Ben and I made sure to update the Shanghai team on our progress every step of the way. At this point, we were further ahead of anyone in our industry for a live IoT solution. Every one of our partners had PowerPoints and speeches prepared on how many billions of devices would be out there in 2020 but anything they had in terms of "solutions" was vaporware. When updating the team back in China on our progress, we would always include how his legacy SFA software was the key component in this solution, which was true. There was mutual praise initially, but the lines of communication would soon get out of hand. We did not handle the communication wisely. There were too many moving parts and massive egos in the picture.

Around this time, Ben was recruiting Chris (Coke's application director) to come work for us. In theory, it was the perfect match because he knew every one of the bottlers and he just happened to live right near our office in Langhorne, PA. As a 23-year-old who was knocking it out of the park, this made me nervous as I didn't want anyone to steal my thunder. Luckily, I had enough mentors at the time who told me the best strategy was to do what's best for the company. Based on the knowledge I had at the time, the best strategy was to bring Chris on.

I closed a few more deals and we were now having to deliver on these pilot projects. To date, we had not sold any of Ace Software's legacy solution developed out of Shanghai, which had been our primary directive when starting the US business. Ben knew we had to carefully navigate this, so I was also pushing heavy to get a sales force automation (SFA) customer implemented. Since the technology was vastly inferior to many other companies (like Marc Benioff's salesforce.com), we really couldn't get any traction with large customers. All the Shanghai software could do was take Coke orders. I had found a few small customers to keep the team in China busy, but the team couldn't successfully give a demo whenever I would meet with customers in the US.

Every time we wanted to do a demo of our SFA software, it would fail. Here I was staying up all night with the developer team 7 days a week for months, but to no avail. The head of the Shanghai team was also becoming more and more irrational. The head of the operation would frequently initiate conference calls at 3 am simply to yell at everyone in Chinese.

After a few months, we finally signed a new SFA customer — Coke Japan! This was huge in the Coke world as Japan was known as being the most advanced technically out of all the bottlers. We got invited to Tokyo to help implement the solution and tried and pitch IoT as well. The first day onsite, the Japan team looked into the code of our SFA solution and found more bugs than an NYC garbage dumpster. They were not happy. Around an hour before my presentation, their whole system crashed and sales reps across the country had no way to book any sales. Despite this, the Japanese executives were so respectful they still sat down to listen to my hour-long IoT presentation. Needless to say, they did not call me back.

During this time, Ben was getting more convinced that IoT needed to be a separate project from the Shanghai software operation. We both knew the cooler technology was the only real-world live IoT solution on the planet for Coke at the time. If we got a major customer rolled out, it could be worth billions. Deep down the leaders of the Shanghai office knew this as well, but it was not something that they developed and that hurt Jon's ego.

We needed the Shanghai team as they had strong relationships with Coke executives at the time. So, we needed to continue to operate as a part of AS if we wanted the Coke account. We continued to pitch an integrated solution from the Coke Cooler IoT device sending the data back real time through sales rep mobile app, something nobody had ever done before. The only trouble was getting AS's mobile app to work in a customer setting.

It was around this time I started realizing that the Shanghai office was broken. We would get calls would call me in the middle of the night Shanghai-time and the top guy would be intoxicated. People would spread rumors, trade on gossip, and slander people's work. This was right out of an episode of The Office or Silicon Valley.

By this time, the technology from the Shanghai office was causing China customers to have technical issues. The CIO of the world's largest beer distributor's (also our customer in China) refused to communicate any more with the Shanghai office. Communication between the office in Pennsylvania ran by Ben and the office in Shanghai (Jon) broke down. Fears of sabotage and recrimination were rampant. Ben and his IoT team began to have private meetings away from the Coke executive he had just hired. Jon also now started inviting Chris — someone who we had hired from Coke — to Shanghai more to try and figure out what was going in. Without knowing it, Chris had become a spy who was out in the cold.

In the following months, I was able to close a few more pilot deals in Asia. At this point, every cloud provider wanted us to put our solution on their platform because none of them really had solutions yet. I even got our US team to put a separate version of the solution on Salesforce's cloud so they would introduce us to their customers as well. I learned as a small fish in a big pond how to use our advantage of innovation and flexibility to partner with big fish. They had deep pockets and customer lists. This was the key to our success. At this time, I was so impressed with Salesforce that I used a lot of my salary to buy their stock. This was one of the great benefits to staying in the traffic despite all of the absurdity of unworkable technology, crazy personalities, and generally bad behavior. I got to see companies on the inside and invest in the ones that were really impressive. Salesforce was one such company.

Chris, the guy we hired from Coke, was a very different personality as even he admitted that he didn't have it in him to "sell". His whole 20-year career with Coke never really consisted of targets or measurable

KPIs so this was a big worry for him. Ben was the exact opposite of this where all he thought about was sales. Implementing and technology to him was someone else's problem. Chris' skill set fell through the technology-marketing cracks. He was neither.

Around the time Chris joined, the pressure was really mounting from China and our IoT customers. Ben would call me Friday nights at 11 pm to talk business and I thought that was totally normal. Our team never got much sleep. Getting cursed out and totally demoralized by my boss and mentor Ben was a regular occurrence, but needless to say it helped me develop very thick skin. I had a girlfriend at the time in Philadelphia who broke up with me while I was at Dreamforce (Salesforce's yearly tech conference) in San Francisco and the reason was just, "I never see you". I remember being sad but knew the potential of what we were doing was so big we had to keep going. Plus, with Ben as a boss, there was nothing we could do.

At this point, I had more real-world IoT experience than anyone I'd encountered in the tech world. Rockwell and a few other manufacturing-oriented companies like GE had been putting sensors in manufacturing plants for a few years, but as for a consumer-oriented setting that was not a controlled environment, nobody had ever successfully done what we were doing. I became an expert at everything from firmware, machine vision, and AI. At 24 years old, Microsoft even invited me to give a presentation to a meeting at their Seattle HQ of CIOs of Microsoft's 50 largest customers.

Throughout this process, I had several turning points in personal confidence. I still remember being in the presenter's booth when Benjamin recognized Nestle's CIO from across the room. After pointing him out to Benjamin, he gave me a look and I knew what I had to do. I walked right up to the CIO of the world's largest CPG company and introduced myself, and to my surprise he invited me to Vevey, Switzerland to personally meet with his executive team. The mean-spirited behavior of the owners did toughen me up.

The Downfall: Shortsightedness, Poor Leadership, Bad Hiring, Awkward Personalities

One day, Ben and I got a call from someone named Ivan at Coke's European division. It was about an IoT RFP for coolers. At first, we didn't think much of this, but then I looked up Coke Europe and realized they were the largest division globally at the time spanning 20+ countries in Europe. Ben and I immediately had them send us the 100+ page request for proposal (RFP). They had invited us to map out a response to a rollout of over 10 million coolers across 3 years.

Finally we had it — the opportunity that would allow us all to hit it big. 10 million coolers even at as little as $1/month was minimum $100 million a year in revenue. Needless to say, we immediately shifted our focus to this deal which we believed to be the biggest IoT contract awarded in 2013.

At the same time, I had also sold two different clients in the US on our SFA solution. They were small CPG+ branding companies that needed a solution to do in-store audits and some basic reporting. What should have been a layup for the China engineering team proved to be quite problematic. Here we are with a potentially $120 million deal for an emerging technology with the largest Coke division on earth and I had to stay up all night fixing bugs in code that could have been written by a 4-year-old. The team and the leadership in China were not delivering and we were having to put Band Aids on what was looking more and more like terminal cancer.

The engineers in Shanghai weren't bad people or incompetent. I would learn here that with flawed leadership not even the brightest people can make a company successful. With several major customers I already signed up for our IoT solution, Ben had dozens of investors willing to give us an incredible valuation. Ben tried to convince Jon in Shanghai to take money from the venture capital firms offering (great deals) but Jon wasn't willing to give up even 1% of control in this project. *Lesson Learned*: Toxic or narcissistic leadership at the top will always ruin a good technology. We did not recognize this.

At this point, Jon was teetering on the edge of deep irrationality. He regularly cursed people out in the office. The only thing that really kept the company going was his relationship with the top executives at Coke who had invested in Jonathan's company. We knew if we wanted to win the deal with Coke, we needed a partner who could actually deliver. Ben asked some of our friends at Microsoft who we should talk to and they referred us to Accenture. Even for a big company like Accenture, when you mention a $120 million contract for IoT work, they come running.

Accenture Enters the Picture: From PowerPoint to Actually Making a Product

The next day Benjamin and I were in Accenture's Atlanta office with all their senior executives for North America and the CPG vertical. Within 48 hours, Accenture called in experts from everywhere — from Italy to

Brazil — to read and analyze this huge RFP. That's where I first met Joseph. Joseph was the senior director responsible for the RPF response on the Accenture side. To this day, I've still never seen anyone navigate the bureaucratic machine as well as him in order to get things done.

With over 100 pages, the response that Accenture helped up prepare was very complex but also comprehensive. At this point, I was willing to do whatever it took because my contract explicitly said I get 1% of ALL Internet of Things revenues generated, which at the time could have been over $1 million. We proceeded to respond to each individual piece as thoroughly as possible. Their RFP processes were very strict and could only communicate with one person in all of Coke Europe. That's how I met Alex. He was the director of IT for Coke Europe based in Sofia, Bulgaria.

Before taking off for Sofia we had to finish a few things up in our Pennsylvania office. Chris had called Ben who as usual was doing five things at once. Benjamin answered the phone not really paying attention and then gave me the phone to talk to Chris. While handing the phone to me it accidentally ended the call, and that's when our former Coke IT director finally lost it.

Figuring it was just a bad day or something I ignored Chris over the weekend and went to the office on Monday to get some things before heading off to Bulgaria. When the door opened, I knew it would be awkward, but I never figured what was about to happen. Chris walked in and proceeded to come to my desk and actually get in my face, continuing to scream at me seeming like he just went on the internet and googled "how to curse at someone", you could tell it was his first time but nonetheless he wasn't fooling around.

I told him "Chris I understand you're under a lot of pressure and its ok" which made him even more mad as he wasn't interested in admitting he made a big mistake leaving his cushy corporate job at Coke. After what seemed like 5 minutes of provoking me to try and fight him (this is a 48-year-old man with a daughter) I finally stood up, looked him dead in the face, "Go sit down Chris" and pointed to his desk. I don't know what came over me or him, but he went and sat down.

It All Sours in Bulgaria: Greed, Poor Leadership and Mismanagement can Sabotage Technology

The next afternoon Rajesh, the lead developer on our IoT team and I arrived in Sophia. At around 11 pm that night, we realized we had a bug in the app that caused the camera not to recognize Coke's #1 competitor as a "foreign product", a functionality Alex specifically requested to see. Rajesh and I decided to get room service and stay up until 4 am to try and fix the bug. Finally, as the sun was coming up the bug appeared to be fixed and I went in to setup the cooler in Coke Europe IT headquarters in Sofia for a demo later that afternoon.

When Alex met me at the front door that morning, I was pretty scared to say the least. I hadn't seen a single person smile in the 24 hours since arriving in Bulgaria, and Alex looked like he could kill me with one hand tied behind his back. After showing him the successful demo, we finally saw our first smile, and even got invited out for Bulgarian barbecue.

Jon flew in from Shanghai that night and seemed to be happy, but the next day he went right back to a manic state. The company was running low on cash and he was unwilling to raise any additional funding as it would dilute his ownership stake. Even though we had customers ready to pay for his SFA solution, he just couldn't seem to execute on the software. We continued to progress in our bid with Accenture and even made it to the third and final round of the RFP. I was working with Joseph and top Accenture leadership on a daily basis putting together the response. On top of that, I was training all the "experts" they brought in from Italy, Spain, Brazil, and Germany.

Our final bid for the contract was $120 million. We knew we had two competitors, but nobody had a solution close to ours in terms of technical capability. Believe it or not, Accenture was actually the weak point of our solution as their main interest was upselling analytics services which Coke Europe did not want at the time. The further we progressed, the angrier Jonathan became that this solution was not his baby, even though it could 10× his company's yearly revenue in the first year.

Then one day, conveniently prior to learning the results of the contract being awarded, my salary did not show up in my bank, commissions from sales I made were also not being deposited. I knew this was the day we had been fearing for a while. Jon had finally lost it. Ben and I even found out he had called the Indian IoT Engineers and tried to force them to provide their source code and hardware specifications to his China team. He also threatened to cancel every single deal with Coke in AS's name, which was every deal at that point. Right out of a bad episode of Silicon Valley. Why? Jon had found out from his Coke contacts we won the RFP, and he didn't want to share any of it.

So, the work of this millennial was for nothing. The owner of the company had some inexplicable tie to Coke and when the Pennsylvania team won the contract, it was taken. In my contract, there was a 1% commission which would have been $1 million. It was gone in a puff of smoke. The months of hard work was for nothing.

Even though AS still hadn't paid me for expenses and commissions from the sales I made I decided not to be involved with Jon anymore. I negotiated a job with Accenture and decided to take a 3-week trip to South America with no cell service while we waited for Accenture's legal team to extract me from my current company and move to the Atlanta office.

Workshop 1: Millennials Have Great Compassion, Understanding, and Acceptance for Other Millennials. But can be Harsh and Judgmental on Boomers. They Even Have a Dismissive Phrase for Boomer Advice: "OK Boomer"

Issue: How should millennials upward manage boomers and how should boomers reverse mentor millennials?

1. Millennials often think that the boomers, through selfishness, have (1) wrecked the financial system and have no solutions, (2) aggravated climate change and (3) intentionally destroyed multilateral institutions without any replacements. They perceive the "over 45" set as intolerant of difference, whereas millennials display great acceptance to each other when it comes to racial, ethnic, and sexual difference.

2. This seems to be the nub of the generational divide. Millennials see older people as intolerant, unwilling to change or learn, insensitive to the level of maturity shown in high levels of tolerance, acceptance, and understanding of difference. Fundamentally, isn't this a result of the reality that there are now more mixed-race younger people than at any time in history? Older people see millennials as intolerant of accepted norms and therefore entitled. They see millennials as far too accepting of sexual differences and, therefore, a PC minefield. They see

---

(Continued)

millennials as demanding a more fluid work–life balance (not less work) and are, therefore, not producing.

3. Older people see two sexes. Millennials have more than 10 designations. Older people start at 8 and go home at 6 with an hour break. Millennials do not even eat breakfast anymore. They drink it. There are now more mixed-race young adults than at any time in human history. There is a flexibility and a fluidity to millennials which older adults don't have and often don't like. Millennials frequently see older managers putting them into strict employment boxes which grossly misrepresent their talents. This is a mistake. The newness of technology often means that new employees may bring as much to the table (or more) as a 10-year veteran.

Discussion: There needs to be some form of constant institutional communication among and between millennials to clear the air on what are glaring differences. Some form of standing committee with equal parts millennials and old timers needs to be created to review compensation, hiring, breaks, schedules, and performance review. The old system did not work before and is utterly obsolete now.

Chapter 5

Accenture and IoT: Long on PowerPoint, Short on Solutions

My 3-week trip to South America to decompress ended up being much needed. At the time, I had no assurances prior to leaving that Accenture would even accept me but I figured it would be a lot less torturous of a wait enjoying the beautiful scenery of the Andes than at my mom's house in upstate New York.

For almost 2 years, I put my heart and soul into developing this IoT technology at AS. Benjamin and I hadn't had a day off since we started and after having Jonathan just tear it all down out of pure ego, I felt like my head was about to explode. I was so distraught I insisted that Accenture moved me to Atlanta where Joseph and the RFP response team were. I thought a change of scenery would help me start over. I knew living in the US full time would be a big change, and really wanted to make sure I didn't lose my Chinese abilities I had worked tirelessly on for the past 4 years. When it came time to finding a place to live all I really cared about was finding a Chinese roommate.

I figured my highest chance at finding a Chinese roommate was Georgia Tech student housing. When I called the housing director and asked her if she could recommend a Chinese roommate, she almost hung up on me after saying, "we don't allocate roommates by race". In my panic, I somehow managed to think of a great way around this. "Can you please send me a list of the students' first names and phone numbers looking for new roommates?" I asked. "Sure" she said. I proceeded to add everyone on the list who had a Chinese name on WeChat and ended up finding my roommate Ming from Shandong.

Some good that happened in all of this was I managed to live on a student budget and, in addition to paying off a lot of my college loans, I used my life savings to buy a few of the companies I worked with like Salesforce, Facebook, Tableau, and Apple. By this time, each of those had more than doubled and although I was not playing with a lot of money, this helped me to pay off all my student loan debt just 2 years after college.

The day after I got back I packed up my Honda fit (yes I drove a Honda Fit) and brought my whole life to Atlanta. Originally Accenture wanted to offer me $80,000 and I was firm on $100,000. I even listed Benjamin as my former employer, and he told them I was making $120,000 at my last job even without me asking. To this day, I still think it's ridiculous that corporations in America value you based on your previous salaries. Here I was negotiating a $120 million deal on an emerging technology nobody was really doing successfully and they couldn't get over my years of experience. This is a common refrain for millennials. Why are they put in salary boxes which are decades old when they often have better skill sets than their managers? This automatically creates bad blood and sows the seeds of early departure.

I managed to negotiate up to the max for my "experience bracket" which was 90,000 and they also included a $10,000 starting bonus and I

Workshop 1: Why Do Fortune 100 Companies Still Use Systems from 50 Years Ago to Hire Millennials?

Issue: A common refrain for millennials is: Why are we put in salary boxes which are decades old when we often have better skill sets than my manager. This is because new technology favors the young who are early adapters. This automatically creates bad blood and sows the seeds of early departure.

1. Managers stick highly skilled millennials in these "experience limited" boxes either while negotiating their pay or even on projects after they started. Now it is easier than ever to switch jobs and each time you bring a new employee on it costs the company thousands of dollars to recruit, etc. Why not do the right thing from the beginning and pay people what their skill sets are worth — not what your box says they should be worth.

(Continued)

2. Millennials need to realize that it is ok to be a very tough negotiator with potential employers. Many just take the first offer and are afraid to push as to not upset the employer and lose the offer. The key I've learned is to be tough but respectful in the process. I do this by expressing gratitude and excitement at each phase of the negotiation.

3. "Thank you for this offer, I can't wait to join the team and am positive together we can hit our targets for 2020. Given my skill set I think I can add a great deal of value to this team and if you can come up 30% we would have a deal right away." This is a line I've used countless times. Most employers want to know you are a fighter because that means you will fight for them too. If they can't move on salary due to some kind of obscure HR rule about "experience" than you can negotiate other things like a starting bonus, higher 401,000 match or more vacation days (you can trade them for dollars if you leave).

Discussion: Flexibility is key. Firms need to have a sandbox for experimental hires as many banks and central banks have to accommodate new products and services. If central banks can have sand boxes, you can too. HR must be in the habit of experimentation as the old ways have miserably failed. Millennials offer new skill sets, new technology, and new methods but are very anxious because older people have broken the climate, the banks, and the government. They have solutions. Question? Should HR help them achieve these with HR programs? Have an open discussion blog on apps for sleep, meditation, mindfulness, nutrition, and trauma. Should HR create a committee of millennials and older adults to create flexible hiring practices?

even got $5,000 to move. Since I think I spent a total of $88 in gas on the drive down, I was pretty happy to have doubled my income in a little over a year to over $100,000.

At this stage, we were in the third and final stage of the $120 million RFP that I had no personal way to benefit from anymore. However, Accenture would look good on the resume and it got me away (so I thought) from Jonathan. We got to work right away.

The first day in the office with Joseph was great. He was the most organized person I have ever met and seemed to know exactly what to do.

While working for Ben, I became a technology expert and gained enormous confidence in sales after working with so many C-Level executives so early on in my career. What I didn't have at this point was finesse. I could get pretty much anything done by just bulldozing through obstacles, but I needed to learn how to "keep in line" and learn how to do a more consultative sales process.

Accenture is separated into technology and industry verticals. I was hired into Accenture Digital under Joseph for my expertise in IoT. We had another Managing director Fabio who was responsible for Coke in Italy and he had just moved to Atlanta. We were the three leading the response team on the Accenture side and had gotten a lot of exposure internally.

In addition to the $120 million RFP for Coca-Cola Europe, I brought on several other opportunities. Accenture was very interested in the implementations of IoT at Coke in Mexico, Vietnam, and Cambodia. Accenture primarily had the same interest as Microsoft and every other large technology company at the time. They wanted to go from writing PowerPoints about IoT to actually doing it. PowerPoint only gets you so far.

Joseph and Fabio reported to Ken who was a Senior Managing Director. Ken owned the entire consumer goods vertical at Accenture and therefore the Coke account as well. For all intents and purposes, he was God and we were his disciples. On the second day, Joseph regrettably told me that Jonathan had actually personally called Ken after I left AS to try and convince him not to hire me. I was so angry at the time I had no idea how to handle it. I'll explain more on this later.

The following weeks during the RFP responses and implementation, Joseph and Fabio did their best in leaving me out of all direct AS interactions. This was until one day when Joseph accidentally copied me on an email chain in which Jonathan was also copied. The next morning at 3 am Shanghai time, Jonathan decided to write another email to Joseph threatening to cut Accenture out of any future Coke deal if they even copied me on another email. It wasn't enough that Jonathan didn't pay me any of the money he owed, but now he actually tried to ruin my career even after I left. At this point, I'd been all around the world and met countless wonderful people, but Jonathan was vindictive, and I knew this wasn't good. The situation was getting out of hand, so we decided we needed to leverage our own Coke relationships. Ken had plenty of those.

By this time, Ken was well aware of the craziness coming from Jonathan. We all continued to keep in touch with Benjamin in Pennsylvania who let us know how the IoT implementations I sold were failing miserably after Jonathan had taken control of the project. Ken was not about to let hundreds of millions in new business slip away, so he arranged a meeting with the CEO of Coke's largest division by revenue, who at the time was #3 in the entire company.

Joseph and Fabio arranged the meeting once Ken requested. Both of them were some of the nicest guys I've met in corporate America, but they still followed the traditional ladder. When I found out they didn't invite me to the meeting, I was crushed. Here they were going to talk to the CEO to pitch a technology that Rajesh, Benjamin, and I developed and sold, of which they knew nothing about. Still, I knew I had to suck it up and continue to contribute where I could.

On the morning of the meeting Joseph, Fabio and I reserved a meeting room so I could help them prepare. They even brought in another managing director who was an "IoT expert" with 20 years' experience. Unexpectedly, Ken walks in the meeting room and starts asking questions. "How many pilots are there currently? Who is the responsible person at Coke in Vietnam?" he asked. After a five second awkward silence, I decided to speak up. "Ajay" I said, "and he is the one CIO I am closest with, so we can leverage this relationship."

Joseph and Fabio were shocked I had spoken up. It was not common at Accenture for analysts to even be in meetings with SMDs, let alone actually talk. After a few second pause, Ken looked me dead in the eyes and proceeded to change my career and life. He then looked at Joseph and Fabio and said the most satisfying words I've ever heard, "Is he in the meeting?" Ken asked. "No" Joseph responded looking like he just walked in on his parents in the bedroom. "What the hell are you thinking? Make sure he's there" Ken demanded. I tried so hard not to smile but I couldn't help it, I don't think I'd ever been so happy.

We arrived at Coke's office in Atlanta around 4 pm. Getting off the elevator was like nothing I'd ever seen before. The C-Suite office was all mahogany, with several secretaries who met us after leaving the elevator.

I discovered very quickly that meeting with CEOs are much different than CIOs. CIOs are usually technologically oriented people who first want to learn more about the technology and how much money they can save comes into the picture later on. When Aiden walked into the meeting with his COO, he made a joke how a meeting with Accenture always seems to cost him a lot of money and we all laughed. When he shook my hand, he had a certain look in his eyes. I couldn't tell whether it was admiration that a 24-year-old ended up in this meeting or just smiling because he was a nice guy. All the other people in this meeting were men at least twice my age.

Aiden started the meeting by saying, "What do you have for me today and how much is it going to cost me?" Ken opened as he had the relationship, but he didn't know anything about the technology. He quickly handed it off to Joseph and Fabio who introduced it as any good consultant would — they introduced the technical features. Aiden generously pretended to listen for 3 minutes (which felt like an eternity) and finally stopped him mid-sentence, "You want me to pay $120 million for a device that can tell me what temperature my cooler is? For that amount of money, I can build a new factory in Cambodia, Munich, Buenos Aires and still have enough left over to buy a few thousand new coolers to replace the lost ones!"

The meeting went silent. It was obvious that this was a much higher-level discussion than even Joseph and Fabio were used to. After an awkward silence, I knew I had to say something. "Sir you lose $400 million a year in Asia alone just from store owners selling Competitor products in your coolers" I blurted out. "And what the hell is a camera going to do to convince these shop owners not to sell competitor products in my coolers?" he yelled in a very scary Irish accent.

I responded, "Well, in my time in Vietnam with Ajay, in Japan with Tagomi San and in Mexico with Jose and his team, this is what I learned. When we go on store visits, we realized that the majority of problems occur from simple lack of visibility into the actual problem at the individual store level. The salespeople tend to know what's going on but their managers have no clue."

"But we already know the damn problem, how do you solve it?" He replied.

My retort was, "The difference is not only our device and machine learning algorithms we use to get the data, but also our integration with the processes of the sales reps. I personally have shadowed these reps in over 20 countries and know what they go through on a daily basis. They have all told me that by making the data actionable, we can achieve a 50% decrease in most of these issues. For example, if we prioritize the rep's day by which coolers/stores have the biggest issues, they can be more efficient and solve the biggest problems. This could save us a $50 store visit to a 711 with no issue."

The whole room, including Aiden, paused, and just as I thought I was about to get fired, he smiled and yelled, "Now this is a guy who knows what he's talking about! The thing I hate about technology vendors is they don't understand our business." The rest of the meeting Aiden just talked directly to me, all the while with a smile on his face. It got to the point where I knew even though Ken was happy, I had to turn once in a while to Joseph and Fabio to allow them to contribute out of fear they'd somehow retaliate later.

Towards the end of the meeting Aiden looked at me and said, "You ever been to Vietnam?" "Yes, once before" I responded. "Good because you're going there soon. Prove to me this works in Vietnam and you've got your deal."

Workshop 2: Developing a Case for IoT

Issue: How do you develop a case for disruptive technology (a first mover problem) and get sign-off from people who have an entrenched set of beliefs?

1. Get the facts from the people who were on the ground and carefully explain that data to management with Python and great 3D graphics. The truth is big companies really have no idea how much money they lose monthly to these types of inefficiencies. They know it's really bad, and sometimes they hire consultants to come in and give them PowerPoints with information they already know that is not accurate. These recommendations, anyway, never seem to get implemented.

2. Go around with the sales reps (even if it means getting in the truck or on the motorcycle in Vietnam). Watch. Listen. Learn. If this means going to Mexico City or Hanoi, go! Offer concrete and data-driven observations with results to the head of the business unit. Make a pitch directly to the CEO. Hit the upper management from different directions

3. Ask for resources for further testing and data collection. In the case of Coke, one in 10 coolers were out of stock. This is huge lost incremental revenue and the sales can be calculated by the number of times the cooler door is opened. Some of the reps won't care, shop owners won't

(Continued)

(*Continued*)

change their stocking schedule, etc. That's fine. BUT, the point is even if 50% of the problem is solved by rerouting the distributor or the sales rep, the biggest out-of-stock stores can be serviced better. There are other big advantages to implementing this system of sensors: additional sales from a cold and lighted cooler and more sales from coolers with only Coke. Since this data had never been collected before, a big selling point was that reps could also use this data to convince shop owners to better follow Coke guidelines as it was to their benefit. Turn the IoT into a math problem that either cut costs or increased sales. That helped to get all the corporate professional non-risk takers to take a risk and implement a disruptive solution.

Discussion: The world is passing by those who do not believe in IoT. IoT is not only valuable from the point of view of inventories and product distribution but also offers important data for a location, a demographic, and a city. It offers cross-selling opportunities. It spots trends before others can see it. It increases employee efficiency. It makes for happier consumers. It guarantees product safety. China is in a runaway race on this by integrating consumer with smart cities. This connects to working capital activity and then creates collateral opportunities for vendors who can borrow since there is detailed live data on their revenue. This will create a live and integrated view of SMEs which have been forever starved of credit. People who act as a second mover (waiting until a competitor has something) will tend to panic and overspend, implementing something without even consulting the business units who have to use it.

Note: As a result, often times it either goes unused or becomes a never-ending tech project. American companies — especially banks — need to get moving quickly. Public–private partnerships are key. So are consortiums. Regulators need to get on board with this. Look at what China did. It knew this and created a super regulator rather than many different fiefdoms.

Chapter 6

IoT in Vietnam and Cambodia

When we got back to the Accenture Atlanta office, to Joseph and Fabio's credit they did not hold a grudge and went right to work to arrange the Vietnam trip (a shining example of good leadership, no ego). Aiden didn't directly control Coke Europe, but he was on the board, so a successful Vietnam pilot was key for this RFP and our other deals with the whole Coke system. From the very beginning, it was clear that Joseph and Fabio didn't want to ride around Vietnam on a motorbike for 6 weeks installing Internet of Things (IoT) devices on Coke coolers, so they left this largely up to me. Now the question was how do we get someone who holds the rank of analyst (me, the lowest rank) at Accenture to get internally approved to go live in Vietnam and Cambodia for 6 weeks? The Vietnamese division also managed Cambodia operations at the time and wanted to test both markets simultaneously, which made my life a lot more complicated.

Luckily for us we had Joseph. He had me go through the internal approval process (which took 2 weeks) and finally at the end I got a call from HR asking me why the hell an analyst needed to go to Vietnam and Cambodia for a "Smart Cooler IoT Pilot". I handed the phone to Joseph who basically explained we were going to do the first ever Accenture IoT pilot and this was directed by the CEO of Coke's largest division, which got us an immediate approval. At this point, our days were long. Everyone at Accenture was throwing resources at us to try and get their division's name on this. I was almost untouchable. Even though Jonathan continued to badmouth me to everyone, Joseph and Fabio had my back. They knew this was their ticket into Ken's office one day.

Around this time, we got a new intern named Matt and a recent graduate from India named Amita. Matt was doing an MBA at some big university and Amita was here on a H1B visa. Every day Joseph would rent a conference room in the Atlanta office and we'd be there from 8 am to 8 pm working on our plan for Vietnam and Cambodia.

It was a complicated operation. Each country wanted to test 200 coolers and each cooler was in a "store" that looked something like the below pictures.

We had different solutions with different functionality, I will try to explain as follows:

Smart Vision

Embedded with a camera for cooler snapshots and purity analysis. 3G connected

Smart Tag

Cost effective Asset Tracking solution transmitting through BLE

At the time, we had a Smart Tag which was a Bluetooth Low Energy (BLE) device. This is the same technology everyone uses for wireless

headphones today. But in 2015 it had not yet been widely used in this type of application before. The Smart Tag did not have a camera or the more advanced functionality as a cellular modem and monthly plan made the device more expensive. We reserved this device for the markets where the cost of a sales rep visit was lower ($4–5) whereas in markets like Japan, Germany, and USA it was more like $80–100.

The Smart Vision however had a camera and came with a cellular modem (gateway) which could send pictures to the cloud so we could run our machine vision algorithm and analyze to see if there were any Pepsis or "foreign products" in the cooler or not. Summary of the functionality is listed as follows:

Functionality	Use	Business Value	Smart Tag	Smart Vision
Bluetooth Smart	Asset (Cooler) Tracking Consumer Engagement	• Alert if cooler is lost, stolen or removed • Direct interaction with end consumer (digital couponing, digital content)	×	×
Temperature Sensor	Cooler Health	• Alert if cooler is not running properly or not plugged in	×	×
Light Sensor	Cooler Health	• Alert if light is not running properly or not plugged in	×	×
Humidity Sensor	Cooler Health	• Alert if dehumidifier is not running properly	×	×
Sound Sensor and Speaker	Cooler Health Cooler Detection	• Alert if compressor needs servicing or air filter change • Predictive maintenance	×	×
Movement Sensor	Location Cooler Health	• Alert if cooler has moved from first location in the store • Track vibrations from compressor for predictive maintenance	×	×
Door Sensor	Cooler Stock Consumer Engagement	• Predictive analytics for potential stock issues • Monitor consumer traffic in multiple cooler locations	×	×
GSM/CDMA 3G Modem	Real-time Data Upload	• Monitor cooler status remotely	—	×

(Continued)

(Continued)

Functionality	Use	Business Value	SmartTag	SmartVision
Cooler Machine Vision	Cooler Purity Cooler Stock Picture of Success	• Alert for cooler purity issue • Alert for out-of-stock issue • Monitor against picture of success	—	×
Stock Monitoring	Real-time Out-of-stock Monitoring Automatic Ordering	• Alert for out-of-stock issue • Monitor against picture of success	—	×
Mobile Integration				
Full Mobile App Integration	Cooler Repair Module Actionable Analytics SFA/DSD/Supervisor Module RED Integration	• Compliance to picture of success and RED • Increase visibility to health of coolers • Increase sales rep field efficiency • Reduce cooler theft	×	×
Phone App with Camera	Cooler Purity Compliance	• Increase sales rep efficiency • Monitor against picture of success	×	N/A
Real-time Alerts	Purity, Stock, Health	• Proactively manage customer issues	—	×
Optional Add-ons				
Digital Signage	Dynamics Promotions	• Increase customer awareness and brand strength	—	×
Electronic Pricing	Compliance	• Ensure pricing visibility compliance • Confidential do not distribute • Allow remote management of pricing	—	×

Since Cambodia and Vietnam didn't want to pay for a cellular connected device, we had to train these devices to connect with the sales rep's phones when they did their weekly visits to the stores. At this time, the device would download all the data saved from the last week to the reps phone and they could see: (1) how many times the door was open, (2) if the cooler was moved, and (3) temperature trends (many store owners would unplug to save electricity). Through analytics even though we didn't have a camera we could still make an approximation if the store owner was using the cooler for their own personal purposes because we knew the average amounts of door opens per sale was around 1.5 and if it was over this we knew there was an issue (for example the shop owner was selling non-Coke products out of the Coke cooler).

In terms of operational capabilities and both knowledge and experience in our given industry, we were years ahead. Many people were trying to sell cooler monitors into Coke and other CPG companies, but they were all missing two key pieces:

1. How to make the IoT data collected actionable; and
2. Develop a concrete business case. I will explain each one further in the below case studies.

Workshop 1: How to Make IoT Data Actionable

Issue: After you make a case for the technology, you must talk Coke into installing a lot of IoT devices to launch a global initiative to revolutionize how the company monetizes data.

1. The IoT solutions that become successful have to make it through two stages: (a) Proving that the solution can actually work to collect the data; (b) actually turning the data into something that either saves the company money and/or earns more revenue. This requires a great deal of imagination and also the ability to use inexpensive test markets that are more "primitive" in order to implement experiments quickly. This is because these markets, processes, and consumers are not contaminated by processes and regulations that prohibit (and are designed to prevent) new entrants. Also, these new markets are not swarming with lobbyists and lawyers who impose barriers to new entrants.
2. Coke used Vietnam for just this purpose. Most of the 14 million coolers globally are put in retail outlets that it does not own or control. They are given to shop owners for free in exchange for only using them to sell Coke. For IoT to be successful, an IoT sensor needs to be installed in each one. Shop owners could try to take this device and sell it, so they included a lock so it couldn't be removed. Shop-owners would be likely to unplug the coolers (to save electricity) when the Coke sales rep wasn't in the store but plug it in the morning before he/she would visit so they designed a battery backup that would allow the device to still collect data even while the cooler was unplugged.

(Continued)

(Continued)

3. For the second stage of making the data actionable which is probably the most important factor in why we won out against all the competition. Many IoT vendors develop devices with a (1) sensor and (2) a basic independent, non-integrated app that shows the temperature and location of a given asset. But, they forget what they are actually selling. They think they are selling a monitoring device when what the customer actually wants is *ICE cold Coke* in all their outlets. They totally forget to explain and plan for how to actually *solve the customer's problem*. The key is to focus on exactly what the Coke sales rep is trying to achieve. Even though we had the technology to enable this, solving the problem was 80% going to be on the sales rep who visited these outlets regularly, so we had to account for this.

Discussion: At this early stage in IoT, it is *still* rarely practiced and implemented as an end-to-end solution. Everybody is making PowerPoints and fake dashboards, but not actually creating any value or solving the client's real problem. At Coke, we solved this by making the hardware to collect and software to report the data, and it also integrated the data into their sales app so that when the reps woke up, their schedule was automatically organized by an algorithm which prioritized the biggest issues that represented the highest sales (and many other factors). Previously, the sales reps followed a 7-day schedule and often times visited stores that did not need to be visited. Now, the visits were determined by data (inventory issues, fewer door openings, temperature problems, and cooler location questions).

Tech Geeks Must Interact with Marketing People to Make IoT Work

Most IoT devices and applications were (and still are) developed by tech people. The ones that become successful have to make it through two major stage gates: (1) proving that the solution can actually work to collect the data, and (2) being able to actually turn the data into something that can be used to actually improve the process and either save the company money and/or earn more revenue. For both parts of the "actionable" component, it was critical we had Rajesh and Manoj (our development team) who not only had years of experience working for top-tier pharma companies, government agencies, and hospitals right in Washington D.C., but also grew up in India. Both these guys' technical knowledge was unparalleled, however, growing up in India I believe gave them a huge advantage, as they were building the technology, they foresaw things that tend to happen in developing markets like Vietnam that I didn't even consider long before we ever tested in the field.

A perfect example of this for the first stage gate of making the devices successfully collect the data was that Rajesh and Manoj anticipated things the shop owners would and wouldn't do, in addition to conditions of the retail outlets nobody could have predicted. Most of the 14 million Coke coolers are put in some kind of retail outlet that Coke does not own or control. They are given to the shop owners for free in exchange for only using them to sell Coke, keeping the light on and plugged in, etc. Rajesh and Manoj would realize things like the potential that shop owners could potentially try to take this device and sell it, so they included a lock so it couldn't be removed.

They also foresaw that many of the shop owners would be likely to unplug the coolers when the Coke sales rep wasn't in the store to save electricity. They would likely plug it back before a visit. So, the tech team designed a battery backup that would allow the device to still collect data even while the cooler was unplugged. There were hundreds of these examples that allowed us to have the #1 device on the market and handle any customer objections. By us making these devices ready and rugged enough to handle the developing markets, we were a slam dunk in the developed markets in the west.

For the second stage of making the data actionable which is probably the most important factor in why we won out against all the competition. While many IoT vendors develop devices with a sensor and maybe a basic independent, non-integrated app that shows the temperature and location of a given asset, they forget what they are actually selling. They think they are selling a monitoring device when what the client actually wants is *ICE cold Coke* in all their outlets. They totally forget to explain and plan for how to actually *solve the client's problem*.

The way we did this better than anyone was relentlessly studying the people who had to actually use the data to tell the shop owner to remove the fried chicken from the Coke cooler or plug it in 24/7 or else they would put the cooler in a more profitable outlet. Even though we had the technology to enable this, solving the problem was 80% going to be on the sales rep who visited these outlets regularly, so we had to account for this.

Installing IoT Sensors in Vietnam

I arrived in Ho Chi Minh City on a Sunday in July of 2015 and it was really hot. When I got in, I was met by Khanh, the applications director for Coke Vietnam. Khanh was around 30, must have stood around 5′8″ and was the nicest guy you'll ever meet. We had talked on the phone quite a bit so we were already like old friends. He took me to my hotel to drop my bags and we went out right away for some street food.

The next morning Khanh picked me up to go to the HCMH office which was their headquarters in Vietnam. I went in and met Ajay the CIO, and then met Andre who was the CEO at the time. Both of them were very interested in this project because their boss Aiden was very interested. I tried to listen as much as possible to them while also sharing a little what we had learned in other markets like Mexico. I knew if we wanted to get the Coke Europe deal, we would have to make these guys happy and build a credible business case to be extrapolated to the rest of Coke.

That afternoon Khanh and I left to go on a few store visits. Visiting the stores in Saigon was nice and the city was loud and vibrant. We spent the day getting ready for our trip the next day in Da Nang, which was where they requested the pilot take place. Da Nang was apparently Coke Vietnam's "innovation hub" so I didn't really have a choice in the matter.

My motorbike in Da Nang

The first week was all about planning with the local team. Khanh and I went first thing to meet with the reps during their normal daily sales meeting before they started going out on store visits. Naturally I understood nothing, but Khanh was nice and helped me translate. Once we collected the feedback from the reps, we went back to the hotel to make our installation plan. That night Khanh helped me rent a motorbike because it was much easier to get around. We also stopped at this sketchy place to eat more street food, which I knew was a bad idea as I hadn't lived in Asia for over a year and my stomach wasn't used to it, but agreed to go anyways.

Our first sales meeting with the Da Nang team

Since the Smart Vision devices were more expensive and required a cellular connection, Coke decided not to use them in Vietnam. So, we needed to deploy 200 Smart Tag which was definitely the easier device. Since the Smart Tag was a BLE powered device, we would have to pair it with a sales rep's phone upon installation and log the cooler's location, temperature, etc. We would open and close the door to test the device and as soon as it is registered in the app, we knew we were in business.

Of course, we had problems at every store we went to. Jonathan in Shanghai had gone and made sure that the project wouldn't happen unless everything was integrated to his software, which Cambodia and Vietnam were using at the time. By now Rajesh and Manoj's hardware was well tested in all conditions but Jonathan's team still couldn't develop software that would integrate. By 3 pm on the first day, we might have completed five or so installations. By this time, it was over 40 degrees Celsius and I was in the middle of my first experience with food poisoning. I found an excuse to go back to the hotel and didn't leave for the rest of the night. That night I talked to Joseph and Fabio about the issues with AS's software and they basically told me to just document everything and get these things installed no matter what.

Khanh and I were in full gear the next day. I haven't been to Da Nang since, but in 2015 it was not a place one could easily find food suitable for an American getting over food poisoning. I managed to eat some bread from the hotel for breakfast and we were on our way.

Khanh and I installing the coolers in Da Nang

We picked up the pace on day 2 and got 15 units installed ourselves. Now that we had a rhythm going, we were able to train local technicians on how to install and activate the devices so we could focus on data collection and training the sales reps. Initially, we would consider it a success if the reps could simply arrive at the store and have the device synch with their phone, which for the most part they did.

We were now getting all the data on door openings, temperature, and if the cooler was moved or turned off. I even wrote an algorithm to determine if the cooler had a purity issue without the camera. We started to know based on comparing the door openings by time of day to the overall weekly sales data whether or not the store owners were opening the door to go get their chicken for dinner that night or whether it was a customer buying something. We also found that some owners turned the cooler off as soon as the sales rep left to save electricity.

Installing IoT Devices in Cambodia

After 2 weeks of installations and training for the team on the ground, we had to go to Cambodia to do the whole thing over again while the coolers in Vietnam continued collecting data. Cambodia's sales director Meas met me on the ground there and we were at it again. Each team in both Cambodia and Vietnam were some of the nicest, smartest people I've ever met. Being on the ground in both these places, I could really see the progress by the day. Each of these organizations were installing new software systems, well versed in IoT, and completely technology driven. The only thing really holding them back was actually Coke, and that their HQ had the biggest say in major decisions for technology, etc.

When being on the ground with the teams, I learned quickly as it had been for me in China that the most important thing was to gain the trust of the local teams. In addition to technical knowledge and experience, the best way to accomplish this was to really hangout with them and interact in a non-judgmental way. Since I didn't drink, I basically had to go out with these guys and eat local food all the time to prove I was open to get out of my comfort zone to better understand and appreciate their culture. By me driving around on a motorcycle in the 40-degree heat while going through horrible food poisoning, it gave me credibility most foreigners wouldn't have, and I'm not just making this up, both Meas and Khanh told me this almost every day throughout this project.

Workshop 2: Booze, Brothels, and Millennials

Issue: Many people I come across with addiction issues think that in order to be successful in business, especially in Asia, you have to drink and do things like going to brothels with your clients.

1. The political winds are blowing cold now and various governments will be looking for ways to trip up technology in competitor countries. Minor infractions such as visiting a brothel can be used to sabotage someone's credibility or reputation.
2. Take the tale of a Chinese British millennial who went to Shenzhen for business in the middle of 2019. He was not necessarily detained for stirring up trouble or smuggling contraband. He was detained for several days because there was video of him entering a brothel not once but 3 times. The Chinese government arrested him on a legitimate (albeit absurdly common) misdemeanor and tried to compromise him. All governments do this — and will do it more as the new tech Cold War heats up. His career was never the same.
3. One of the oldest tricks in the book is to compromise a business associate so you have them under your control. You have dirt on them and so can corrupt them to your way of thinking or acting. If you have dirt on them, they can't expose any corruption for fear of reprisal and exposure to a spouse or loved one for sexual hanky-panky. Why go down this road if you don't need to? It's not just good morals. It's good business. Mixing booze and brothels leads to problems. When has it not?

Discussion: The use of booze and brothels to generate business is something of a distasteful topic for millennials. There is greater attention to mental health and awareness of addiction issues at a younger age. It's a badge of honor to be a "Sober millennial" these days. Austin said: "I have sold millions of dollars' worth of disruptive technology all over the planet and never had to be forced to drink or do anything that goes against my moral code." In addition, it is a curious phenomenon that millennials are having less sex, anyway. If you let people know who you are from the beginning, they will respect you and if they don't, you can't be afraid to walk away to uphold your values. As Bob Dylan said, "the times they are a changing".

Once our sensors were up and running in both countries now the real work started. Collecting the data was the first part but now we actually had to show business value. We knew the basic metrics in most of the stores in terms of what percentage of the coolers were turned on, etc., and now we needed to see if we could make improvements in those stores, which would hopefully lead to improvements in revenue.

I spent the following few weeks going back and forth between Cambodia and Vietnam riding around on a motorbike dealing with the local teams during the day, then up with Joseph and Fabio all night on the phone building our business case for Aiden. I'd met a girl from Puerto Rico in the elevator of my building in Atlanta (let's call her Jane) before I'd left for Vietnam and if I didn't pass out after talking to Joseph and Fabio I usually give her a call. To this day, I couldn't imagine what she thought initially talking to a gringo who was off in Vietnam installing smart coolers for Coke.

Toward the end of my trip in Vietnam and Cambodia, some of the Coke big shots including Aiden came to visit. At this point, we had most everything up and running so I went out with the guys in the field and showed them how it works. What happened next will surprise you.

Aiden and the Coke leadership really liked the technology. At this point, they all knew that AS was a bad investment and Accenture was the only one keeping this entire project alive. This was by far the most successful pilot Coke had ever done here because we were the only ones to demonstrate the coolers with the monitoring actually sold more, whereas most of the other tests they had done were purely for technical ability (only collecting data).

By now, the 8-week project had come to an end, and that was time for me to go home to Atlanta and debrief with the Accenture team.

The first day back in the Accenture office in Atlanta was an interesting one. I remember Joseph, Fabio, and the team waiting for me as I entered the conference room and Joseph even gave me a hug as he was so happy to see me again. They asked me all kinds of questions about how the trip was, the local teammates, and how horrible AS's software was. I probably exaggerated a little bit, but overall I gave them a good summary and so now we had the task of summarizing all the data and showing a sustained increase in sales. We were continuing to collect data even though we were not actually in the country anymore.

Every day we would analyze the data with the team during the day and at night I would be basically on the phone all night with the two teams in Cambodia and Vietnam giving them instructions on what actions to actually take to improve sales in these coolers. While this was going on, we were continuing to push for the European deal with Coke, but they were still waiting for the official results of the Vietnam pilot. Finally, after around 3–4 weeks of hard work analyzing this data, we got invited for a call with the chief development officer of Coke and also the chief technology officer, which out of the blue, we kind of had a bad feeling about.

First on the call was a woman named Gladys who did not really know much about technology but somehow, she got a high-tech position in a Coke. Following that Roberto joined, who notoriously did not like us and had a reputation in the industry as being cheap. Joseph and Fabio allowed me to sit in on the call again (very nice of them considering I was technically "junior" in Accenture).

Gladys got on the call first and wanted to wait for Roberto to join in order for us to start, which we knew was a bad sign. When Roberto finally came on, he did not let us introduce anything or even state our case. He did not waste any time and said something like, "we have decided not to work with you on this project and thank you very much for your time and effort." Yet another big blow after another tireless year of working day and night to move this IoT project into production at a mass scale. When Roberto said that, I mean, being a boss of all of Coke IT, we knew it was over.

Later that day, we found out as well that Coke Europe had decided to not choose us as a partner but still choose AS, so AS did in fact got the deal for their hardware and software. Of course, Rajesh, Manoj, and I did not see a commission for even though all the work was performed by us as Jonathan thought he could handle the implementation all with his 400 people in Shanghai. I remember that day like it was yesterday, walking out of the office totally defeated. I even went to the expensive restaurant next door to treat myself to something nice. It was a nice Atlanta day and the only thing I could think about was "what the hell am I going to do now?"

To my knowledge, Coke never ended up scaling any of these IoT projects. They may tell you in the news of all the things they are doing for technology, but if you look in the coolers at any 711 in the US you will likely not find the devices. I can only imagine this is due to either Jon's ego, or the typical corporate over-thinking and bureaucracy of big, US companies. It's similar to how they have all these "environmental initiatives" but when you go to any river or lake you are bound to see some Coke or other CPG company's plastic bottles or packaging. My experience has taught me mostly all these things are really for show and by the time they implement anything it is already too late.

The good thing was that I was still at Accenture and I had a good salary plus benefits, but at Accenture you have to actually apply for projects internally even once you are an employee there. I was still going to have to apply for jobs on different projects and so I figured since I had this IoT expertise, it would be easy. I would come to find out that Accenture was not doing as much with IoT as they had let me to believe.

Workshop 3: Is Expertise of Older People "Dead" Given that New Technology Favors the New Young Entrant? If This is the Case, What Do Consulting Firms Full of Older People Have on Offer if They Do Not Develop the Da Vinci's?

Issue: Because there is so many new types of knowledge, new sciences, and new technologies, is experience a liability? Do young people have a leg up because everyone (young and old) are learning the same new knowledge?

1. Of course, the answer is yes. In his book *Da Vinci*, Walter Isaacson makes the point that we are in a period of time like Da Vinci's. In these times, there is an explosion of new technology, inventions, and new ways of doing things. It is an upsetting of the old order. This kind of works favors the young who have strengths in multidisciplinary sciences. Even the expertise of the young can be a liability. There is a great need for people — young and old — to connect new arrays of hitherto unidentified dots. There's definitely an art to maintaining balance, calm, sanity, and poise during times of great uncertainty.

2. These times call for a kind of (admittedly) exhausting return to generalist learning about everything. We don't know what is going to be important. We don't know what will work. We need to experiment. Hence, Da Vinci's constant experimentation was with paint, bronze, masonry,

(Continued)

(Continued)

munitions, flying machines, anatomy, marble, tile, etc. On the way, he became one of the most influential people of the millennium.

3. Da Vinci had mentors. He had benefactors. He had political support. Without all of these, he would never have succeeded, and he knew how to cooperate, although he was notoriously fidgety and prickly about projects. He was left-handed, gay, moody, and scatter-brained. We need the creative and innovative in these times, although these people, by nature, do not fit into traditional corporate boxes. Does the maturity and judgment of the old really count? Of course. It counts if they have the maturity and flexibility to know that times are changing, and that different temperament and diverse arrangements are necessary to discover new ways of doing things.

Discussion: Millennials are changing the ways we traditionally learn, perform tasks, interact, work, and are motivated. Do they change jobs because firms do not understand this? Because these firms have done the same thing for 50 years? Millennials recognize down time and work rhythm. They have a healthier view of what money means. Yet, very little has changed in hiring practices, flexible time, incentive structures, physical job space, interview protocols, fundamental discussions of motivation, or ethics. Many companies are trying to do things on the surface to pretend they have made big changes but cultures where innovation is discouraged and unethical leadership still remains in place much of the time. We recognize ideal millennial behavior — and even applaud it — yet corporate culture rarely reflects or rewards it.

This stretch of time is where I had to do something I particularly hate, which was waiting. At Accenture, when you are not currently involved in any project is called on "the bench" just like baseball or football. When you are on the bench, you are supposed to apply to different projects and interview with the internal managing director who is responsible for that project. For someone like me with 2 years of work "experience" at the analyst level is supposed to be billable 90–100% of the time while the higher-up executives can spend up to 60% of their time doing non-billable business development.

By this time based on I'm very confident that I was one of the very few at Accenture or at least in my IoT team that had real-world IoT implementation experience. There were plenty of people who had designed sensors, made strategy PowerPoints, and put together solutions + business cases on paper. Until this point, I had not yet met someone who had actually built a solution from scratch, coordinated the installment of devices, and integrated the data so it was useful to the end users. So, at this point in time, even though by their marketing efforts you could not tell this, it appeared Accenture did not have any actual IoT projects active at that time.

So, therefore, my team instead of only being called the IoT strategy team, was called "Mobile Internet of Things Strategy" team. Our mobile projects were essentially doing analysis for firms like Procter & Gamble on how they could better develop enterprise apps for their employees to log their timecards, file HR complaints, etc. So, what I realized was I was the only one before this doing real IoT work and most of the around 40–50 people on my team were doing this kind of mobile strategy work. This essentially consisted of making PowerPoints telling companies what they could do with "mobility".

I knew that I could not risk going backwards and doing a non-IoT project so I applied to the only three or four projects I could find that had "Internet of Things" in their title in Accenture's backend project portal. I found out later on that these were not actually real IoT implementations similar to what I had been doing but "IoT strategy" projects. I soon also discovered that none of these were actually sold to the client yet so they were essentially making PowerPoint pitches to companies on the benefits of IoT, so non-billable and useless to my KPIs.

So, when there is an unpaid project at Accenture, it is classified as "business development". In these cases, I would not be billable right away, so my team lead didn't allow me to apply. What I realized was there were not actually any active projects in IoT at the time however, like many other consulting firms were working like hell and try and get clients because their marketing all said they were IoT experts already.

Joseph and Fabio were managing directors, so they got reassigned almost immediately. Joseph started working on some kind of digital customer experience for a large cruise line and I am not really sure what Fabio was doing, but he pretty much ignored me from there on unless he wanted me to do something for him. Joseph tried to get me on his new project but they did not really have a budget or an IoT component so that did not work out. The managing director of my IoT team's name was Ian, who was a nice guy, but he also knew that they did not really have much in my wheelhouse at the moment either. So, he just tried to give me something to get his team's billable hours up so I was not dragging down the team's PNL.

Here I was again, a 24-year-old or so who spoke Chinese, was an expert in IoT in a company that was marketing itself as a digital IoT company, and I could not get a job.

I have been in these situations before obviously and knew that I could not give up. I knew that I had something special to offer and it just did not seem like there was a good fit within Accenture, but I kept going because the salary was good and quite frankly, needed the money. I did very well and continued to save around 70% of my income living like a college student. This would end up being very important later on.

I then started reaching out to everyone at Accenture that had anything to do with China just like I'd done after graduating Drexel. The first person I reached out to was someone named Robert who was a managing director for IoT in China. Like me, he claimed to speak Chinese, so I told him my story to see if it would resonate and maybe lead to an opportunity. It was similar to his story, but he just really didn't seem to be interested in helping me. His exact words were "Chinese people won't do business with a white guy who is under 40, it just will never happen." I was so mad; people had now been telling me this for 5 years and I couldn't wait to prove him wrong.

I noticed that it continued to happen more and more within the company. I reached out to different managing directors and senior managers within Accenture and passionately told them my story and where I could add value. To their credit, they would always take the meeting with me, but a lot of them either could not do anything or just did not care enough. Most were more worried about how they were going to look to their boss the next time their performance review came up and were not as interested in sticking their neck out for a junior person.

I had a girlfriend at the time who helped distract me from the pain from the universe seemingly now pushing me in a new direction. We lived next door to each other, which was funny considering we met in the elevator of my building. On the weekends, we took trips to the surrounding places of Atlanta like the Smoky Mountains or some random beach in Florida. I remember it being one of the better times in my life until that point. However, I was getting more and more worried about my career and knew that even though Accenture was stagnant I had to keep moving forward.

Jane was from Puerto Rico and spoke Spanish fluently. So, I figured that if I was not going to be advancing anymore in my IoT experience, I might as well add another language that 500 million people globally speak. So, I enrolled in Spanish classes at the Atlanta Latin America Association. I started going to classes 3 days a week, which was useful to start. For me staying stagnant is the same as going backwards. If I'm not moving forward at a rapid pace, I just can't sleep at night. To this day I don't know why this is, but it usually causes me to have quite a few crazy ideas to work on simultaneously.

While this is happening, of course, Ian (the MD of the mobile strategy and IoT at Accenture) is trying like hell to get me a billable job so I do not drag down his team's P&L. Finally, they called me one day and told me there was a spot for a financial company outside the suburbs of Philadelphia, Pennsylvania to help them do an analysis of their internal mobile applications. When I heard about this project, I immediately wanted to jump off the 10th floor of my building due to a lack of excitement. However, I figured maybe I could learn something new, so I decided to go forth with it.

Workshop 4: Huawei Mexico: Does the American Monroe Doctrine Lead to the Chinese South Sea Doctrine?

Issue: The United States implemented the Monroe Doctrine in order to eliminate the possibility of European powers from trying to recolonize their old dominions. When Austin walked into the AT&T offices in Mexico City, there were wall-to-wall mandarin speakers all over who were from Huawei. Did this reality get back to Washington and cause the government to have a "Monroe Moment"?

1. On December 6, 2018, Sabrina Meng, the CFO of Huawei and the founder's daughter, was arrested in Vancouver Airport. She was transiting to Mexico City for work with Huawei. Huawei was building out 5G equipment for Mexico. Until May 2018, that is. That was when Huawei's partner, Altan Redes, suddenly changed vendors for 5G and gave the buildout for the northern part of Mexico City to Nokia. Huawei's 5G buildout was relegated to the southern half of Mexico.

(Continued)

(Continued)

2. The US government said that Huawei was an untrustworthy agent of the Chinese government. It said that all data from Huawei could be accessed by the Chinese military for nefarious purposes. It implemented a program throughout Latin America to try to extract Huawei from the region. This went beyond Latin America and included any NATO ally. Altan Redes said it made the decision "exclusively on technical and economic optimization criteria".

3. The attempt to exclude Huawei from the US and Latin America is hypocritical, according to Peter Frankopan in his magisterial work "The Silk Roads". He said that "the US decided that Huawei and ZTE "cannot be trusted" on the basis that they are too close to the Chinese "state influence and thus pose a security threat to the US" — paradoxical given the subsequent revelation that the National Security Agency set up a clandestine programme named Operation Shotgiant to infiltrate and hack Huawei's servers" (p. 518).

Discussion: Should the US still run the emerging markets "neighborhood" in a brutal imperial way? Is this behavior from another century? The US interfered in more than 20 countries in Latin America with coups and installed military governments. Is this behavior past its "sell by" date?

Leading this project was a consultant, which was one rank ahead of me at the time and this guy, Tony was my boss for this project. This finance company in PA was essentially paying us, Tony and I, $500,000 to make them a PowerPoint containing the different definitions of the components of a mobile strategy. At the time, our team had a nine-tier or nine-component mobile strategy framework, they called it. I don't remember what the nine components were, but I remember it didn't seem like anything groundbreaking.

I remember one was something like "stakeholder engagement", so my first task was to develop a theory about how this company needs to do stakeholder engagement around "mobility". This was for an internal mobile HR app that nobody used in the company anyways. I remember feeling so bored that all I could think about was learning more Spanish or suddenly leaving to become a Sherpa in the Himalayas. My Spanish classes started at 6 pm. So since most of this project was remote, I basically spent all day at my house pretending to do work with these PowerPoints. If I had a conference call, I would put the call on mute while driving to class.

Even though I was not getting much from my work, life overall was still good. I had some really good friends in Atlanta but I knew that I needed something else to happen. I really enjoyed learning Spanish and I was starting to get pretty good at it. As with Chinese, I knew that if I wanted to get really good that I had to go and move to a Spanish-speaking country because as nice as my girlfriend was, she was not willing to speak Spanish with me yet. I must have made all my mentors crazy because I had been calling them for weeks, telling them I was sick of doing PowerPoints, I just wanted to do something that made me feel I was moving forward, I could not stand to be stagnant. I had to accomplish that goal no matter what so I decided to move to Mexico and study Spanish.

Before I had a chance to tell my boss Ian at Accenture, I suddenly got a call from him. I was a little worried as this was the first time he had ever actually called me. "Hey Austin, quick question" he said, "you speak Spanish, right?" "Yes" I said, "I mean enough to get around", which was a total exaggeration. He continued to say, "I have an Internet of Things project in Mexico City that I think would be perfect for you." He explained that AT&T was buying the third and fourth largest communication provider companies in Mexico to try to get rid of the monopoly that Telcel had there. What they needed was someone to manage the integration of their IoT program with the providers in Mexico, and he thought of me for that! It was a total eureka moment, not only would I get to lead a huge IoT project but would also get to become fluent in Spanish! I said yes immediately and moved to Mexico on Monday morning.

Chapter 7

AT&T and Huawei in Mexico City

Our Internet of Things (IoT) project kickoff meeting took place in the W Hotel in Mexico City in the basement. When I arrived there, there was a huge table filled with guys in suits along with Joe who I met for the first time. Joe seemed like an ordinary IT geek from the south. Everybody was pleasant and while they were introducing themselves, I felt right at home. I knew that based on our interactions that day, Joe would either accept me or not as the project lead for this initiative. The good news was I knew he did not really have any interest in the day-to-day execution. At the time this was actually a relief because execution was my specialty.

As the meeting started, I realized I had no idea at the time what this project actually consisted of. I just knew it was an "Internet of Things" project in Mexico City so I immediately said yes. Joe began the presentation, introduced the project, and essentially, we needed to connect the IoT networks and the backends of AT&T and the two companies that they acquired, which I had no idea how to do. My area of expertise in IoT at the time was sensors, software, user applications and analytics. This project, however, was focused on the integration of the backend of three telecom providers. Even though the meeting was in English, they might as well have been speaking Spanish the whole time because I had no idea what they were talking about. Right from the start the meeting turned very technical. Hearing words like HLR's, SMS, IoT core had me starting to get very worried.

There were representatives from different teams in the meeting. The IT team, which I would be working the most with, had someone named

Ekton and Donizetti. Juan Carlos and Carlos headed the network team and Antuan and Roberto managed the sales team. Joe got up and then explained in very technical terms what needed to be done with the integration of these three companies. The technical details of this I am not allowed to share, however, I will give you a broad idea of the culture and what went on behind the scenes of the actual project.

I had considered trying to impress Joe with my IoT background, knowledge and skills but something told me that he just wanted someone that he could stand to work with and not necessarily the technical expertise. I decided when we were on our lunch break to start by asking about his family and then mentioned something about football. Joe was from the countryside in Georgia and from his response it seemed he was more or less refreshed to hear a normal conversation. Whatever I did must have worked because within a couple of hours I got a call from Dustin, the AT&T Account director from Accenture, who had told me that Joe absolutely wanted me to lead this project from the Accenture side.

That evening the Accenture team in Mexico City invited me out to dinner. We went to an American restaurant, which I thought was slightly strange (we were in Mexico City). The team mostly consisted of people in their 20s and 30s who seemed to be to me a little bit stuck up. Most of them went to colleges like Georgetown and got their MBA from the University of Chicago — and liked to remind people of that.

Under Accenture's typical consulting contract, the project did allow you the usual option of flying to Mexico City on Monday morning from wherever you lived in the US, and a Thursday evening flight home. So, all the people in this project (I think there were around 30–40 of them) chose to do exactly that. Most of them did not speak Spanish and I was the only one that I could remember had any intention of learning the language and more about Mexican culture in general. I was also the only one who seemed interested in talking with the locals working on the project to learn more about the big picture in where this project and Mexico in general was heading.

To me this seemed crazy because I thought this was an awesome opportunity to learn a culture shared by 130 million people and a language shared by 500 million people. Even though most of the team didn't want to adventure outside of the Accenture group, I knew exactly what I was there to do. So, I asked Dustin if I could stay in Mexico City on the weekends using the excuse it would save money. They seemed to think this was strange, but ended up agreeing in the end.

The first official day of the project was Tuesday and I was forced to go to one of AT&T's old IT offices way outside of CDMX. It took around an hour and a half to get to from my hotel in downtown with typical Mexico City Traffic. I went inside and met with Ekton who was my partner on the project and a really nice guy. Ekton's English was fluent, which was a good thing for me at first because I really did not know any Spanish at the time (even though I pretended to in order to get the role). By this point, I had already found out from my previous experiences whether it was technology or learning Chinese, the best way to learn something for is just to throw yourself into the shark tank, and that is exactly what I was going to do with both for this project.

Ekton took me around the office and introduced me to everybody. In Mexico there is a real brotherhood among coworkers that you do not see in the US. Every single person that you meet if it is a man, you definitely shake their hand and possibly give him a bro hug, and if it is a woman you give a kiss on two cheeks even if you do not necessarily work with them every day. In any given day in the office you can kiss between 15 and 20 people. Everybody is extremely friendly in the office environment, which I thought was great. It felt as if everyone was more like friends than colleagues.

There were probably 500–1,000 or so people in this office and one thing I distinctly remember walking through there on the first day was that around a quarter of the people in this office were Chinese. So, of course, I asked Ekton, "What are these Chinese people doing here in Mexico City?" and he replied, "Oh! Those guys work for Huawei they are building out our network infrastructure."

I was so surprised that right on the border of the US that Huawei would be doing a huge network buildout (this theme will continue to play out later in the story). I will say, in every developing country I have been to since Mexico, Huawei has been there building out there 3G, 4G, and 5G infrastructure. One thing in particular I noticed about the Huawei personnel that was distinctly different than any Western partners at AT&T was they kept such a low profile. Anyone in the office from Cisco, Ericsson, Accenture, or Tech Mahindra always wanted to be seen. They were always asking for meetings with the CEO, etc., but Huawei employees almost seemed like they didn't want to be noticed. It felt like they just wanted to complete this project before anyone really realized that a Chinese State-Owned Company was building out this wireless network just a few miles south of Texas.

Our first day was essentially filled with meetings in Spanish of which I understood maybe 2%. People talking about extreme technical details of how we are going to do this integration. To be honest, I wouldn't have understood even if it was in English. One thing I did know we needed to have if we wanted to be successful was a good project plan. Luckily I had just finished working on a very large, complex project with the best project manager to this day I have never seen (Joseph). I immediately gathered all the materials that Joseph produced to manage the project with Coke and then translated them down to fit our project.

This is also another golden rule I have. To be clear, I don't want to advocate stealing or copyright infringement, but one thing that the Chinese do very well (that I have similarly adopted) is the following: if you do not have to start from zero and it's possible to learn from someone else, then do it.

I saved probably 2 weeks of starting from scratch on a project plan by just using what we had done with Joseph previously. That Tuesday was filled with meetings, of which the productivity level was questionable at best. However, in Mexico City if you want to get anything started, it is a very, very political process. We had to invite someone from every department to a separate meeting to make them feel included. The topics we were discussing really didn't impact them at all, we just needed to make sure they didn't cause any problems for us by complaining after their egos were hurt by not feeling included.

So, then when 1.30–2 pm came around, which the universal lunchtime in Mexico, Ekton and Donizetti decided on going out to Hooters. The women in our team came along as well and it was totally normal for them to choose a place like Hooters. It was not a chauvinistic thing, they just happened to like Hooters' fried chicken wings. The whole team also managed to have 2–3 beers each in the over 2-hour "lunchbreak". After watching an entire football game by the time we got back to the office it was already 4 pm.

I would say that the first day was not the most productive day ever, but it definitely gave me some insight into what the next couple of months was going to be like. That night I got back to my hotel room and the first thing I did was to find a Spanish teacher. There was a website I found that had tutors available, but my problem was the only time I had free was early mornings before work, by the time I got home my brain was fried. At this point I came to realize how difficult it was to find someone to work with you at 7 am in Mexico City. After calling dozens of numbers, finally

I found a tutor that was willing to meet every day at 7 am. Her name was Maria and she had fled Venezuela some time back.

From then on, my days consisted of waking up at 5.30 am, taking a shower, putting my suit on, going downstairs in the hotel (I was lucky enough to stay at the W Hotel for a year, major Starwood points). From 6–7 am I was doing my Spanish homework and eating breakfast, then when Maria showed up at 7 am, I basically forced her to talk to me for 1 hour in Spanish before heading to work at 8 am.

My Spanish improved very rapidly because of the strategy I employed. All day in the office we had meetings in Spanish. Every time there was a topic or even a word that I did not know a lot about I would write it down and review with Maria the next morning. Say if the topic was "software integration". The following morning at 7 am with Maria, I would make the topic of our hour-long conversation about software integration.

She would make up random questions like, "how long does it take to integrate the new CRM system with SAP? What are the phases of your project?". Then usually I would proceed to try and sell on some type of implementation plan in Spanish to which she would respond with the questions that a typical buyer would ask. We did this every day for eight months repeatedly until my head hurt.

The days were very long and for those of you who have never worked in a foreign country in a different language, it takes an extra toll on your body and your mind. Every day by 2 or 3 pm, I felt completely mentally exhausted because not only was I working on a project that was technically challenging in a different culture, but I also had to process these things in Spanish. That being said, I was living my dream. I was doing exactly what I was supposed to do and could not have been happier. I was learning about new technology, new culture and new language.

The project we were on moved painfully slow. Joe ended up really checking out after the first initial meeting. During the second week he invited me to go out drinking with him (barking up the wrong tree) so I went out with a couple of our colleagues and after refusing to drink for the 5th time, he decided that he did not want to hang out with me anymore. This was a price I was willing to pay for putting my physical and mental health first and avoiding alcohol or drugs.

Each day that passed was very similar to the last in terms of what we have to do for the project. There were meetings, which everyone showed up late to, followed by a 2-hour long lunch with beer and tacos, followed by more meetings, and then we went home. I started to realize that telecom companies (both US and Mexico) are pretty disorganized — and very inefficient — which caused them to ultimately fail to add real value to the IoT.

Around this time in 2015, it was undeniable that IoT was going to be bigger than ever. The large US carrier's core competency has always been the data side for cellular connected devices. As the number of cell phone users in developed countries started to peak (because you can only have so many cell phones) these providers needed new ways to grow their business and so they looked to IoT to do that. The problem is/was the real value in the IoT is in the actual data collected and user application where that data is analyzed, to later be put into action similar to what we were doing with Coke.

However, the telecom providers did/do not have real expertise in software or really understanding their customers' businesses, so they constantly struggle to find where they can add value in IoT (this story will play out over the rest of this book). Unfortunately, it has taken far too long for the telecom providers to actually understand this, even though the writing was on the wall very early. So they decided to stick to what they knew and ended up providing the data for only cellular connected IoT devices, which are actually a small percentage of overall IoT devices.

However, as we said earlier, with the Coke example, most companies try to avoid cellular connected IoT devices because they do not want to pay for the cellular modem, which at the time was around $40 extra for each device. In addition to the added hardware cost they do not want to pay the monthly data plan, which is between US$5 and US$10 a month depending on how many devices you roll out, and it made the cost of most IoT applications unsustainable. There was no return on investment in many cases if you have a cellular connected device. At this point, AT&T understood the Mexico business was way behind, so, our project was mainly focused on just getting the technical systems able to simply retrieve data from IoT devices. They weren't even close to being able to develop software that would actually add value to an end user of an IoT application.

So, in order to get AT&T's IoT network built and integrated, it required a great deal of collaboration between the IT, network, and sales team. It was very apparent to me very early on that this was not going to happen. I wished somehow, I saved the endless email chains with so many people copied on each of them. The only way to possibly describe this in a way anyone could understand, it was extremely political and disorganized.

To this day I do not think I have ever seen an organization waste more money on a given project for internal political reasons than what I witnessed in Mexico City. The thing was that AT&T knew that they were not able to execute this, which is why they were spending $120,000 a day plus five-star hotels and weekly flights from Mexico City to anywhere in the US for 40 Accenture senior people who were basically doing it for them.

Everything we needed to get done with this project required approvals from all three of those teams — IT, networks, and sales. Each one of the directors of the network, IT and sales team seemed to be involved in a competitive political struggle to please the CEO in Mexico. For the first 4 months of this project, I do not think one deliverable from my project was completed. You could look in this as a poor reflection on me as the project manager or you could choose to believe me when I said that nobody could have gotten this project done, no matter who they were.

In many instances, we would get half of the system built on the IT side, but the network team chose a different vendor that was not compatible because they wanted to build a separate system. In these cases, the directors would usually spend 3–4 weeks arguing, then we'd have to start over with a new vendor. All the while, Huawei was working like hell in the background. They had rented out an entire building next to our office and even had a Chinese chef for all their employees.

I, however had to focus on what I could control, and what I could control was my positive contribution to the project. One of those was learning Spanish to better communicate with the engineers below me. By the third month of this project, I was fluent enough to work and conduct meetings in Spanish. I made project plans in Spanish, had conference calls, and I was happier than ever that I could now communicate with 50% of the world's population.

I knew even though I had to struggle a great deal in month #1, #2, and #3, but from my experience learning Chinese and anyone interested in learning a language can benefit from this advice.

Even though the project was moving slowly Joe and AT&T were giving me great reviews. Having me 100% billable on the project helped Accenture's PNL and I was as a 25-year-old leading a team of 30 people in a technical project and language I didn't understand initially proved to be challenging early on. After much pain and frustration in addition to learning Spanish I also learned a lot about IoT networks and backends. Having to navigate the internal politics of AT&T Mexico was almost as difficult as selling IoT to Coke.

Even though I was actively managing 30 people for a project that cost in the tens of millions of dollars I was still the lowest rank that existed at Accenture. I would often joke that if Mark Zuckerberg came to a big consulting company, he wouldn't even be a managing director because he didn't have enough "years of experience". I pushed Ian hard for a promotion and I could tell he wanted me to have it because he loved taking credit for my projects internally. My method of managing up is different than most because I'm not afraid to speak honestly. Politics is not my strong suit, but I am in general pretty aggressive when it comes to my career and Accenture was no exception.

I started to also make a backup plan in case Ian couldn't deliver on the promotion. I would get daily LinkedIn messages and would go on interviews to keep my skills sharp. In addition, I kept close to Joseph and other managing directors. I even tried to switch to a team within Accenture that specialized in manufacturing IoT in exchange for a promotion, but Ian found out and squashed it.

Finally, after one year of working like hell on Coke and 8 months in Mexico, it came time for the company to announce promotions. It was clear to Ian at this point that in order to keep me at Accenture he had to help me in some way. Technically to move up to the next rank of "consultant" the requirement was 4 years of experience which I was short of by around a year. Finally, when the day came, they announced the promotions for the team and I wasn't on it. They all went to guys with 4 years' experience doing mostly PowerPoints and conference calls. While they were announcing Ian messaged me and apologized. "Sorry, Austin, by the time these approvals get to HR they are like robots and don't care about the value you create. I'm getting you approved now for a retention bonus so we can promote you next year."

I give a lot of credit to Ian for trying but by then it was too late, I was already starting to write this off as something that would take the rest of my life to really move upward, and I didn't have the time to play Accenture politics until my hair was falling out.

Chapter 8

Verizon

One day as I was going back and forth to Mexico City, I received two LinkedIn messages, one was from an MD I had known at Coke and the other from Verizon HR in the US. I paid $30 a month for the premium feature so I was getting a lot of inquiries from human resources people around the country. At this point, I was taking a wait-and-see approach, but I was not going to leave Accenture unless I got a big offer for a significant higher amount of money.

Both of these roles were Internet of Things (IoT) related. For Coke I was going to be the national manager of IoT projects for the US bottlers. That would involve me going around the country to different bottlers and consulting them on how they can extract more value out of the IoT. Verizon had just started an IoT solutions sales team and were looking for people to come on and sell actual end-to-end IoT solutions as opposed to just data plans, they were doing until that point.

Both Coke and Verizon had initially said the starting salary for the position was US$200,000 to US$300,000, which was much more than I was making at the time, so I was very interested. Coke ended up offering me the job, but the offer was much lower, and they said it was due to my "experience level". So, I decided to go with Verizon, who had stuck to the original target number. Even though they had actually given me an offer that was twice my previous salary, I still managed to have the guts to negotiate for even more. To my surprise, they called me back and agreed.

Verizon had a mandate to recruit a 100 people in 2 months to ramp up this IoT program that they started because they knew that they were falling behind with their enterprise customers. In addition to the pay, I just had too many bad memories at Coke and I knew they were still working with Jonathan in Shanghai, so I finally decided on Verizon.

We had a kickoff meeting (one of many kickoff meetings) with the Verizon team of 100 people that were recruited in the previous 60 days. Around 60–70 of these people were previously either Verizon salespeople with backgrounds mostly in selling handsets and data plans to enterprise clients or salespeople from AT&T, Sprint or TMobile doing exactly the same thing. So, 70% of our team really had no background in IoT solutions or software at all. The remaining 30 were men (I think out of the 100 people there must have been only three women) like me from various consulting companies and big outdated technology firms like IBM and Oracle.

It was clear from the fact that Verizon recruiting 100 high-level people making that much money within 50–60 days that they were quite desperate and knew they were behind the curve. More likely than not all of these people were evaluated as well as they should have been, but that being said you couldn't ask for a nicer group of people. However, in terms of selling and implementing end-to-end integrated IoT solutions with software and hardware, I probably had more experience than most of them even though I was the only one under 40 years old.

These 100 people were split up into three different verticals manufacturing, agriculture, and smart cities. Each of these verticals were ran by a managing director, who on average had 3–4 sales managers divided by region. Each of the sales managers had 5–10 IoT sales architects like me on their team depending on the region. At the top stood our Vice President, Ron.

Verizon is basically two companies, the main company is responsible for wireless, which has all the cell phones, data plans, network, etc. The other company, Verizon Enterprise Solutions, owns the fiber networks and a few other small enterprise businesses. Verizon Enterprise Solutions (VES) was much smaller and less profitable than the wireless business unit by a significant degree. VES also had a "professional services team", which was Verizon's version of a consulting business so they decided to put IoT within professional services.

The logic behind putting the 100 IoT people on my team into the professional services department was sound because IoT Solutions typically need professional services around them to integrate into existing client systems to make them relevant. In addition to that, most IoT solutions require sourcing together different pieces of the solution like the sensors, software, API development, etc. Ron was a smart guy, but I could tell from the opening meeting, it seemed a little bit fake. It seemed they did not really know what direction they needed to go yet. It just felt like more of a motivational speech on why Verizon was great rather than actual concrete technical reasons on why we had a competitive advantage in IoT solutions.

Verizon loves to talk about how many "assets" they have and how they are the largest company in terms of capital expenditures yearly within the Fortune 500. However, in my experience, they really only have one asset which is the network. In short, what happened was when wireless was being first introduced, the US government only allowed a certain amount of spectrum to be used and Verizon was able to buy a lot of that spectrum in the early days of wireless. This gave Verizon and AT&T monopolies in wireless and allowed them to be extremely profitable charging very high fees compared to other countries. However, this caused their competitive advantage to become lobbying the Federal Communications Commission (FCC), buying spectrum, and acquiring smaller companies to create an anti-competitive environment rather than competitive advantages like customer service, software, flexibility, etc.

Workshop 1: A Millennial's Take on Whether ATT & Verizon can Deliver 5G

Issue: This is important in many ways today because the US is mostly relying on AT&T, Verizon, and now the combined TMobile + Sprint (with the merger that should have never been allowed) to lead them into the 5G world. This may sound good to people who don't know and understand these companies, but my experience has me concerned about this as a strategy for the US for a number of reasons:

1. The Chinese Government is not just hoping their top three telecom companies lead the country into 5G. They are directly helping Huawei, China Mobile, and China Telecom to develop this technology and build hundreds of smart cities much faster. There is an absolute mandate to get this done ASAP and they all work together for one common purpose rather than three separate short-term agendas. The Chinese government

(Continued)

(Continued)

even encouraged the most innovators in the country to join the boards of the old telecom companies in order to give them a "kick in the arse". This is controversial and smart.

2. China Mobile is just as profitable and has almost the same dividend as AT&T, Verizon, and Comcast while carrying a far lower debt load. Despite this, in Shanghai, I pay a combined ¥200 (US$30) per month for Wi-Fi in my apartment in Shanghai, unlimited calls and data on my cell phone, and cable TV with China Telecom. In the US, my mom pays $200/month for cable, over $100 for Wi-Fi, and $120 per cell phone per month and these companies still can't earn higher profits than Chinese telecoms.

3. Chinese telecoms have only one purpose set by the government which is to advance 5G and communications for all of China as fast as possible no matter what. In the US, you have a series of failed acquisitions into the media space which are distracting and will slow down the 5G transition even more. On the other hand, Cisco, AT&T, Verizon, and TMobile are all public companies with short-term dividend conscious shareholders. This keeps management very short-term focused while China is playing the long game and investing big.

Discussion: Which country has state-sanctioned monopolies? China Mobile has less debt than AT&T. It has a far lower price for its cable services. It has better margins. Its balance sheet metrics are superior to AT&T. China and the US are both trying to put a fire under the behind of the big conglomerates and force them to get hungrier and more competitive. AT&T has a 60% dividend payout and keeps on buying back its stock. Is this sustainable?

Verizon had chosen six solutions to begin this IoT program. I could tell from our first meeting, these solutions were likely chosen in the same way most of our team was selected and onboarded, way too fast and careless. One of the solutions chosen was called "Share", which is essentially a $200 device that you can put on a car and it can unlock the car with the "Share" app and allow someone to go in and drive it.

I know what you're thinking. Can't most cars already do this? Don't most vehicles in the US already have remote unlock and start capabilities when they leave the factory? Why would anyone buy a $200 device and pay a monthly data fee to Verizon to do the exact same thing? Believe me, we were all wondering.

Another one of their solutions was a GPS location-based tracking system with a $100 device and a backend platform that showed dots on a map of where they were located. We even found out later on that the lovely device had a battery that lasted only 1 year, after the battery was dead, the entire $100 device would have to be replaced. Anyone who knows the IoT industry just based on these two descriptions would know that the devices themselves would not be very competitive in today's market. Using a basic business case proves this, assuming a $100 device fee, $70 technician installation fee, and $10 per month data charge from Verizon, the client is looking at a cost of $290 per year just to know the location of their asset (device had no other capabilities such as vibration, monitor temperature, etc.).

The first thing we did with our team lead Andrew was to identify target customers who would need this solution. Given my sales background in IoT solutions, I recommended we start with the business case and met customers that fit our requirement. Andrew let me build this out and I presented the team something similar to the following:

Assuming a cost of $290 per year and the only value lever of this solution is "knowing location" which you have to assume translates into recovering lost assets (which it rarely does), we were in a difficult situation to say the least in proving the value. In order to find a client that meets the required 3 times return on investment (typical industry IRR requirement for IT solutions), the assumed math would have to look something like this.

Client profile needed in order for this solution to make sense

- 3% of assets per year lost (very high and unlikely but ok)
- 50% recovery rate based purely on the dots on a map solution (also very unlikely)

(Continued)

(Continued)

So, assuming you have a client with the top two conditions, they would also need to have an asset value of $58,000 in order to get a 3 × ROI. ($290 cost per year per device times 33.3 (3% missing per year), times 2 (assuming you recover 50% of devices) times 3 again because a 3 × ROI is needed to be worth the internal effort to implement the solution.

Given that our sales target of $100 million that year (and it was already May), all we had to do was find companies with a total of 344,827 ($100 million/$290) assets valued at over $58,000 of which 3% are going missing per year. Should be easy right?

Needless to say, after seeing the math, the team was pretty bummed out. I can remember at least three of my teammates texting me during the presentation wondering why they wouldn't have calculated this a year earlier. The truth was nobody knew.

The IoT sales architects like me were all brought on to sell these six solutions, however, there was another team who had been "building" these solutions for 2 years before we got there. Our product team was placed under the Wireless division, and was filled with about 70 people also under three different managing directors who again had partners underneath them. Once again, under the MPs were the teams responsible for each of the individual solutions by region. Around 90% of the product team were former network engineers who were nearing retirement so none of us on the sales team ever felt they were really motivated.

Originally we, the IoT sales team thought these solutions were all developed by Verizon and we could gradually improve them as we progressed. We later came to find out that each one of these solutions were not actually built by Verizon, they were white labeled from other vendors. Which as you probably already guessed meant that Verizon had 70 former network architects full-time dedicated to being middlemen in six poorly chosen IoT Solutions that were to be sold by a completely different team and a completely different organization.

The product team's role was never actually clearly defined anywhere, which would lead to a lot of conflict later on. Both my teammates and I knew right away that this was not a good setup, but I was making so much money for a 25-year-old. Every 2 weeks when my paycheck arrived, I ignored the fact that the actual business was likely not going to go very far, and I should just make the best of it.

The GPS tracking solution had a seven-member product team spread throughout the country; the leadership was based in San Francisco, where the chosen vendor who actually built the solution was also located. Who this vendor was we never actually found out because the product team guarded them like how an eagle guards her nest. They knew if we ever actually found out who they were, there would be no need for the product team.

Most people reading this would probably think, "How could a team of seven senior engineers in 2016 select a $100 device that only shows dots on a map and has a battery life of less than 1 year when you can buy and enjoy a Huawei smartphone to make calls, watch videos, take pictures and include a GPS for less than $100?". Well we asked this question too and the answer was it took seven full-time "IoT experts" on the product team 2 full years to pull this off. Apologies for appearing to be such a downer, I only use these real-world examples to prove a point that the US really needs a different strategy when it comes to 5G and China.

The pressure was now mounting to get sales so regardless of the ugly business case we went out and started selling. As any technology solutions salespeople would tell you, when you present these kinds of solutions to the customers, they will inevitably have a lot of questions. Since we had only been working with the solutions for 2 weeks, we had a lot of questions as well. The only problem was to get a response from any of these seven "very busy" product team members in regard to the GPS solution took around 1 week, and many times the response was "I'll get back to you once I talk to the vendor". You might be asking yourself now, "how could someone whose only responsibility is to be a middleman managing the vendor with a team of seven that has no other responsibilities be so busy? How could anything else be more important than assisting the salespeople in selling this solution to customers? We couldn't figure it out either.

The main problem was there was no accountability from anyone on the product team and nobody in the company could actually do anything about this. It was like dealing with 50-year-old children in a boardroom. Our IoT sales leadership would complain that the product team did not really do anything and the IoT product team's leadership would complain that the sales team did not sell well. The truth was that the sales team as a whole was not qualified to actually build and sell IoT solutions, however, they were still much better at selling than the product team was at building and implementing IoT products. The fact was the product team was made up of 50+—year-old network engineers that had around 5 years left until retirement. These people had really no interest in doing anything innovative and behind closed doors they would tell me as such. This being the exact opposite of my teams in China, which were filled with motivated 20–30 years old technology experts who would refuse to leave the office on a Friday at 4.30 pm even when I tell them it's ok to go home.

Regardless of all of these, we had to get a sale at any cost, so we were going out and meeting with customers every day. There was very high pressure from our sales leadership to demonstrate that we were out there actively selling. So every single customer call or in person meeting that we did had to be logged into salesforce.com — our CRM system. Every week we would have "readouts" with the leadership on how many meetings the team took, the results of those meetings, what stages our opportunities were in the pipeline, etc. So from a sales management perspective, the management did a pretty good job of implementing this system because they had experience selling handsets and data plans to various businesses across the country.

After 3 or 4 months, we had sold nothing. Out of 100 people, we had zero revenue and zero deals in the final stages of the pipeline. Given that the running costs of 100 people making $200,000–300,000 a year while traveling everyday was quite significant, even for a company like Verizon, the head of our organization, Ron, suddenly "retired early". Therefore, Verizon decided to bring in another person who was a vice president of the company's Security Organization at the time, a man named Robert to head the IoT Solution sales team. Robert again had virtually zero experience selling and implementing IoT solutions. However, in typical US corporate style, they chose one of the "good old boys" who had the right relationships with the right people.

As Robert came in, he continued to put more pressure on more people because the higher-ups in the company were obviously putting more pressure on him. There was a sales goal that Verizon made before we were hired to sell US$100 million worth of these IoT solutions in the first year and here we were in month four with zero in revenue and no deals in the pipeline that were near closing. We had weekly calls with my team on how we could find ways to sell more, what the status was with our different customers. My teammates were overall very nice guys, but they were in a very difficult situation so the attitude on the team was very negative.

My team leader Andrew was probably the one with more sense than anyone of these 100-people organization. Andrew lived in Tampa and I would see him maybe once or twice a month at a Verizon function or going with me to customer meetings. He was a career Verizon guy, but he did have a stint as an entrepreneur, which gave him some credibility with me as he knew ways to attempt to cut through the red tape and get some things done.

I liked Andrew and I wanted to do well, so, I worked like hell to sell the first solution. I met with a local taxi company introduced through a sales rep in Iowa. Iowa wasn't technically my territory, but I took the opportunity because I knew even though it was small it would be a huge win to actually close something. The company was interested in implementing a solution that allowed the drivers to change cabs after their shift without actually having to return to the depot as it used up a lot of fuel. While all the other salespeople on this organization tried to use a typical value prop of "strongest network", other high-pressure sales tactics and past relationships, I chose to use the more consultative sales approach Joseph taught me at Accenture. I knew if we wanted to be successful, we had to help clients build a business case around the technology and prove the value through numbers.

Even though the taxi company was not going to be a big deal in terms of revenue, I knew we needed to sell something to actually shed light on the fact that these products were really inept, so that is exactly what I did. I took the managers of the cab company through the different benefits that the solution could bring them then assigned a monetary value based on the client's data to each one of the value levers provided by the solution. We spent days to make a very comprehensive business case which wasn't an extremely efficient use of my time as the deal might have netted $30,000 in revenue. This probably equaled a few trips to Iowa and several hours of my time, however, I did it anyway just so we could get something going. Miraculously, the company agreed to implement, and we had sold our first end-to-end IoT solution ever at Verizon.

One of the things I noticed was as we got closer and closer to really closing this deal, the product team was getting further and further away from being willing to actually help us. I know now that the real reason for this was that they really did not ever want a solution to be totally sold and implemented because that would expose the fact that it didn't work. By the time I actually sold this, Andrew actually forced the product team to invite him and I to the company's headquarters to review how we were actually going to pull off this small, but very significant implementation. I still remember that Monday morning, going into the conference room and seeing the entire product team available, which was the first time that had ever happened. Previously they had been far too busy to meet with us, but now that an actual sale had occurred it was a different story.

Workshop 2: How Do You "Slot in" a New Digital Business Run by Millennials into an Existing Hierarchical Structure? Is This Possible and How can It be Done?

Issue: What are the perpetual roadblocks to introducing a new digital business into an organized hierarchy run by inter-generational adults?

(This is from a millennial to a millennial. Assuming a millennial is placed in the same position I was in.)

1. Be humble and be of service. The first thing to do is to establish yourself in the company. For me, this usually took 2–3 months just for people in general to know who I was and about what I could do. My attitude is absolutely the most important thing. People often seek out negative things about you as a millennial, so you have to give them nothing or next to nothing and your attitude determines this. I have found a vital trait is humility. Even if you know you understand a technology or customer better than a baby boomer that has been there for years, you have to place humility first in your dealings with other people who have been in the company for a long time.

   So how does one who knows both business and technology better than their baby boomer counterparts be "humble"? There are some steps I've acquired and the first one is to be of service. When I was at Verizon, I was placed in a team of 10 grown men all in their 50's who had almost no experience selling IoT software solutions. At the time, I was 25 and I was trying like hell to grow a beard so they wouldn't know I was 25.

   The first team conference call we had was debating how to start selling our "track and trace" IoT solution which was based on our industry not a competitive solution technology or price wise, but nonetheless we had to figure out a way to move forward. The first thing I did on the call was offer to help make an introductory PowerPoint for our team. It was

(Continued)

grunt work and all 10 of our guys had their own ideas, so I volunteered to collect all the parts from each teammate and put them into a master document. This had a few advantages, one of which being I got to know each of the guys because we all had to have individual phone calls to discuss their pieces.

Throughout my time at Verizon, I continued to do similar things like help other less-technical teammates prepare for customer meetings, etc. By first establishing myself as someone who genuinely wanted to be of service to the team people looked at me in a much more positive light and listened later on when I wanted to exert influence and make positive changes that got people out of their comfort zone.

2. Next steps: (a) Establish yourself as someone who wants to be of service; (b) polish your own personal brand; (c) prepare yourself for the fight of a lifetime with hard work and long hours while remaining grateful; (d) get a small win. Usually the best way to do this is to sign the first customer of the new business unit. Starting out everyone including your bosses will just assume because you are a big company that has these great customers in your legacy businesses, getting one of them to sign up for your new technology/business unit will be easy, right? WRONG! You have to assume this sales cycle is at least 6 months and has a win percentage early on of 10–20%. What then should you do? While everyone in your company is focusing on the potential big wins like Coca-Cola, P&G, etc., you should go out and sign up a small customer. This will accomplish two very important things that are typically overlooked: (i) It will allow your technical team to have a real-world test and work out all the bugs in addition to making YOU the only real expert in your company on the technology. By actually going through an implementation (even a small one), you will learn everything you need to do to prepare the customer for what is coming. This will be a huge asset to you later on when you land a large customer. (ii) This will give you immediate credibility in the company, especially with top management who are making the decisions. At both Verizon and Accenture, I was always the one called in as the subject matter expert

(Continued)

(Continued)

both for internal meetings and external meetings with client CEOs because they all knew I'd done this before.

3. Find a mentor and give them the credit. At Verizon and Accenture, my mentors were my direct bosses, both of whom were really nice people and also wanted to really make a difference. When I accumulated wins early on, it was very important to give the credit totally to them externally with other people in the company, but also make sure they remembered it when they were deciding my compensation at the end of the year. For me, it was very important to very actively manage my career upwardly. I was always totally transparent with my intentions to rise up fast in the company with all my bosses.

Discussion: How can we better?

Some say I switched jobs too fast and didn't give each opportunity enough time to really play out. In one case, I was offered a 100% increase in base. Is the quick switch worth it? The biggest struggle is with attitude and humility. Sometimes when I have an objective, can I turn into a bulldozer and leave some collateral damage in the wake of what I am going after. There were times at past companies where I just disregarded other people's feelings to accomplish a goal. Is this effective?

In addition to that, I would take it personally when people made decisions that hurt the overall goal of the business unit making progress to protect their empire. I viewed this as wasting my time, which I consider very precious. When our CFO or CIO would block something purely out of ego, I would get very angry. Do I have an outlet to prevent me from taking things personally? What's the point of gossip?

Meanwhile, the first cab installation was beginning, and we soon realized very quickly that everything was about to go completely wrong. It was one problem after another. The cabs were different make and models and so we found out that on some of the models we had to install an additional $200 device to make our devices compatible. This put the cost of the solution through the roof but our company offered to pay for it anyways because we desperately needed a showcase customer in order to be able to move forward with other clients.

We started with two test cars and in our pilot phase. I can't say I remember a time where either one of these was working at all. I had built up a good relationship with the client and turned the delivery mostly over to the product team. This was mainly because of the following: (1) there was nothing I could do to change the solution technically and (2) I really did not have time nor energy to fight with the product team anymore. As this solution was failing, I actually managed to sell another one to a nonprofit organization in South Carolina, which I realized later on was a mistake on my part as the first customer was still struggling with an implementation. However, we needed the Workshop and I made sure we put in the contract that our company would cover the cost of any faults or failures in the solution.

So now me, a 25-year-old on a team with 100 people whose children were mostly older than I, had sold the first and the second ever end-to-end "IoT Solution" in the entire company history of Verizon. I felt good, and they treated me like a superstar. Receiving recognition from leadership was nice, however the constant politics was really taking a toll on my motivation to get up every day and go to bat for the company.

By this point, we were about 6 months into Verizon's IoT experiment, so Robert had now been running the team for 3 months or so. Then one day out of the blue we receive an email saying Robert had now been "reassigned" and the IoT sales architect team would be going through the first of many restructurings. In corporate America jargon, this is basically what big companies do when they do not want to admit an initiative failed, and they need to shuffle all the people to different roles and titles but continue on generally the same failing strategy. Our team was then reshuffled to Verizon Wireless, so now, we were in the same organization as the product team was, however, and it did not help us very much.

I began to enter a very difficult period in early 2016 as within a month's time my girlfriend of 2 years who was struggling with severe depression left, my grandfather who had helped raise me died, and one of my best friends who was also sober relapsed and killed himself.

I can remember having to tell the doctor pulling the plug on my grandfather because my mom was too sad. He was the greatest man I had ever known, and at 80 years old, moved in with us to help raise me even though I was an absolute disaster of a teenager with zero gratitude for many years. I was however happy that over the last 5 years I was able to be a good grandson to my grandparents. Right before he told me that my recovery was the biggest turnaround he had witnessed in his life and he was incredibly proud. To this day, this felt better than any monetary success I've ever had. I knew I needed to keep going but I started to feel as if I was slipping into another black hole.

At work, I was praised for being the only one actually making sales. I was even called by the various vice presidents in charge (there were many of them) to begin training the other sales executives how to properly sell IoT. I was making more money and traveling more than most people I knew but, on the inside, I felt totally empty. Thank God I had a huge support network that really save my life (for the second time). I was in a similar place to my last year in college before getting sober. I knew I had the ability to do great things and I had to get away from the death and alcoholism that was around me.

Finally in June 2016, it all came crashing down. A few months had passed, and I was still nowhere near over my last relationship. I was also completely devastated as my family was falling apart after the deaths of my grandparents and still dealing with the death of my friend Bill. I knew I needed a change but didn't know what to do. I was making good money at my job but I was again at the point where I felt I had hit a ceiling and there was no getting around it in my current position.

Up until this point in my life, I learned that each seemingly hopeless situation I found myself in was usually around the time at which life will turn in different a direction I didn't even consider a possibility. Whether it was before getting sober in college, learning Chinese, getting my first job as a sales director after being rejected repeatedly, getting randomly assigned to go to Mexico, and chase my dream of learning Spanish (these were just the career-related instances of the universe looking out for me, there were many more we don't have time for in the book). Even despite these past examples of being taken care of in what seemed to be the worst situations I'd been in, I always seemed to forget that no matter how dire things were, they tended to work out ok. In fact, they typically worked out incredibly well in some way I didn't even consider as a possible outcome.

Despite being totally devastated on what was going on with my family this ended up being the kick I needed to actually get up and do something about this. I knew I needed a big change but didn't know what specifically to do. I wanted to be an entrepreneur and now I had some money saved up, although I didn't feel it was enough to start a company, plus I didn't know exactly what I wanted to do yet. I knew it should be technology related and knew I had to get back to China where everything was happening but had no idea how.

Finally, I decided to call one of my most important mentors James, who was the father of one of my American friends in Shanghai from college. James is an American businessman in Shanghai that owns a large conglomerate that does over $1 billion in revenue. James was a nice guy and would always take my call when I reached out. Usually I would contact his secretary every 6 months and setup an appointment to catch up. Whenever I'd meet him in his office, I would see pictures of him with Presidents Obama, Clinton, and even Xi Jinping, the President of China.

James was my hero. I wanted to be like him in every way. He had come from a family and economic situation similar to mine, learned an Asian language, moved to Asia with nothing and created a billion-dollar empire. All while having a seemingly ok family life based on the fact that his son, who was my friend, didn't hate him.

On the call, I laid out the entire situation both personal and professional. I told him I knew I was meant to be an entrepreneur and be in China. I knew I had to do whatever it takes to get back there. James came back with good advice, "What you need to do is find a high-level position in a small to mid-sized company in China, take a minority stake and grow the revenue like crazy. Once you save up $1–2 million you will be ready to start your own company, I'll even help fund you" he said.

This was music to my ears, "But where am I going to find this company in China?" I asked. "Why don't you come run my company?" he said. My head felt like it was going to explode I was so happy. I honestly only wanted advice and didn't expect an offer like this. It took everything I had to play it cool, but I managed to end the call without screwing it up. James connected me with his CEO named Henry to try and work out a deal. Henry was a Harvard corporate lawyer who James hired to be his CEO while James was traveling with his other companies. This began my next China chapter at Cashew International.

Chapter 9

Building an IoT E-commerce Business in Shanghai

Henry was a Harvard corporate lawyer that had never worked as a CEO until James gave him this opportunity, and it showed even in my early interactions with him. He grew up in the Boston suburbs in the wealthy neighborhood of Brighton Mass. Both his parents were successful psychologists so I can only imagine the kind of pressure that would put on someone to grow up and become successful. Henry was around 40 years old and had a family living in the US at the time so I could tell he was dedicated to his job in Shanghai.

Over the following few weeks, we came to a deal that included a lower fixed salary but with a percentage share of our net profit in addition to a percentage of the company's shares each year over a 3-year period. Overall I was happy with the deal and trusted them to honor it. After all, James was my hero.

The first day in Shanghai was an adventure, to say the least. After my experience in Mexico City, I initially was very concerned with going back to a "developing country". My memories of Shanghai from 5 years ago were similar to Mexico with inefficiency, traffic, beeping horns, trash on the sidewalks, and overall lack of healthy food options. To my great surprise, I came to find Shanghai was a *completely* different place in only 5 years. My first day back an old Shanghainese friend took me aside and had me download several apps which were TMall, Alipay, WeChat, and Didi. I later discovered that in Shanghai you can literally do anything with these four apps. It was like instant gratification on steroids. That morning also I took the metro into the office, to my surprise it was completely clean. The streets had absolutely zero honking, and Shanghai just felt different.

I reached the office around 8 am and to my surprise there was nobody there. The maid said people usually don't start arriving until 9.30 am so I sat and waited. When 9.30 came around, I was treated like a king. Henry had given me the title of Director of Revenue and aside from him I was the only other foreigner in the company.

James had been trying to start a premium food e-commerce company in China for around 7 years now but had failed several times with different teams at Cashew. Around 7 years ago, James bought a controlling stake in a premium seafood company supplying five-star hotels and restaurants in Shanghai and Beijing owned by his Norwegian friend, Yon. Yon and James both lived in Shanghai during the somewhat more difficult years to be an expat. In these days, it was very difficult to find reliable, safe food of any kind in China and there seemed to be a new scandal every day. Whether it was water being injected to make things weigh more, babies dying from chemicals in milk formula, to products produced in China but companies slapping an "Imported" sticker on them, everyday it was something new.

James was a typical ultra-wealthy leader where he always had a grand vision of what his companies were to become. His conglomerate owned over 30 different companies and he tried as hard as he could to have them work together. James' first successful company had been an infomercial company he started in Korea 30 years ago. He ended up growing this into a substantial business and decided in the early 2000s to do the same thing in China. The Chinese company — let's call it Cashew — was very successful at first and they went public in New York at a few billion USD valuation. However, after a few years, as China became a more e-commerce-focused economy, Cashew failed to make a transition and suffered greatly. Most of their products were cheap infomercial products like exercise equipment and cooking pans. They did however have one product which was a neck massager that was so famous that its name in China became synonymous to the likes of Kleenex or Google.

Cashew at this point was being held up by this neck massager product, which was extremely profitable, however that was the only successful business within the company. Cashew also had a team of people working in a call center calling on retired people to buy collectables, another team selling oxygen purifiers, and one working on telemarketing insurance plans. Aside from the neck massager, the company really didn't have any other revenue, so they needed someone to build new businesses and bring them into the digital age. So I figured, who better than me?

In the beginning, we were setup to be a complete success, with James as our chairman and a motivated company with a lot of cash I figured there was no way I'd fail. The first business James wanted me to revive was the premium food e-commerce company called Cashew Fresh (CF). The idea was similar to Hello Fresh or Blue Apron in the US. Since we already had a premium Norwegian seafood company owned by James, we started with what was readily available. Many of you may be thinking, "Seafood…yawn". However, I can assure you in China it's a huge business. Plus, we didn't see ourselves as a seafood business, we were in the e-commerce business. Our vision was to start with what we had and eventually turn into a subscription health food company for Chinese families.

Initially James had an exact vision for what the company was to be. He wanted us to build our own subscription platform and sell our products on a monthly basis to wealthy consumers in Shanghai. He envisioned we would expand from there and become a billion-dollar business. James wasn't around a lot, but whenever he walked in everyone would stare as he walked by, he always said hi to everyone but it was easy to tell he enjoyed the respect and attention. "The minimum price I'm willing to accept is 600 RMB per order" he said in our first meeting, which was around US$100 at the time. James had a very specific idea of how he wanted the business to be ran and was very unwilling to accept anything other than his vision at first. This annoyed me but I figured it was his money so what the hell, let's give it a try.

My first employee was a Chinese man we will call Frank. Frank was in his late 30s and was a traditional Shanghainese man with a 5-year-old son, wife, and grandparents living together in an apartment he bought up the road from our office. Even though I was technically his boss, I always considered him my partner. In the beginning, the days were long and hard. We would stay in the office until 9 pm working out pricing, sales plans, storage, and logistics. When we go to the company, there was virtually no infrastructure to setup this company. On top of that, due to the previous failed attempts of Cashew Fresh, nobody wanted to work with us even including our supplier Yon, Shun Feng (China's largest cold chain company), and the different teams within our own company. To say we were starting from zero was a complete understatement, we were starting from negative 20.

Every day was a fight. Henry and James claimed to be entrepreneurial, but I couldn't understand why they setup Cashew in such a hierarchical and bureaucratic way. Although we were essentially a startup at this point with only one successful legacy business they still seemed to want the company to appear to be a structured, large organization. It was still early at this point, so I didn't know whether it was ego or some other reason, but I had a good contract that was dependent on winning and that's exactly what Frank and I planned on doing.

Our dealings with Yon and his team were very hostile at first. Yon, who was supposedly James's friend and partner, seemed to overtly hate us from the very beginning. As we would ask him questions about the products, he would even refuse to give us product info. Frank and I would tell this to James and he said we should just use single-frozen as our pitch. Single-frozen meant that the food was only frozen one time, by the time it reaches our consumer to be eaten that is the first time it was to be defrosted. The idea being that if it is frozen during the whole supply chain there is no opportunity for any harmful chemicals to be added, etc. The only problem was Chinese people had no idea what single-frozen meant, nor did they really seem to care.

We knew we would need other information on where the food came from, what the health benefits were, etc. if we were going to start generating any sales. However, any time Frank or I asked Yon or his team this information they refused to provide us. This caused a lot of anger on my part because my deal was performance-based and Yon seemed to be set on making us fail. On top of that, all of China's delivery companies refused to work with us due to the previous Cashew Fresh teams doing things like selling outdated inventory and not paying on time. So due to the past team's mistakes we had zero way to deliver our product for the first 3 months of CF's existence.

James however didn't care about any of this, to him they were small formalities. When he visited the office, we either needed to show progress or get yelled at. In the beginning, even though the meetings with James were filled with yelling I still learned a lot. Aside from being a bit of a jerk, James was still a marketing genius, and ultra-wealthy so I just listened and tried to learn what I could.

On top of our only supplier and delivery companies refusing to work with us another problem we had was Cashew's approval process to get any contract executed by the company. In a company of fewer than 200 people, each document needed eight approvals which consisted of two different approvals from Henry the CEO, CFO, legal department, and myself the business lead. Those reading this book intending to start a business in China should know that in order to get any business off the ground it requires a lot of different contracts to be executed, and each of these contracts need to be signed by the company's legal representative and stamped by the company's official stamp. The stamp was something from ancient China that was used to ensure documents weren't fake. It seems a little ridiculous now that they still feel a simple stamp can't be faked, but nonetheless it is required in any legally binding document in China.

It felt like Frank and I were getting nowhere in the first 2 months, and I had to go into pure bulldozer mode to get anything done. Neither the finance nor legal department would even respond to our emails because they didn't think the business would be successful based on past failures. I couldn't really blame them, as premium food is a hugely competitive business in China, probably more than anywhere in the world. I didn't care, I would sit right outside their offices for hours until every contract we needed signed was complete. The most surprising thing through all of this was how little Henry, our CEO, cared as well. Frank and I could tell from very early on he didn't think we would get anywhere either, he'd also seen this play out before. Finally after calling Shun Feng's cold chain manager every day for 3 months, they finally agreed to deliver our products.

This was a huge step for us and now we needed to sell. TMall and JD.com were and are the largest e-commerce platforms by far in terms of traffic and GMV (gross merchandise value) in China. In the US, people will go to a firm's website to see if a firm is trustworthy, but in China ".com" websites are pretty much irrelevant now. The first thing people do when they want to buy something regardless of where they see the product is to check out the firm's TMall page to see the sales and comments about the product. In our business if you didn't have a TMall page, you essentially didn't exist.

One of the past CF teams had also opened up a TMall page and failed to gain traction so when we informed James of our strategy to go back on TMall, he became very angry immediately. When James would yell at us, it was more than just criticizing what you did wrong, it was more of a personal attack that left you feeling useless afterwards. He was the boss and wanted to make that clear, it seemed he liked it when people feared him. We definitely disagreed on this key issue, but James had helped me so much in my life as a mentor before Cashew and I would do whatever he said at this point. He was more than my mentor, he was my idol, and if he wanted to try a different strategy we would go along with it.

His idea was to go to international schools in Shanghai and sign people up for 600 RMB/month subscriptions. I remember staying up all night for weeks looking up every single international school in Shanghai and Beijing. I called them up and was rejected over 70 times. James still wasn't satisfied with this so I started showing up and trying to get them to agree to promote our service. It was humiliating but James wanted us to try so I figured the faster we brought him the data proving his strategy was wrong, the faster he would let us do our strategy.

I even went to the international school fairs pretending to be a parent so I could meet the head of marketing and work my way in that way.

Brochures from the Shanghai international school fair

Henry would sit in on the meetings in James's office. He never had much to say when James was around and it was pretty obvious that James preferred people working for him that were agreeable, and that's exactly what he found in Henry. James would usually arrive at the office around 11 am, yell at Frank and I until 1 pm, then go on and have a meeting with Henry where he probably yelled at him too. I didn't think it was the most effective strategy, but it got him to where he was so we more or less blindly trusted it would work.

Weeks and months went by and James wouldn't allow us to sell on anybody else's e-commerce platform. He insisted that we build our own and drive traffic to that. He almost acted as if it should be easy to build an e-commerce platform and charge people US$100 a month for seafood, when competitive products were priced at less than half. I'm not sure whether it was an act to try and motivate us more or he really believed that, but he was wrong. In China, people rely on customer ratings in TMall to make purchase decisions, and if you didn't have any on TMall, it was almost impossible to get sales. We made the argument to him that it would be best if we could just start the application for a TMall store just so we would be relevant to people searching based on reviews but James still wasn't even willing to let us fill out the application to even open a store. In addition what James didn't seem to understand is it was much cheaper to acquire customers on TMall because they already go there to buy things like food so the number of clicks to get a customer to buy is much less than if we built our own app and acquired customers there.

My job again became fighting all day and night. I woke up and fought with Yon to give us better prices and service because we were 2–3× the market price and many of the deliveries were returned due to quality issues. I fought with James about letting us sell online where our customers already were which would be cheaper and much more scalable than driving customers to our own website, which was a nightmare to build. In the afternoon, I fought with the finance and legal teams to approve our contracts needed to move forward. We had so many customer issues early on that it seemed like every order was a fight.

We had built a WeChat page and had gotten some orders from James' friends early on but couldn't build traction. Every few months James would read a business book and become totally obsessed with the book and make the whole company read it. The latest obsession was Traction. It is actually a great book on how to "get traction" in a startup business. Essentially there are around 17 channels that can be used to get customers early on. What the book recommends is you make small calculated bets on each one of these channels early on and those that fail need to "fail fast" and discontinue and the successes need to be scaled rapidly. Frank and I had made several detailed traction channel plans early on and would share them with James and Henry.

I wish I could say these meetings were useful, but James would take over the meetings and spend hours nitpicking at things like whether search engine marketing should be called a "channel" or a "method". To Frank and I, it seemed completely ridiculous. How could two grown men, one who went to Harvard and the other a billionaire spend an hour arguing with two of their business leaders about the definition of a word in a business plan?

Frank was probably the most positive person I'd ever met. There would be days when James would come in the office and not only demoralize us by cursing us out in regards to the plans we made, and even personally attacking us, but Frank would always keep me going. Even though it hurt having someone you looked up to attacking you personally I just assumed it was intentional tough love to make us better businesspeople. However, James had this ability that even though he would treat people this way, he was able to easily turn on the charm right after like nothing had happened.

We knew Henry was brought in to execute on James's strategy so Frank and I came up with a plan to try and convince Henry to approve our plan without getting James involved. There was a small foodie platform called Xiachufang that had a few million MAU's where people posted recipes and sometimes bought different food products. We positioned it as a small and insignificant "traction channel" to Henry, and since the name of it was not TMall he agreed to let us try the platform. Remember, the only reason James didn't want us on TMall was that a past team hired by him did not succeed previously as they didn't have the proper skill set. Neither of them took into consideration the fact that it might have been the team's fault and not the channel.

Of the few startup organizations I've led, the phase just described is usually inevitable. It's usually a much longer period than budgeted/ planned for and the main setbacks are typically egos and red tape. In my experience, the key to getting out of this "stuck" phase is to begin generating real sales, so that was exactly what Frank and I did.

The one thing nice about working for James was he had a lot of money, and he wasn't afraid to spend it on his ideas. The drawback was that even though he was seemingly a smart guy, many of his ideas were based on an outdated direct marketing via telephone and television mindset and his ego prevented him from seeing that Frank and I were actually right a lot of the time. The only way to get him to go along with one of our ideas to help the business was to convince him it was actually his idea. The fact that he hired Henry as a yes man made it even worse because Henry acted more like a policeman/lawyer rather than a CEO to support his subordinate teams.

After 5–6 months of pushing and fighting, we were successfully onboarded to Xiachufang. For those interested in entering the Chinese market and selling online, you should know that is anything but easy. Most of the platforms have an automated onboarding process where your company has to apply to become a store — all in Chinese. This is usually a 3–4-month process depending on the platform, and if you don't know anyone it can take much longer.

Once onboarded to one of these platforms, it may feel like a huge win, but you are still very far from getting sales. The #1 revenue source on these platforms is advertising and if you want to get any of their traffic, they will want you to pay. Since James wasn't willing to allocate any money to these platforms, Frank and I were initially forced to figure out how to get traffic for free. Anyone in China will tell you this is no easy feat, but we had no choice.

Workshop 1: When, Who and How to Fight in Building a Digital Business in an Analog Company?

Issue: When, who, and how to fight. Fighting is inevitable if you want to start a digital business as a millennial in an established corporation. Once you've laid the groundwork, the big question how to do it without getting fired? The answer is not easy, but it is possible.

1. Most of the big problems with these new business units early on are with the product. Because when any company, even a large one, develops a new product line there are always problems. Furthermore, its more than likely in a big company the team developing the product is a totally different team than the one marketing and selling it. Or even worse the marketing and sales team are even different "organizations" with different KPIs. This is where that first small customer is so important. You as the salesperson know the faults in the product, but the technical team has "worked hard" on this for a long time and you are a new person who

(Continued)

(*Continued*)

is the same age as their kids. How do you convince them to make changes? The answer is to put all changes needed in the context of the customer. If you go to the development team and say "We need these APIs" or "The app needs to be more user friendly", they will likely tell you to go screw off. Then their managers and eventually your manager will also tell you to screw off. But if you put the changes you need in the context of your customer, they have no way to defy you. "My customer needs the app to have less steps to complete an order" or "My customer needs the back end to integrate with SAP" is almost impossible for a company to say no to. This goes beyond technical changes and also works for changes in strategy of the business unit, etc.

2. Even with this strategy, I was still met with resistance from people in the company. Whether it was the development team, finance, James, HR, or whoever. When you expose someone and threaten their empire because you genuinely know how to accomplish the goal better than they do, you will face pushback no matter how logical your argument is. So what to do when this happens? The answer for me was to align with powerful people who had revenue targets because at the end of the day what they want to happen will get done. The CIO and all the other ops teams may have their own budget and separate KPIs that are really ambiguous (they make them that way on purpose) but the leadership with revenue will ultimately make the call. So at Verizon and Accenture what I did was took all my unwinnable battles to the people with revenue targets and brought along the business case for the change I needed in addition to the specific customer demand. Even this wouldn't yield results right away but once they have enough time to go to bat for you, you will win in the end. At Cashew, we had a slightly different strategy as James (the Chairman and owner) was my boss. In these cases, we had to try and figure out how to convince him that our ideas were actually his ideas.

3. Build a personal brand and stick with it. Another important thing to prepare prior to your dealings with co-workers while you are being of service is your personal brand. It was critically important that I knew who I was and that my message didn't change. Many situations will cause us to want to change our brand depending on the situation or just give up in saying

(Continued)

who you are and what makes you unique because you think it doesn't matter anymore as you are already lost in the corporate abyss. DO NOT fall into this trap. At all of my companies I've worked with, I was always the IoT guy who spoke Chinese. It's VERY important to communicate this in a humble way because remember humility is the key, but remember the definition of humility is an honest appraisal of oneself followed by a genuine attempt to become what you can be.

Discussion: The key to your attitude in bringing digital change to analog people is to get ready for a big fight, bigger than you've ever known. Get the small wins on the edges. In order to get anything done in a new business in a large organization, you have to be ready to fight for it every day. There will be totally irrational people that are looking to protect their imaginary empire they've built in their years in the firm and they will not want to give it up. This can be very annoying and even eat your soul. Every day you will return from work and say, "Why am I even bothering? Is this hopeless?". That's why it's important to aim for small wins to track progress rather than measure the success of the entire business unit day-to-day. Go for the small wins each day. They add up.

In China, the e-commerce platforms have people responsible for each category called the *xiao er* (小二) which literally translates to "small two". I have no idea how they got this translation for platform rep, but these guys hold the key to your success in e-commerce in China. Our platform rep was the person responsible for the food category at Xiachufang. The reason these reps are so important is they dictate the different positions on the platforms. It's similar to google search results where if you are at the top of the list you are more likely to get clicked, so we needed to be at the top.

Once you are onboarded to the platform, there is still a lot of work that needs to be done. Each e-commerce store in China has a number of different pages. The most important being the product page and the home page. The product page is where you describe the benefits of your product, pricing, and why customers should buy and homepage is essentially a brand introduction. At this time, only Frank and I were on the team and since nobody else in the company would help us we had to write out a storyboard and design all these pages ourselves. Since most of the products in China lacked a personal feel where you didn't actually know who was behind the company, Frank and I figured we would tell the company story through ourselves to humanize the brand.

The number one reason people don't buy things in China is because they don't trust the brand. It's very different from the US where there is an inherent level of trust due to reliance that the government will help if the brand does something wrong. In China, consumers need to be fully confident the product is real and top-quality or else it might as well not exist. Frank and I figured if we could convince the customers that we were trustworthy, they would trust our products. Since Yon still wouldn't tell us the specifics on why our products were the best, this was our only option. I'd learned in the past if you want to be successful as an entrepreneur you have to be resourceful, nowhere is this more true than in China.

After weeks of learning photoshop, how to write buy-one-get-one free in Chinese and taking the train to Beijing and Hangzhou to meet with our platform xiao ers, the Xiachufang foodie platform rep finally agreed to give us a homepage sales event position. For those interested in e-commerce in China, this is very important. In China, every e-commerce platform has a homepage which is where people land when they open the app. Every day, the platform has different events which consist of low-priced offers that companies pay the platform for, so they can get a lot of traffic and hopefully paying customers. If you can build up enough credibility with your *xiao er* and sell them on the idea, they will sometimes give you the position for free, so that was exactly what we did.

A xiao er's main KPI is GMV generated in their category. Each category's *xiao er* will be awarded between 5 and 10 positions per month by the platform to give to the vendors in their category. Assuming there are 1,000 different vendors in your category, there will be a lot of competition, but if you can demonstrate your product which will have a high repurchase rate and good customer satisfaction, they will sometimes give you a chance. The repurchase rate is important because each time someone comes back and repurchases without having to give an advertisement is considered free traffic generated.

Our sales were struggling up until this point and we were getting killed at every meeting we had with James. His strategy was to yell and keep the pressure on maximum as he felt that was the best motivation tool for us. It wasn't needed because Frank and I were motivated already but it definitely worked.

The big day came and our event was a huge success. We sold 5 times more in that day than we had in the previous 5 months combined. The event took place on a Friday and we didn't have nearly enough inventory to cover the deliveries. We called Yon and told him of our success and for the first time he actually seemed happy. We even got a call from James saying congratulations which was the first time I can remember him saying anything positive to us. Frank and I knew Yon's company would never be able to handle this volume and maintain quality so Frank and I spent the entire weekend in the warehouse cutting and packing fish.

Frank and I in the warehouse preparing orders

Now that we had found a traction channel that worked, the company and our partners finally fell into line. Sales grew rapidly but since it took 6 months for James to approve of Frank and my strategy, we were way behind on our sales targets for the year. Finally we got James to agree to open up a TMall and JD.com store but each of these applications would take 4–5 months to complete. Frank and I knew it was the only way our company would ever scale so we began the long and painful process. In the meantime, we had many things to do to keep us busy.

It was during these 4–5 months that we entered the expansion/scale phase and when I became a true expert in China's new digital world of social media, e-commerce, and payments. As we were waiting to get approved by Alibaba and JD.com, we opened and scaled as many of the smaller platforms as we could. One of the huge reasons e-commerce has exploded in China over the past 10 years is that regardless of what app or webpage you are on, purchasing whatever that page is talking about is literally only two clicks away. Since the overwhelming majority of payments in 1st and 2nd tier cities occur with Alipay and WeChat pay, it is incredibly easy to make purchases online.

In virtually any app you go into, whether it is Weibo, the Chinese twitter, Babytree, the Chinese platform for advice on motherhood, or even Yizhibo, a popular live stream platform, you will find that they are all integrated with both WeChat and Alipay. Whereas in the US, you would have to jump through three user unfriendly non-mobile pages typing in your credit card number, address, and expiration dates, in China all these are saved in your Alipay account and is ubiquitous across any platform (minus JD and Tencent because they hate each Alibaba). In China, every page you would go on is already designed with a mobile-only mindset and your payment information is only one click away. This allows almost any site in China to become an e-commerce site.

In addition to this, the logistics are completely different than in the West. In China, there are giant logistics companies like Shun Feng that can store and manage your inventory, package, box, and ship it across the country at minus 18 degrees Celsius for around US$3–4. About 95% of these packages arrive the next day with a 100% quality guarantee or else they will refund the customer's money. Try doing that with UPS, FedEx or the USPS and let me know how it works out.

Scaling the smaller platforms proved to be a very good strategy because we were able to target super users more effectively and at a lower cost than we would have on TMall and JD. The big trend now in China is that most of these e-commerce platforms are also trying to incorporate a social media component. They do this through things like live streaming and the introduction of influencers on each of their platforms called KOLs (Key Opinion Leaders) in China.

What we started to do was have Frank and I film the chefs cooking our products in a hotel owned by James in Shanghai and then offer this content to the platforms for free in exchange for giving us more events which drove more traffic. We also incorporated KOLs into our marketing by inviting them onto our cooking shows and then having them promote our products through their own social media. Again we didn't really have the support of anyone internally so we had to be resourceful.

As we were in the scaling phase preparing to onboard to Alibaba and JD, there was a lot to be done. James and Henry were pushing us to "over-hire" in preparation for what was to come. I was shocked by the quality of people we were able to find. Within a few weeks, we had 20 people who were all rockstars in their early 20s and hungry to grow our business. None of the people I chose had been to Harvard or even spoke English, but they all had two things in common in that they were experts in e-commerce and very hungry to succeed.

I hired a product manager so we could expand beyond seafood, designer to build all our product pages, inventory manager to interface with Shun Feng, KOL manager to reach out and make revenue share agreements with different KOLs, two customer service reps to deal with customer questions, and four different platform managers to push the different xiao ers to give us more traffic. Our sales were increasing at 50–100% every month and we had a momentum that seemed like it couldn't be stopped.

Then the day came where we finally opened on TMall and JD.com. These were the big fish that can either make your business or take all your money, but we soon found out that succeeding on these platforms was anything but easy.

The sales started off slow, and even though we were succeeding that didn't stop James and Henry from continuing to try and tell us what to do. This caused a lot of animosity from Frank and I because we felt up until this point they had been wrong on every strategy and delayed our success we were now starting to experience. To avoid this from happening again, Frank and I would basically still execute the outdated strategy they asked to make them happy (even though we knew it would fail) and at the same time execute our own strategy, succeed, and then give them the credit to keep their egos happy. We had to do two jobs which was making them happy and actually scaling the business so we could hit our numbers.

Henry knew a lot about business from an intellectual standpoint but was not the best at execution and certainly not a people person. He had an inherent mistrust of anyone other than himself and he structured Cashew so that all decisions went through him. He was pretty much the exact opposite of James and I, which I think was why James liked him there. The neck massager product was still keeping Cashew afloat while CF was going toward profitability. In addition to that, Cashew had ownership stakes in a number of different outside companies from the legacy info-mercial days. Henry mainly spent his time focusing on liquidating those businesses but when James came into the office all he wanted to hear about was how CF was doing — as we were the only new business at Cashew that was growing.

Henry hired a HR director named Doris who was super-friendly when talking one on one but everyone knew was really the grim reaper of Cashew. Henry seemed to enjoy firing people and would typically use Doris to do so. Frank and I always believed growing up wealthy in the suburbs as an only child must have been the root cause of this lack of empathy but we never really figured it out. He would often tell me, "Hire this person to try them out and if it doesn't work just fire them before the 6-month probationary period so we don't have to pay their benefits." It was like people were just numbers to him and their personal life situations and hardships seemed to be irrelevant.

Henry was always focused on structure and he had Doris come up with a rating system for employee performance, which even I had to fill out. In the beginning of the year, Henry and I set metrics weighted in different categories like customer satisfaction, re-order ratios, work ethic, sales, and overall company performance. I specifically didn't put a big sales number target in the beginning of the year because I already had a sense James and Henry would cause us to get off to a slower start than we had anticipated.

We went through our performance review and Henry gave our team a 95% overall rating based on the system developed by Henry. I was happy and all seemed good. However, over the following weeks when it came time to pay my team's bonuses, the company refused. It took 10 weeks of me appealing with HR and Henry to finally get the company to pay what was contracted. I tried to shelter the team from this but it was impossible to completely avoid. Henry continued to avoid me and would respond to other emails about the business but not to ones about the team getting paid what they were owed. At this point, he also owed me a portion of the company's shares as well but I figured I'd only address one at a time to increase our chances.

We had to keep working even though this was very demotivating for everyone. Even despite this, our success with the business continued. We had to hire more people and before we knew it we had a team of 30 people. We had an incredibly differentiated sales strategy which is not easy to do in the premium food business in China. We were selling commodity products at 2–300% over our competitors' prices and still doubling sales every month. When we first started with TMall and JD, even they told us to just give up because our products were too expensive. Until that point, nobody in our industry had ever sold premium food packages at the prices we were aiming at. We knew James artificially inflated the food prices to make

Yon's profit higher (which he owned most of anyways) and then James only allowed us to use Yon as a supplier so we had no choice.

As we started to sell more, Yon and I began to become friends as our consumer business at CF was now bigger than his business selling to restaurants and hotels in Shanghai and Beijing. It was during this time we found out the real reason Yon was so difficult to work with in the beginning was James had basically been treating Yon the same way as Frank and I over the past 7 years of trying to start Cashew fresh and by the time we started he was pretty much ready to quit.

This all made complete sense to Frank and I but also cause us to be even angrier because we saw every bit of progress we could have made that year was really destroyed by James' ego, even what we thought was originally Yon's fault. It turns out Yon was just facing the same treatment as we were, just at a different company.

After weeks of chasing Henry for what the company owed the team, he finally called me into his office to discuss. Henry and James had an incredible ability to give you less than what you agreed on and still make you feel guilty as if you didn't deserve it anyways. Finally he verbally agreed to give the team less than he initially promised, but I took it because it was better than nothing. Frank and I then had to go back and explain why they would be getting less than initially promised, which as you can imagine did not go over well. At one point, Doris had even tried to get me to sign a sheet that essentially canceled the rest of my contract for the following 2 years in order to get the bonus owed to me in year one. It seemed like just as the company was becoming successful Henry had decided he didn't want to abide by our previous agreement.

It was around this time I met my girlfriend Karen in Shanghai. Our nickname for Henry became "the alien" because he had no empathy for people and you really never knew what he was going to do. When I asked Doris about the paper, I said, "you know this is extortion right? If you force someone to sign something forgoing future earnings in order to get something that is already entitled to the person in your contract?" Doris knew, but pretended to be my friend, she had no say in the matter though, and she had to do whatever Henry told her.

During this time, even though our team's motivation was decreasing, the business we built was accelerating at a crazy rate. Frank and I were even invited by JD.com's CEO to receive an award on behalf of Cashew as the "Best Managed Store on JD.com". I was the only foreigner sharing a stage with CEO's of companies like HP and Lego. Despite what was going on, Frank and I were so proud. In 1 year, despite the obstacles we faced we build a business from zero to being the best managed store on the third largest e-commerce platform in the world. In addition to this, we were now the #1 store in our category on TMall in both sales and repurchase ratios. We had built a team of 30 people selling commodity products at 2–3× market prices on nine different platforms with five-star reviews in the most competitive market in the world.

Me with JD's CEO

James and Henry didn't say a word about any of this when Frank and I returned from JD's award ceremony in Beijing, they even yelled at us for attending. This really brought my morale down and it was difficult to hide.

One day when James came into the office he asked to go on a walk with me. He was super friendly at first, and the whole way in the elevator we talked about non-work stuff and even US politics. When we got out of the building he kindly asked me, "What's wrong? I feel like you haven't been yourself lately." He actually seemed really genuine in asking so I explained to him how I didn't like to be treated as I have been with yelling, and what Henry had done with my pay was very concerning.

Immediately after James' defenses were up and the conversation started to turn hostile. James reacted by yelling loudly while cursing at me on the sidewalk in Jing'an (downtown Shanghai) for 90 minutes. James is a big guy and at some point it was like watching a rabid dog foaming at the mouth he was so angry. Granted, I had developed a very thick skin working for him for the past 2 years but this for me was the last straw. I loved this guy like a father, practically worshipped him. There was something about having your idol just totally rip you to shreds emotionally that destroys your soul. I didn't know what to do so for the first time since I can remember I actually started shedding tears while walking down the sidewalk in downtown Shanghai.

It felt as if my whole world had been shattered. The man I worshipped and gave everything I had for 2 years working around the clock had showed me who he really was. I contemplated leaving that day and just forgetting about what they owed both my team and I, but I decided to stay until our team was taken care of.

Frank and I would have coffee every day before the team arrived and try to figure out why someone would do this to the only division of the company that was actually growing their business. The best we could figure was that they couldn't stand being wrong. It seemed like James would rather lose his own money on a strategy he was wrong about than make money on something that was someone else's idea. The interesting part of this was at this point in time the book James made everyone in the company read was called Principles by Ray Dalio. He would come in the office and tell everybody that they needed to leave "their egos at the door and let the best idea win" just like Dalio said. I'm not sure if he heard everyone in the company laughing in the background but to this day, I believe neither of them had any conception of their actual behavior and how it impacted other human beings.

Workshop 2: How Should Millennials Cope with Baby Boomers Who are Their Superiors that are Unwilling to Change?

Issue: Many times, in the workplace, baby boomers can tend to automatically discount what a millennial is suggesting without even knowing it. These are people for all intents and purposes have already "succeeded" in life. If they are top leadership in a large company, they are likely already wealthy, and many times have children older than you. This can cause many baby boomers to miss out on many great opportunities and frustrate many millennials to leave their jobs and go to competitors or even start their own business.

1. Success and experience can be great assets. Having capital to invest is the starting point that enables most ideas to turn into big companies. The majority of the time millennials will not be the ones with capital so whatever job they are doing will likely be funded by a baby boomer to some extent.
2. "It's my money and I've done this for 30 years! Shouldn't I be able to tell people what to do?" Any baby boomer saying this is in fact, 100% correct. When you have the capital, you are definitely the boss. The issue that we want to bring up is how to get the best result for all those involved?
3. After becoming extremely successful, there's a certain point when people become removed from everyday society when they forget what it's like to be a real person. After not driving yourself, not getting your own laundry or food for years and years, leaders of companies can become disconnected with what it's like to be an average person. People get so used to being waited on and the fact that everyone is their employee. In addition after making a certain amount of money, it becomes harder and harder to believe in your own mind that there was actually a significant amount of god given luck to make that happen because believing it was all you makes it feel so much better. This causes egos to spin out of control.

Discussion: In Ray Dalio's book *Principles*, he describes the #1 most important principle as having an "idea meritocracy" where anyone can

> *(Continued)*
>
> question the status quo at any time, and regardless of rank or experience they will be listened to and the best idea will win out. How can established companies entrenched in ego and politics make this change to value everyone's contributions and ideas equally? How can a company like this truly create a system that allows the best idea to win and millennials feel excited about going to work because they can really make a difference?

At this point, I had enough and knew my time at Cashew was over. Being demoralized by someone I really looked up to was really difficult, especially because I never really had a father figure and really wanted to succeed in China as James had. A few weeks later, James for some reason ended up personally sending what I was owed, and my team was paid in full for the previous year in exchange for signing contracts canceling our previous deal for a share of the profits over the next two years, just as we were becoming profitable. I was happy he finally did the right thing but couldn't understand why it came to this. The worst thing about all of it was leaving my team, who I really cared dearly for.

Despite the fact that at the top levels of Cashew we had flawed leadership, it was still an incredibly valuable lesson and experience. After being the head of a Chinese company right in the middle of the e-commerce space in the most competitive online market in the world, you really feel like you can do anything. We put together a summary of how we were successful, which can really translate to any product category online in China.

I vowed never again to work for someone else. I had saved a lot of money through salary and during my tenure Cashew's stock (and my life savings) had risen 400%. It was time for me to be an entrepreneur.

Chapter 10

A 25-Step Approach on How to Crack the Chinese E-commerce Market

ABC's of Breaking into the Chinese E-commerce Business

Ad revenue is important to these companies with powerful platforms. They will basically engage in extortion to get you to spend money on useless ads, but there are ways around it. In order to succeed in this cutthroat arena, there are a couple of hard truths you need to believe to your core. The first one being your brand does not matter and it's totally useless to spend even one RMB promoting your brand. How is this possible you ask? Branding is super important no? WRONG. If you are a well-established brand in the US or Europe, then yes, your brand will absolutely help you in China. Look at Coca-Cola and how well they do. However, if you are a small company or even a small division of a bigger company, trust me when I say any investing you do to promote your brand is likely to result in a poor return on investment. Let me break it down as follows:

Every company we went to do business with pestered us with "requests" to spend on advertising. Initially my partner Frank and I thought, "ok no big deal! We can buy one ad and then we're in". But when we were given a quote to just get our foot in the door, the cheapest "package" any of these platforms had was 3–4 million RMB or US$500,000, and when we asked what we got in return, the platform would respond: "It's important to invest in your brand, so people know you. We will put you on the home page for 1 day which gets 10 million views a day."

10 million views sounds pretty good, no? However, the real number is at least 30% of that. Usually after telling you the view number, they will tell you how they have the best platform because of (1) total user numbers, (2) customers' loyalty, and so on. Many of these numbers are fabricated and have no way of being validated by an external partner.

It was around this time where Frank and I would ask the platform sales people a series of questions: "(1) How many added customers or sales will these 10 million views convert to? (2) Will they offer any guarantee on sales? (3) What is the average order size?" They would say: "Every customer is different, we cannot guarantee." This is the best way to tell in advance on whether the ad they are trying to sell you is questionable.

The key is to be aware that you are a direct marketing company rather than a brand and only invest in advertisements where there is a direct return on investment in terms of sales "early on". Therefore, once you understand that you are a direct marketing company and each ad needs to be attached to a sales target and a selling price that makes it profitable, the next thing is to promise yourself you will never defer from this strategy no matter what. Rest assured that every partner you have in the e-commerce space in China will do everything they can to make you give this up. However, waiting for the right opportunity with ROI is much cheaper and more efficient in the long run.

Workshop 1: How to Set up an E-commerce Sales Operation from Scratch

Issue: How do you avoid the trap of being forced to buy ads and sell at the lowest price possible on Chinese e-commerce?

1. Around 100% of Chinese e-commerce make most of their money through selling ads — not on actual sales and shipping of products. In addition, they all believe (and probably rightly) the #1 thing to attract and retain customers is having the lowest price. Therefore, all these e-commerce companies from TMall to Kaola will basically force vendors to buy ads and sell at super low prices which, of course, makes it very hard to be a vendor like us. Everyone we hired had to have

(*Continued*)

a specific plan on how to bypass this way of "business as usual" for whatever channel, platform, or product category we were hiring them to oversee.

2. First of all, we had to align incentives correctly and reward those who came up with the most creative solution. We ensured that we were awarded all the best promotional positions on the home page when opportunities came up. We had marketing personnel who would buy media on different platforms like keywords, banner ads, influencer (KOL) posts, etc. Our operations team was forced at all times to work across different departments not being limited to their "silo". Procurement, customer service, and logistics were always talking to each other.

3. The ways we got around not buying ads and not being forced to sell at the lowest prices were as follows: "(1) Nail down your story and evolve it — NEVER deviate from your original narrative. (2) JD.com can take 4 months to accept you on its platform, so start with small niche platforms that are directly related to the product category you are in. (3) But the key is to first get us approved to be on the platform so we can begin selling, then we will purchase the ads." (4) Its very important early on to know your minimum price and to NEVER go below it. (5) When you are choosing your traffic product, you need to be sure that your main word for your product on your home page is searched heavily by your target market every day, is clearly differentiated and that your pricing has enough margin when holidays require a drop in price.

Discussion: What other ways can you break into a powerful platform which forces you to buy ads and sell at impossibly low prices in order to make money? There are several ways you can unconventionally do this. As I said previously, these platforms really make or break you and for a small company it is almost impossible to in 2020 introduce a new product and make a return on your investment. Most of the companies on TMall today are well established products what have a much higher negotiating power, ones that consumers will buy no matter what. But if you are a new company it is absolutely necessary to be more creative like we were.

The 25-Step Process to Enter the Chinese E-commerce Market

We list below the 25 ways to growth hack your way into Chinese e-commerce platforms:

1. *Evolve but DON'T Deviate.* The first piece of this is to have your story nailed down and to evolve but never deviate. Just as it was important in the last section to have a personal brand in a big company and let people know who you are, it is also important to do the same thing when dealing with Chinese e-commerce companies. As a small company, you will always be playing from behind with a small amount of resources but the key is to take whatever those resources are and put them into a story that aligns with what these e-commerce companies care about. Let me give you an example of what we did.

   Our company was a part of a larger enterprise owned by our chairman James. We also already had another successful product on TMall already (the massage product). Even though internally at Cashew the massage product was like a completely separate company, when we were in front of the TMall team we would make it seem like we were the same team as the already successful massage products. In addition to this, the frozen food we were selling was already being sold to a few of the five-star hotels in Shanghai and Beijing so we played it up like we were the player for imported premium food in China already in the B2B space. This gave them confidence that we could actually deliver. In addition to this, we had to come up with a story on each of our products on why they were unique and why they should sell for a higher price than similar products already online in China. This is the hardest part because really all these guys care about is price.

2. *Stick to the Same Story No Matter What.* Once you have your story put together, it is very important that you stick to this story no matter what. You may get thrown out of 30 platforms initially but eventually the category manager at one of these platforms will call you back because they will have a need for a quality product with your differentiating qualities. That's also why it's important to add all these people on WeChat and make sure they can see the moments you post on a daily basis to remind them that you are still there. Eventually they will reach out.

3. *Start Small on Small Niche Platforms and Build.* So now that you have a brand and product story you will need to start selling your product on some platform. The only problem is just because you have a product doesn't mean the platform will approve you. For us to get on TMall and JD.com, it took 4 months for our application to be approved after our company chairman finally decided to "allow" us to apply. How are you supposed to go 4 months without sales? The answer is to start with small niche platforms that are directly related to the product category you are in. Since our product was premium frozen food, there were essentially two niche categories we fit into. The first one was foodies and the second was mothers who buy premium ingredients for their kids because they don't trust food safety standards in China. Therefore, what we did was find the two platforms that were the go-to places for Chinese foodies and mothers in China. In China, there is a social media app for every kind of niche you can think of, so the key is to find the one with the most loyal following and reach out.

4. *Get Personal Wherever You can but Don't Act Desperate.* If someone on your team or any friends know someone at that platform for an introduction that's the best-case scenario, and I recommend you start there. If not, all these apps have an application section for their e-commerce stores on their website. Use the contacts — any contacts. Once you find the application section, have one of your Chinese teammates fill out the application and get the contact of the person responsible. Usually they provide their QQ contact info but the key is to get their WeChat as it's more personal. The person responsible for this is more than likely someone very junior on the procurement team. This person likely cannot do much for you so it's important to have your junior team member play you up as a big boss and say you'd be willing to speak to the boss of the procurement team at some random time on Tuesday afternoon. It's very important to give a specific time so they think you are important and never make the time on a Monday as e-commerce companies in China always do reviews with management on Mondays and have a ton of customer requests. Now that you are connected with the VP of procurement, it's important to act as though you are not desperate and have other opportunities when really you are depending on them to allow you on the platform. Now is where your pitch comes in.

5. *Don't Fall for Their Demand that You Buy Advertising.* Once you give your pitch, they will give you a long phony speech on how they only

accept the best products on their platform. The reason I say this is phony is because you already know that your competitors are already selling totally fake and/or low-quality products and are only allowed on because they have big ad budgets. Nonetheless, you need to play along and give them face. "Yes of course, your platform is well known for quality and that's why I reached out to you before your competitors" I would always tell them. This brings me to another important point which is that Chinese e-commerce platforms HATE their competitors more than any other place on earth.

6. *Play the Platforms Against Each Other.* The ecosystem is basically divided between Alibaba and JD/Tencent. Most of the niche players you will find are either controlled directly or indirectly by one of them. Most of the people working at these places are very smart and rational until you mention their competitor, then they turn into little kids and make bad decisions to spite their competitor. Frank and I used this to our advantage many times by telling Alibaba that we were the best-selling premium food last month on JD. This made BABA much more likely to give us favorable positions on their homepage.

7. *Avoid the Ad People and Get to the Product People.* Usually once you convince the VP of procurement that your product is of ok quality, they will either let you on the platform directly or give you another stage gate which are the ad salespeople. These are the toughest people to deal with as their only target is to sell ads. It's much more preferable they hand you off to the product category lead but more times than not you will first have to fight with the ad people.

8. *Do Not Give into the Ad People No Matter What.* These meetings with the ad people usually go as I previously described. The key is to NOT give in to them. If the procurement people already like your product, this means you are already basically in if you can hold out long enough. What I would do is tell the ad people I was VERY interested in buying their ads and I had a big budget for next quarter. "But the key is to first get us approved to be on the platform so we can begin selling, then we will purchase the ads." They will continue to try and strong arm you for a commitment prior to going live on the platform but if you hold out they will usually let you on within a couple of weeks. Once you are in the key is to just avoid the ad people and focus on your relationship with the procurement team and the category lead (小二 *xiao er*).

9. *Know Your Minimum Price and Do Not Ever Go Below It.* The *xiao er* is the one who is responsible for the GMV of their category. My category was food but all the categories pretty much ran the same way. Every e-commerce platform I've worked with will separate ads from GMV, but this also creates another challenge. Since the xiao er's only target is GMV, they don't care how they get there, and the fastest way for them to reach their GMV target is to force their vendors to sell at very low prices, prices that will make your company go bankrupt. It's very important early on to know your minimum price and to NEVER go below it. All these platforms remember your "lowest price" (低价) for every one of your main SKUs. What they will do when 11.11 or some other shopping event comes up and you want to sell at say 99 RMB but the system remembered your first week on the platform you had a promotion for 79 RMB they will force you to sell at 79. The platforms will tell you the system only remembers the low price for 1 year but it's actually longer than that. If you can avoid pricing mishaps early on, it will serve you well in the long run. The key is to maintain your minimum price and never go below it. If you stick to your value proposition and never falter, eventually the *xiao er* will call you with a homepage opportunity.

10. *Consolidate All Smaller Diversified Channel Successes and Blast Your Success.* Now that you are successfully onboarded into one or two smaller platforms that are likely controlled by JD or Alibaba you need to begin the application process for BABA and JD right away. In your application, it's important to emphasize all your certifications and your sales with their other brother and sister companies. Whatever your product category is you can usually pay 30,000–50,000 RMB for some reputable third party inspector to give you some kind of industry quality certification which are very important in China because people naturally assume things are fake. The key to my success in e-commerce was expanding channels rapidly and not depending too much on one platform because they can end your business very fast if you get a bad comment or one of your competitors raises their ad budget.

11. *As You Grow, Resist Ads. If You Must Buy Ads, Only Do It on JD or TMALL.* Once you are on JD, TMall and a few other niche platforms now the key is how do I start getting sales? It's better to get it out of your head that they will magically start happening as the process is long and painful. Again, the platforms will continue to insist that their ads are the key to building your brand and we now know from

my experience that it's not true. The only platforms in China that I recommend spending money on ads is JD and TMall. This is because they are the only platforms that people actually go with the intention of buying things so it's easier to convert to sales and track your ROI. Especially Alibaba makes it very easy to track ROI on every investment made on ads. However, the smaller platforms are not the case. They need to be won in a different way.

12. *Be Clear About Your Target Market, Differentiate at All Times and Focus on Your Lowest Selling Price.* After getting on TMall and JD, the first thing to do is to identify your "Traffic Product" (流量产品). Many brands make the mistake of thinking all their products are great and people will search for them. The fact that most people don't realize is that especially in the beginning, 80–90% of new store sales on TMall and JD are from the store's main traffic product. This is because most people do not understand Alibaba and JD's algorithms and how traffic flows on their platforms. Most of the traffic on each of these platforms comes from searching for a specific product through a keyword on the homepage. Therefore, when you are choosing your traffic product you need to be sure about the following: (1) it is searched heavily by your target market every day; (2) it is clearly differentiated; (3) you have enough margin to price it super low for sales events and not go bankrupt.

13. *It's a Game of Lost Leader Traffic, Product Placement and Price.* This traffic product will be very important because it's how people enter your store on TMall. First, they will search for your main product, say "Australian beef" then they will come into your store after adding the beef to their cart and see all your other products. But if you did not have an attractive offer for the beef they would have never some in your store and seen the seafood or your other "margin products" (利润产品). So in order to win at the game it's important to understand that this is the way it is played. Your traffic product will be the one used to acquire customers and your other products will be used to make money. In time, your other margin products — if popular and searched enough — may become traffic products.

14. *Focus on Search Data — Not on What People Need.* When doing product development, I recommend to completely ignore what products "you think" the customers need and purely focus on the search data.

The fastest way to gain traction is to sell highly searched products, if nobody is searching for them you will never earn a return on investment because the customer acquisition cost will be too high.

15. *Alibaba 'AIPL' Model Dominates — JD is Second.* Now that you've decided on your traffic product, start generating traffic to get sales. When it comes to e-commerce traffic in China, there is Alibaba and then there's everybody else. If your business doesn't figure out TMall, it will never be a big company. JD.com has traffic and dedicated customers but it's nothing compared to Alibaba despite what they may tell you. In order to succeed at getting traffic, it's important to first know how this is looked at in China. All traffic in the Alibaba is analyzed in terms of AIPL Aware, Interested, Purchase, and Loyalty.

TMall's definition of each of these is never 100% clear but it's something like:

Aware = Someone who has seen either an ad for your product or passed by it in a search result.

Interested = Someone who has clicked on your product between 1 and 5 times but has not yet bought.

Purchase = Someone who has purchased your product one time.

Loyalty = Someone who has bought your product two or more times.

Alibaba Watches Billions of These Data Points. This traffic is all analyzed in Alibaba NEWLY developed databank. Databank is a system unlike anything I've ever seen before that tracks user behavior across every app or platform that Alibaba either controls a stake in or is even a partner to. They then use this data to get a 360-degree view of everything the customer does online and create a digital profile of that customer. Because Alibaba is so powerful, they can force partners to share data with them. BABA representatives once presented me the list of all the apps they collect data from — it ended up being over 100. NOT only does Alibaba have the most valuable data in China, which is people's buying behavior online, they also have their offline buying behavior from Alipay, what they watch on TV from Youku, what their hobbies are, etc. It makes the data google collects look weak at best because Alibaba is involved in every part of a Chinese consumer's life. Below is a screenshot of what I would look at on a daily basis when I got up in the morning and opened up my store's Databank back end.

In the top left in the following chart, the 10.8 million impressions you can see how many customers are in each of the categories of AIPL. Then within each of the AIPL categories it breaks customers down into a much more detailed set of demographics and buying behavior.

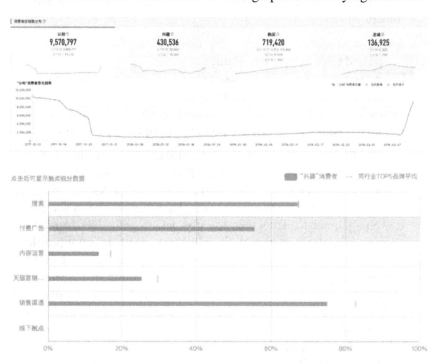

Once you get the AIPL breakdown, the amount of detail you can break the data down to for further analysis is truly unlimited. Above you can see the "Interested" customers and how they became interested. Many of these customers were obtained through "search" as you can see in the earlier chart.

Here you see a breakdown of what else these people are searching for. This goes much further to break down by age, buying behavior, and even has a system to give different ads to different customer demographics. Truly the most advanced ad analysis and delivery system I've ever seen. Note that JD claims to have an equivalent system but it was largely unavailable as of August 2019 and I have never actually seen it up and running. Alibaba is years ahead in this arena which is why I personally don't see JD being able to survive much longer independently.

16. *Know How to Optimize Traffic.* Now that we are on some of the platforms, have a sales pitch + traffic product and understand how to analyze and optimize traffic it's time to learn how to generate purchases in the most efficient manner possible. This is where the creativity of my team really came into play. As I said before, I divided my team into sales channels and sometimes product categories that the people were responsible. I also had two data scientists, Frank and myself almost full time analyzing and optimizing our databank traffic flows, and we quickly realized this was the key to our success.

17. *Seek Out Event Slots.* To get more A through P customers, we had many creative methods. The most basic and most effective is to convince the xiao ers to give us event slots on either the platform or the category homepage. Chinese e-commerce platforms are much more advanced compared to Amazon in terms of the social experience of buying and the diversity of ways people can sell. To give an example, every platform in China has the technical ability to allow people to get

a discount if they bring a friend to buy something and they can track it automatically through the link. In addition, they have buy one get one free sales, hot products, live stream sales events, discounts for posting on Weibo, discounts for writing a review, discounts for joining a WeChat shopping group, and using their QR code, and onto infinitum. This makes the options for putting on different sales events far greater than Amazon. *Then Use Price to Get into Big Events.* The platforms have events like this every day and slots for these events (page positions) are divided among the xiao ers according to the overall GMV of their category. How big your category is determines many positions there are to be awarded and how valuable they will be. Typically, the closer to the top of the page the better the position. The key is to clearly know your minimum price and make it known to the *xiao er* that you really want to be included in the next event. For the first few events, the *xiao er* will try to see how low you can actually go on price by making a ridiculous offer below even your COGS. The key is to resist until they get in a jam and need something fast. Now you are ready, but you still need to make sure that you are able to do the following: (1) sell a lot of volume and (2) get good reviews. So if your logistics haven't been figured out yet, don't do a huge event as people will give you bad reviews for slow delivery. Doing events like this with your traffic products will increase your numbers of A through Ps which will then allow you to target existing customers to become "Ls" or repeat customers which are the least expensive conversions you will find.

18. *Find Influencers to Help You.* In addition to homepage events, the platforms also care deeply about KOLs or influencers. Now in China there are thousands of useless influencers that would be happy to take your money, but the key is to find influencers who can convert views to sales or as we say in Chinese (有转化的 KOL). Since Alibaba is already huge and gets KOLs like Taylor Swift to perform at their 11.11 show, influencers will not mean a lot to them. However, if you can bring an influencer to a platform to attract what they call outside traffic, they will usually offer you a good position in return. The question is how do you convince an influencer to work with you for a reasonable price and how can you be sure it will payoff?

19. *Most Influencers are a Waste of Time except WeChat.* After working with hundreds of Chinese influencers over the years, I like to think I've found the answer. In my experience, there are really only two kinds of influencers worth dealing within China and that is those with

WeChat stores and those on TMall. All the other influencers on Weibo and Xiaohongshu (Little Red Book) are a complete waste of time if your end goal is sales. The reason for this is largely because the vast majority of people don't go on Weibo or Xiaohongshu to buy things. They go to TMall for this. For specialty items that we sold, they will sometimes look to Wechat influencers so I would definitely consider them a valuable channel as well. Our bestselling channel for our products was a KOL called Nian Gao Mama (年糕妈妈), who started as a random lady posting articles about her kid on WeChat and turned into a 500 person company that was a one stop WeChat ecosystem for everything parenting related.

20. *Get Your Product in WeChat Stores.* These KOL's on WeChat typically have their own stores, so the key is to get your product in their stores by going through procurement and promising to buy ads like we did for the other platforms. Then you have to negotiate a deal with procurement at a price that has you making money and still incentivizes them to push your product over a competitor (easier said than done). A key way I found that made it easier to do this was to produce content about your product. Most of these WeChat "Official Accounts" or (公众号) are followed by people who are interested in reading their content, so these platforms are in constant need of new content to share with their followers.

21. *Avoid Ad Fees and Create Fun Stories About Your Product via WeChat.* Therefore, Frank and I decided instead of paying 3–4 million RMB per month in advertising expenses, we hired a good copywriter for 14,000 RMB per month to write really useful articles relating to each one of our traffic products to help the WeChat KOLs increase sales. After a while, you can easily do several million a month with these platforms, the bad news is they usually take 30% of the sales so it is pretty low margin. However, there is a key way to overcome this. Out of each of these, WeChat KOLs that sells your products, very few of them will choose to handle the logistics piece of it, especially for perishable products. They don't want to take the inventory risk (unless it's for clothes) and delivery is too expensive. Therefore, they will send you a list of the customer names, addresses, and phone numbers at 4 pm each day so you can organize the deliveries for the next day.

22. *The WeChat Data is Invaluable.* The good news is that Alibaba's Databank allows you to upload people's phone number, Weibo username, WeChat name, or anything you can think of and cross reference

it with anyone in their database of close to a billion customers. Since everybody in China has an account on TMall, Databank can find the customer's Tmall account and help you deliver ads to them. Then in this way the smart vendors can slowly start to convert customers from WeChat to Alibaba (30% commission vs. 2.5%) so you can make more profit long-term.

23. *Avoid KOLS Who Demand Upfront Fees.* In addition to WeChat KOLs, TMall also has KOLs that can be very effective for acquiring customers. I personally have been on the top three TMall KOLs live streams multiple times and on an average day we would sell between 300 and 700k RMB worth of products just for a 3-minute slot. Like anyone, most of these KOLs will want to charge you a huge up-front fee to sell your product, guaranteeing them money regardless of sales. It's very important as with other platforms to avoid doing this. I have personally been burned by KOLs who lie about their followings and once you pay them the money is gone for good.

24. *Instead, Offer KOLs a Percentage of Sales.* The key is to confidently give them your value prop and not give in to the temptation to do a cash up front deal. Hold out until you get a KOL willing to take a percentage of your overall sales, even if it's a high percentage to make sure you don't get burned. We often gave buy one get one half off or free deals to get even more customers to buy. One time when I was invited to the #2 KOL's broadcast I even paid the chef she hired an extra 100 RMB to cook our product on low heat so it took longer and we acquired an extra 3,000 customers in the additional 2 minutes we were on air. Even though these events don't produce profits they allow you to gain 6,000–7,000 A-Ps in 5 minutes time, of which 20% will likely become Ls if you can break down the data correctly in Databank and give them a new ad in 12–15 days' time.

25. *The Key is to Get to Loyal Customers.* Loyal customers then becomes the most important factor for the xiao ers to give your store future events because repeat orders is the key metric they measure their category stores by. Each repeat order your store generates for the xiao er's category is additional GMV that TMall did not have to use either an ad or spend any money or resources to initiate. This is what they call "free traffic" or 免费流量. Once you have made it here, then it's just a matter of increasing free traffic as a percentage of your overall traffic week after week until you hit profitability. The higher percentage of free traffic you receive the more you can spend to go out and

market to new customer groups in Databank and potentially expand to new traffic product categories that may require operating at a slight loss initially to start up as your first traffic product did. Finally, Morph The Sale into a Buying Experience for your Loyal Customers. Once you get more Ls another key thing to do is create a social buying experience for them. One thing we did was collect all the phone numbers from each platform and be sure to alert them whenever we had a sale or any kind of new product announcement. In China, it's very easy to buy a text message system, which we did at first but in the end we transitioned to solely use Databank's text message function. The technology ecosystem to manage customers developed by Alibaba was so advanced eventually it didn't make sense for us to have our customers transact on any other platform besides Alibaba. At the end, Alibaba made up over 80% of our sales and continued to grow.

Part III

Will the US Militarize Technology like the Cold War Years of 1960–1990?

The corona virus crisis reinforces the need for centralized policy and federal government support for basic services among many governments globally, who have hitherto taken a "government is bad" approach. The lessons from the virus will, we think, reverberate through the system and cause us to rethink about the role of government as a source of support and proper incentives on the edges of the body politic for science, technology, healthcare, mental health initiatives, and other types of actions needed to catch up with China.

In fact, we have noticed more federal intervention in technology starting in 2019, despite this being anathema to the thinking of the current regime. Through the Congress and the Pentagon, officials in the White House have developed several initiatives to deal with the virtual absence on the global stage of any US companies in payments and/or e-commerce, for instance. It also deals with the lack of significant progress in quantum technology, AI, disease diagnosis, industrial robotics, and autonomous cars.

So, the US administration proposed $134.1 billion in federal spending for AI technology and R&D and Congress instead granted $156 bn for the year 2020. The administration asked for a further 10% increase for the year 2021. Meanwhile, China has committed more than $150 bn for its semiconductor industry and has planned to develop a completely autonomous chip capacity by 2026. We think this is really the heart of the trade war. Why is this so? This is precisely the way the US is behaving — the administration understands that control over the advanced chip software and hardware is a central key to maintaining economic hegemony. Hence, the all-out offensive to sink Huawei.

Another specific battle royale in global hegemony is in quantum technology. In the US, there will be a doubling of spending for quantum technology to $900 mn. There will be a 70% increase in the National Science Foundation alone for AI-related grants (foreigners need not apply) which will be allotted a budget of $850 mn. This will include significant research for quantum technology. This does not include the spending for quantum technology in the Pentagon. We remind readers that China is pouring $10 bn alone into a crash program in quantum technology and has already launched a quantum communication satellite in space while the US does not even have terrestrial quantum communication capabilities. Supremacy in quantum technology is vital in any area, not the least of which is its importance in code-breaking.

On the social front, the Federal Government is slowly catching on to the mental health crisis in the US, especially among millennials. It is clear that more Americans die from alcohol, drugs, and suicide every 2 weeks than all of the American deaths from the 18 years of war in the Middle East. And the millennial soldiers returning from these wars have suicide rates which are five times higher than the average population.

This is happening at a time when federal mental health services have been gutted, given ideological dislike of the centralized government which prevails in Washington DC. Initiatives that are being put forward by the Democratic candidates in the US primaries include a kind of domestic Peace Corps for students to work off student debt by receiving basic training in areas such as drug and alcohol counseling, working with the homeless or distribution of food, goods, and services to the needy. This service could last a year of 16 months. It is patently clear that philanthropy is insufficient to deal with the epidemic of mental health problems among the US population, especially among millennials (see Part 1 for abundant data to support these claims).

This section will explore the rapid developments in federal intervention in major R&D in many areas of technology, primarily in China and the US. In essence, the US will have no choice but to embark on a national "AI policy", the kind of which it frowns upon in China.

Chapter 11

Conclusion and Recommendations

We advocate a series of policy shifts that are necessary to reverse the decline: (1) an Apollo-like program to tackle the technological challenges for rolling out 5G in hundreds of cities in the US; (2) another Apollo-like project to tackle social issues in creative ways such as runaway addiction and alcoholism, student debt, high school gun violence, climate change, the use of prisons as a cure all for mental health issues, and 18 years of endless wars in the Middle East.

1. Big bloated US companies simply can't and don't want to innovate. Where there is no will, there is no way. This should change.
2. The US government is totally divided and at a virtual standstill. Public–private partnerships can't work in a toxic anti-government environment. This should change.
3. The problems faced by millennials in the US are NOT going away. Social reforms are necessary to help them become more productive. We advocate a domestic Peace Corps for drug addiction treatment where millennials can work off student debt for 18 months in return for some training in drug addiction treatment and offer assistance to millions of addicts, especially those who are incarcerated or homeless.
4. The US and China relationship is likely headed into deeper trouble after the 2020 elections. The current round of negotiations ended with a Phase I agreement which was largely what China recommended 2 years previously.

5. China is rapidly moving away from the US and rapidly creating a separate internet, financial system, etc. and will NEVER put itself at the mercy of the US again. This is unlikely to change.

6. China will move into emerging markets with a commitment to avoid politics. US intervention in local politics has been a disaster, so it needs a better narrative.

Right now millennials see the US government taking the same strategy with China as the taxi companies did with Uber. When Uber took over the transportation market and the taxi companies couldn't innovate fast enough, what did they do? Rather than innovating and coming up with a competitive service, they did whatever they could to halt Uber's progress. They used government relationships to ban Uber. They claimed "safety" as the issue with their service. They said it was unfair competition. Yet is there really anyone who has ever ridden in a taxicab that can honestly say they felt "safer" than in an Uber? Did they have a more comfortable ride? Did they get a taxi quicker than an Uber? The answer to all these questions is "No!".

Big Bloated US Companies Simply Cannot Make the Transition

Aside from a few special cases like Goldman Sachs, Apple, Amazon, and Microsoft, we see the majority of US large corporations being disrupted. The telecom sector is definitely at the top of our list in terms of a sector that needs Apollo-like assistance in order to be able to compete internationally in the world of 5G and IoT.

Over the next 10 years, new US companies without a legacy infrastructure such as Tesla and Salesforce will continue to replace many of these older companies domestically. The old guard will simply not be able to innovate fast enough. Internationally, it will be a combination of these companies from the US — in league with large Chinese multinational companies — which will replace systems that the US dominated. These include transportation, energy, and finance. If you don't believe it, take another look at Austin's story. Verizon, AT&T, and Coke are all too short-term focused and lack big visions. Let us return to some examples:

Payments

Why was China able to completely leapfrog credit cards and go to ubiquitous mobile payments? In China today, anywhere I go I can either use WeChat or Alipay for anything by scanning a QR code. Even old ladies selling corn for 1 RMB in Tibet accept Alipay. Why can't the US do the same?

I went into a CVS a few months back in Atlanta and just for fun asked if I could use my Apple Pay. The clerk proceeded to tell me they didn't accept Apple Pay, but only "CVS Pay". In Starbucks, they also have their own mobile app. How can someone be expected to download a different payment system for each store they visit?

When asked why they don't use QR codes in the US, the common response is "security" (Just like taxi companies used for Uber). But in all my years living in China I have never once heard of a QR code causing a security problem. But ask yourself, is having 10 different mobile payment apps linked to your bank account any safer? Do you trust that Starbucks and CVS are unhackable? I don't...

The big banks and credit card companies in the US can't even be creative in their excuses for lack of innovation. They needed to steal "security" excuse from the taxi companies. Is it more secure to link my bank account to 19 different mobile apps and trust Starbucks and all these other companies with my financial information or trust one company who is a fintech specialist like Tencent?

So what is the real reason the US doesn't have ubiquitous mobile payments? The big banks and credit cards have monopolies (just like Verizon, Comcast, and AT&T), and they use their government influence to halt progress because they can no longer innovate fast enough to compete. At least $3 goes to the banks for every $100 you spend with a US credit card. Why is this? Is this not easily replicable by a new fintech startup or Alibaba?

In Africa, more and more places are accepting Alipay over Visa and Mastercard. Most countries in the developing world are tired of being beholden to the US treasury being able to freeze assets, banks taking huge fees for transferring money, etc. When China's blockchain and payment system goes global, it will continue to lessen the influence the US has globally and will be replaced by China.

Chinese premier Xi Jinping recently made a big speech on block-chain and how it is of utter importance to China. On top of that, the PBOC is busy developing their own digital currency. Meanwhile, the US congress is interviewing Mark Zuckerberg trying to dismantle Libra because they don't understand it. While all this is happening, China will continue to spread their financial system across the Belt and Road countries.

Electric/Autonomous vehicles

From 2014 to 2018, China's electric car market grew much faster than electric vehicle sales in Europe, the United States, Japan, and the rest of the world combined. In 2018, Chinese sales topped 1.1 million cars, more than 55% of all electric vehicles sold in the world, while the US's sales were a little over 350,000. According to data from "Inside EVs", for the first 9 months of 2019 the traditional US automobile companies (excluding Tesla) have delivered a total of 24,528 electric vehicles in the first 9 months of 2019. This is compared to Chinese companies deliver-ing over 600,000. How is this possible? Yes, Tesla is a US company but the only reason they have survived is because Elon Musk has enough money and star power to buck the corrupt, non-innovative system. Tesla even had governors in states like Michigan blocking Tesla's from being sold in the state because they go direct to consumer (doesn't every suc-cessful company do this now?). By coming out in 2003 with a mission of only producing products that are eco-friendly didn't have the legacy infrastructure that the traditional US car companies have.

Was it a secret that electric cars were going to be important? Absolutely not. So then how could Ford and Chevrolet miss the boat this far? This all happened while the US government was debating whether or not global warming was real. While democrats and repub-licans were debating this China, with the directive of the government developed the largest electric car fleet in the world by far. In October, it was also announced that China was developing a nation-wide, charging network at the direction of the government. This all while the US is waiting on the private sector to act. How many charging sta-tions do Ford and Chevy have? How can we expect these companies to develop autonomous driving technology if they can't even build an electric car?

Pl	Global Brands	September	2019	%	P.'18
1	Tesla	49821	257082	16	1
2	BYD	13003	186195	12	2
3	BAIC	12689	107478	7	3
4	SAIC	9155	97700	6	6
5	BMW	14289	90168	6	4
6	Nissan	7209	64130	4	5
7	Geely	3873	61771	4	14
8	Volkswagen	6833	57730	4	10
9	Hyundai	9858	55927	3	8
10	Kia	3761	42651	3	19
11	Toyota	4670	41839	3	16
12	Mitsubishi	4528	40661	3	17
13	Chery	3415	37791	2	7
14	Renault	3626	35155	2	9
15	Great Wall	1877	34295	2	NE
16	JAC	407	33168	2	13
17	Changan	599	32219	2	NE
18	Volvo	4120	29285	2	20
19	GAC	4010	25116	2	NE
20	Chevrolet	2041	24528	2	12
	Others	77440	536218	33	
	TOTAL	183393	1608909	100	

5G

If you live in the US, it's hard to go 5 minutes without seeing a commercial for Verizon's 5G network. Let's ask ourselves, if this 5G network is really so great why does a $750,000 commercial need to be aired 20 times a day to tell people that? I remember being a Verizon employee and Verizon running commercials about IoT every day. There was only one problem, none of their IoT solutions worked.

It is somewhat shocking that the US does not have a single 5G major rollout yet while China rolled it out in 2019. There is plenty of finger pointing going on inside the US about this. But AT&T has been busy trying to reduce its debt load and cutting costs. It had its eye off the ball as it tried to improve a balance sheet that had a runaway debt problem. Presumably, 2020 will bring more focused solutions when it comes to 5G. But China already instituted 5G last November in 50 cities. A year head start does, indeed, make a big difference.

On the opposite side of this, we make the argument that the opposite is true in China, where big companies are innovating in a big way. Whether China Mobile and Huawei with 5G and smart city rollouts or Alibaba with e-commerce and ubiquitous fintech. There is a real desire in China to drop the old way of doing thing for the common interest in advancement of an entire society that supersedes egos and peoples existing attachments to their comfort zones.

The US Government is Totally Divided and at a Virtual Standstill

While Donald Trump is undergoing impeachment hearings and Russia probes, China is laughing all the way to the bank. China is totally unified in their strategy to dominate the world in terms of technology.

This book is in no way advocating for a one-party system, however, if you are going to have only one party, having one that is totally unified and dead set on world technological domination certainly has its advantages if your goal is being #1 in terms of technological power and GDP.

Confusion on how to regulate/support American technology companies

The authors have been working in China for over 8 years now and not once have either of them seen an article about the possibility of the government breaking up Alibaba or Tencent for reasons of a monopoly. The reason is that China likes duopolies because they are forced to compete in everything and it gives them more control of the industries. By having Tencent control everything to do with social media, it makes it incredibly easy for the government to regulate and control. Since the US cannot have the same degree of control over corporations operating within their borders, the only way to be more effective in controlling them is to break them up. While there may be a case to do this to increase competition, etc., making these companies smaller may hurt their ability to invest in quantum computing, 5G, and internet of things (IoT) as we have discussed the infrastructure requires a substantial investment.

The recent technology hearings on Capital Hill have been somewhat comical to say the least. The fact that American regulators do not understand technology has a great impact on why they have chosen a "destroy" strategy rather than "compete and innovate" strategy with China. While most American politicians are lawyers by trade, Xi Jinping studied engineering at one of China's top schools. Xi's engineering background gives him a leg up over virtually any US politician, some of which thought WhatsApp was used to send "emails" in recent congressional hearings with Facebook. Again this is not advocating any political support or criticism, the objective is just to put the information and let the readers decide.

US politicians cannot agree on anything. The system is setup so virtually no progress is made on policy on 2 out of every 4 years. Donald Trump isn't the only US president to face a divided congress. While the American system allows for generally more freedoms than the average country around the world, China's one-party system is more efficient for getting policy through.

The exact opposite is true in China. While they do have their own mostly secretive way of competing for top political positions within the party, China does not have nearly the amount of disagreement on each individual issue. One big reason for this is because Chinese politicians don't have to worry about swaying public opinion on every new policy that is enacted. They only have to convince other politicians that this is the best course of action and the policy is changed. Furthermore, there is a lot of debate in the background for a year about the course of each Five-Year Plan, but once it is agreed upon by the State Council, the CPPCC, and the Politburo, it is set in stone for all to follow for 5 years and not even Xi Jinping can change it.

To give an example: Back in July 2019, when I was living in Shanghai a new policy was implemented that called for people to separate their garbage between "wet" (food) and "dry" (everything else) garbage. Once the decision was made, it was announced about 1 week before with signs and advertisements posted all over Shanghai. Since the government controls garbage collection, they were instructed not to pick up any garbage that had not been separated.

On the day the program began, EVERY one of the 26 million people in Shanghai began separating their garbage immediately. It took some getting used to, but the transition happened incredibly fast. Can you imagine trying to implement a program like this in the US where people were forbidden by law from putting food in the same garbage container as plastic or their garbage wouldn't be picked up and they would even be subject to a fine?

I'm in no way advocating for an authoritarian-like approach to governing people. The point of this example is that when you have powerful leaders who are actually motivated to do the right thing, in this case help the environment, a lot can be accomplished very quickly. China is doing the same thing now in the shift to quantum computing, education, and 5G.

The Problems Faced by Millennials in the US are Not Going Away

American millennials are suffering from addiction brought on by broken families and gun violence and the data suggests this is worsening. After graduating college, many have big dreams that get overshadowed by seemingly insurmountable debt loads. Still some do have dreams of making a difference with their career and overcoming the debt. These optimistic millennials (like Austin) may finally get their chance and realize they have entered a workforce ruled by baby boomers focused on short-term profits.

In China, the exact opposite is happening. China does also see rising rates of addiction and mental illness but they are starting from a much lower base. A big societal difference is the family unit in China is much more intact than the US. This is also changing in China but it will take at least a full generation to really change materially.

In addition to this, with things like health care costs in the US continuing to spiral out of control and all the other various corporate scandals millennials have a fundamental mistrust for the system in general. It's almost impossible for a millennial to comprehend why they would have to pay 4x the cost of the same medicine in New York than it would be 5 minutes from the border of Canada, or why college costs 3x more than it does almost anywhere in the world. It is almost impossible for the average millennial to comprehend why people would deny climate change, block Uber from being available in their city for "safety issues", or to block Tesla because they sell directly to the consumer.

When millennials see that gun violence in schools and incarceration are more severe than any other country on earth by an order of magnitude, it causes a great deal of discouragement, and eventually will lead to action against the establishment. Is this what has allowed non-traditional candidates like Donald Trump and Bernie Sanders to do so well in recent presidential elections?

The US and China Relationship is Doomed

At the time this book was written, President Trump has just signed a bill into law regarding sovereignty in Hong Kong. Right now, there are huge protests in Chile and at least a dozen other countries. There are probably 50 other countries in the world where citizens would like to have fair voting rights. However, the one chosen by the US is Hong Kong. Why was Hong Kong chosen? These kinds of actions continue to suggest that the US would rather take a course of destabilization than competition with China. What about Kashmir? The Indian Army has occupied Kashmir and shut down the internet. India recently put forward anti-Muslim immigration legislation. What about Russia? More than 50 Journalists have been murdered by state-led actors. For this reason, China will continue to move away from the US in every area possible regardless of any trade deal that is to be made.

Earlier in Chapter 2 of this book, we explained why China is the way it is in terms of mindset and social structure. Many Americans — especially many in the executive and legislative branch — still simply refuse to try and see the world from China's eyes. Even though China has shown no signs of wanting to overthrow a foreign government or cause any outright harm to the US — or other sovereign nations — the US assumes that China thinks like Americans do. The truth is that China does not see in only black and white. Would China like to have the #1 economy in the world? Of course! Does the average Chinese citizen wish harm on the US so they can achieve that goal? To date, we have not witnessed evidence to support this. It is the opposite. Most Chinese we know have (or had) great admiration for the US. This good will is quickly fizzling.

For the same exact reason that these legacy US companies cannot change, the government is not likely to change in this area either. Both the administration and both houses of Congress feel it will be easier to destabilize China than to compete (Uber and taxi companies' example). Even as the phase 1 trade deal is reached with China, it won't much change the inevitable outcome. Too much has happened for China to ever trust the United States again.

China is Moving Away from the US Creating a Separate Internet, Financial System, etc. and Will NEVER Put Itself at the Mercy of the US Again

So in the previous point we discussed why the relationship is doomed. Now we will go into what will happen as a result of this "doom" for the relationship.

As we mentioned in Chapter 2, China has a long history of being held back or hurt by foreign powers. Whether it was the United Kingdom taking over their biggest port city and force feeding the population opium or the Japanese invasion during World War II, China along with much of Africa and South America has a hatred for foreign powers interfering and holding back progress. The difference now is that unlike South American and African countries, China now has the resources to make a stand, and that's exactly what it will do.

Unlike the US, China can sell the concept of short-term pain to the general population in order to achieve a long-term goal. That pain right now consists of tariffs from the United States and lack of access to certain products needed by companies like Huawei and ZTE. While it is definitely having an impact on Chinese exports, China is not just sitting around and waiting for it to go away. Through diversification of their economy and establishing themselves as the dominant manufacturer all across the belt and road countries, China will make themselves much less vulnerable to the US if another dispute were to inevitably erupt in the future.

In the writing of this book, the authors have interviewed several executives at the top semiconductor companies around the world who all believe China will have its own chip mass-production capabilities by 2024. In addition to this, Huawei has already produced a version one of their mobile operating system to replace android. It may take a lot of time and investment but all available information suggests these goals will be achieved.

The pundits and analysts in the West still evaluate China by traditional metrics like manufacturing output. Hence, they think China is in an incredibly weak position at the time this book is being written as manufacturing PMI has been declining slightly for the past several months. What these talking heads fail or temporarily forget to realize is that China is already well on its way to being a consumption and services-led economy. It has already moved its low value-added manufacturing to Vietnam and South Asia. The decline in manufacturing in China is yesterday's news.

Misjudging the Chinese economy is exactly what China wants. While the west thinks all is going to hell because manufacturing is decreasing slightly, China's internet, e-commerce, IoT, smart cities, high-speed trains, and fintech sectors are booming. China knows this is the future and have planned for this for many years.

Manufacturing is still an important factor for China, but even though it is decreasing, it isn't decreasing to the magnitude you would expect during an all-out trade war with the world's largest economy. Why is that? The answer is because they planned for that too. Another thing to consider is that China is really good at manufacturing. If you don't believe it, take a look at the Tesla plant in Shanghai that went from a large swamp in Pudong to producing 1,000 electric cars per week in 357 days.

While the Belt and Road initiative has been shown as a disaster in western media, on the ground in these countries, it is starting to benefit all those involved. China is creating a network of other countries to sell their products to across Africa, Asia, and South America. Soon China will not need the US. The authors have spent a significant amount of time in places like East Africa in recent years and it's obvious the USA doesn't have the same influence anymore. China lends money with no strings attached and in return they get strategic influence. Upon interviewing several top government officials and technology executives on the ground in East Africa, it seems the local people and governments adore China for five main reasons:

(i)   China has introduced cheap, good quality products to Africa that were not available previously.

(ii) China and Chinese companies offer loans, build infrastructure project, and conduct all other business with only one goal and zero ulterior motives, to make money. Africans trust the Chinese far more than the west, and so do the Latin American countries. European countries have devastated Africa for centuries. As a result of Slavery, the Berlin convention and the assassination of Muammar al-Gaddafi, the African community completely mistrusts the west.

(iii) The United States has the same situation with Latin America. China is building out their wireless networks, selling cheap affordable products to their people, buying their natural resources, and not demanding any political conditions in return. Compare that to your average World Bank loan and these are relatively easy decisions for local leaders.

(iv) China is creating a completely separate financial system with their own mobile payments and even cryptocurrency.

(v)   From the beginning, China has had a completely separate internet, this will continue.

Is China's Move into Emerging Markets, Primarily Africa, with a Commitment to Avoid Politics Smart? Yes. US Intervention in Local Politics in Latin America, Middle East, Asia or Africa Over Range of Past 50 Years Has Tended to be a Disaster and All too Often Reverts to an Imperialist Mindset

In Africa and South America everywhere you look there are Chinese people building roads, bridges, stadiums, and airports. China has somehow been able to come in and do something the US never did which was get a strong foothold in a country economically without causing political upheaval as a result.

While the World Bank grants small loans filled with conditions like women's rights and democracy, loans from state-owned banks in China come with zero conditions. In private conversations with both government officials and businesspeople in the region, the one thing that is clear is that nobody wants to talk about democracy. What people love about doing business with China is their only intention is to do business and make money. When your partner's intention are well known, they are much easier to do business with as you understand exactly what they want.

In his book *The Elusive Quest for Growth*, Bill Easterly spells out the problems of politically motivated aid. He knows of what he speaks as he was the Chief Economist for the World Bank. He makes the point through many examples that introducing political motives to aid causes perverse consequences as incentives are maligned in favor of ends that have nothing to do with welfare, economic growth, or poverty reduction. In too many cases from the 1960s to the early 1990s, World Bank aid was given to countries who shared an anti-communist view and aid was withheld from countries who cozied up to the Soviet Union. It was an "us vs them" view of distributing aid. Paul saw this with my own eyes in Indonesia as an advisor to the Minister of Finance. Whenever the World Bank would stamp its feet and swing her hips over misappropriation — or theft — of aid funds, top people in the government would bring out the communist boogeyman argument and the World Bank people would go quiet. Both sides were using each other for political ends rather than directly aiming to reduce poverty. Vast amounts of resources were wasted or ended up in Swiss bank accounts by co.

Now the Good News...The Schmidt Committee is Capitalism with Socialist Characteristics

A national commission headed by Eric Schmidt of Google made a series of recommendations to keep pace with China's massive investment in AI as well as its significant strides in public–private cooperation. After reviewing the commission's report, as well as another report by the Congressional Research Service on AI, we have done PowerPoint summaries of both reports (The URL is: http://www.schulte-research.com/east-vs-west-ai-and-national-security/). We conclude that the US intends to go down a road of "China-lite". It just might be capitalism with socialist characteristics. This is neither good nor bad. It just is. It is probably a smart thing, but it will cause a stir on the right wing of the Republican Party who believe that government will only ever make things worse — never better.

The evolution of thinking in the Trump Administration over the last 3 years seems to have shifted dramatically. The new Republican administration entered Washington with an intention to roll back government intervention in the economy with respect to banking, securities, environment, fracking, oil and gas, coastal development, offshore drilling, and so forth. So, it was a new era of "hands off" government. It was a move toward traditional Republican thinking: "The government that governs best governs least."

The problem is that, over the course of 2 years, leaders in government and industry came to the conclusion that the US economy required a wholesale upgrade in its infrastructure (indeed, its superstructure) from analog copper to high speed digital. There was a very slow recognition that the private sector by itself, for an assortment of reasons, was incapable of doing this. Getting this upgrade done requires very heavy lifting from several points of view. Put simply, it requires some organizing body to get states, universities, think tanks, military, regulators, bankers, capital markets participants, investors, and shareholders to change their mindset to see that a common goal of upgrading the US was in the national interest and required sacrifices and compromise. This is precisely the conclusion of the Schmidt report.

In essence, the Trump Administration will need to walk back much of its criticism of China which revolves around the use of direct state power and resources to manage technological progress, fund projects, inject military personnel into private companies, and/or divert federal and provincial manpower to achieve infrastructure projects which benefit publicly listed companies. We summarize the main conclusions of the Schmidt Committee. These recommendations and their detailed programs seem to bear feint resemblance to the China 230 program to become an AI leader in innovation.

Global leadership in AI technology is a national security priority

Fundamentally, the Schmidt Committee believes that while American companies play a significant role in advancing AI research and development, the government retains a core responsibility to steer advancements in ways to protect the American people and foster basic research environment.

What China is doing: This same core belief seems to drive much of the goal of China to become the world's premier AI Innovation Center by 2030. China already increased its R&D national Budget by 30× to 2.5% of GDP (or about $180 billion), far ahead of the US which is at 2% of GDP.

Adopting AI for defense and security purposes is an urgent national imperative

In light of the choices being made by strategic competitors, the United States must also examine AI through a military lens, including concepts for AI-enabled autonomous operations. In other words, what's good for the goose is good for the gander. If China can use Huawei as a national champion with shady connections to the military, the US now seems to reserve the right to do the same thing. This may include deeper connections between the Pentagon and Google, GE, Palantir, Facebook, and Apple.

What China is doing: China has been doing this with Huawei and other companies, as does the UK, Germany, Australia, and other countries.

Private sector leaders and government officials must build a shared sense of responsibility for the welfare and security of the American people

The government must strengthen industry by articulating clear standards and policies for responsible use, rebuilding trust through greater transparency, and offering a vision of a shared purpose. In other words, there seems to be a recommendation that government may need to be larger. It may need to rebuild its trust with the private sector. Governing best may include more interaction with the private sector, especially in helping to build a compelling narrative that public–private partnerships are, indeed, vital for national security, especially in the area of AI.

What China is doing: China's internal narrative is precisely built on this foundation.

People are still essential to government–university relationships

America needs to encourage that talent to come, contribute, and stay. Within government, recruiting, training, and retaining AI-talent will be essential to maximize AI's potential. This means that a major push must come from the government to offer scholarships and funding to universities to increase tenured professors, increase scholarships, pay for new departments in the area of AI to train both civilians and government officials to pump out higher numbers of AI-literate graduates which need to number in the millions.

What China is doing: China has been doing this for 15 years. Way ahead in this. It turns out 10 times more STEM graduates than the US and is ahead in facial recognition, ID confirmation, digital ledger currency, financial technology, advanced e-commerce, among others.

The power of free inquiry must be preserved

The US must protect intellectual property and sensitive technology to ensure that American technology and innovation is not exploited to advance adversaries' militaries or undertake human rights abuses. This means that, in order to receive greater government funding for

AI, universities must agree to greater scrutiny from the FBI in order to maintain funding. So, the FBI reserves the right to create dossiers on overseas Chinese students as well as first generation Chinese students. The benefits of actionable intelligence may not be outweighed by feelings of alienation among Chinese graduate students.

What China is doing: China is seeing a reverse diaspora of mainland Chinese who are returning to universities in China for research and development in the area of AI and other cutting edge technologies. As the US lifts the drawbridge on cooperation, China is doing the same thing. It is imposing state-sanctioned agendas on universities and, in line with Cold War tactics of the 1960s–1980s, deciding what is productive debate, worthwhile R&D and viable spending to further the agenda of the Five-Year Plan. This essentially involves China having near autonomy in most technology so it is not at the mercy of foreign powers which can turn off the technology tap at any time.

Ethics and strategic necessity are compatible with one another

The US sees an ethical imperative to accelerate the fielding of safe, reliable, and secure AI systems that can be demonstrated to protect the American people, minimize operational dangers to US service members, and make warfare more discriminating, which could reduce civilian casualties.

Everyone desires safe, robust, and reliable AI systems free of unwanted bias, and recognizes today's technical limitations.

What China is doing: Both China and the US are deep in preparation for future AI warfare which can inject zero hour bots in any system to shut it down: power, water, oil pipelines, airport control towers, train systems, etc. This can cripple critical infrastructure without dropping one bomb. The zero hour bot war is already here. Russia, the US, and China are leaders in this technology.

The American way of AI must reflect American values

The US military must find ways for AI to enhance its ability to uphold the laws of war and ensure that current frameworks adequately cover AI.

What China is doing: Few countries are talking about this vital element of AI. AI is a new weapon akin to nuclear power. It needs something like the IAEA or the Geneva Convention to regulate its vast and intrusive power. AI can sway elections, cut off power supplies to vast populations, destroy fresh food supply in 48 hours, alter bank records, change stock prices, cause an entire fleet of civilian aircraft to become blind from 1 minute to the next. AI has the power to do vastly more damage to civilian populations than any atomic bomb.

Congressional Research Service Report on AI: Weaponizing Artificial Intelligence

The very recent CRS report (December 2019) on AI and IoT is perhaps a bit more provocative in that it takes a more hawkish view on AI and suggests that public–private projects need to be accelerated as soon as possible in order to incorporate AI in all fields of military endeavor. Again, this goes to the heart of the objection to Huawei's military connections. So, it puts the US in an uncomfortable position of being hypocritical toward China. The following seven recommendations will go a long way to advancing AI, and the biggest beneficiary will be the military–industrial complex. (Our full summary of the CRS report can be found at http://www.schulte-research.com/east-vs-west-ai-and-national-security/).

Again, it has taken a long time, but the penny is finally dropping for the US. Coordinated efforts with the private sector, universities, states, federal government, and the military are vital to create a new infrastructure for digital services and AI. This is smart. It has socialist characteristics. It is the only way to go. It will happen. It's how the US government operated during the Cold War of the 1960s–1980s. If this new Cold War is that much more technologically dependent, we should assume this will happen in a more intense way. Unfortunately, the trade war that the US started with China — and which has caused so many poisoned relationships among and between the G7 — is precisely based on forcing China to abandon the things which the US will now do. This pours hypocrisy on top of what many see as bullying.

Intelligence, surveillance, and reconnaissance

In coordination with Google, Project Maven team is incorporating computer vision and machine learning algorithms into intelligence collection cells that would comb through footage from drones and automatically identify hostile activity for targeting. In addition, IARPA (The Intelligence Advanced Research Projects Activity) is sponsoring several AI research projects — developing algorithms for multilingual speech recognition and translation in noisy environments, geo-locating images without the associated metadata, fusing 2D images to create 3D models, and building tools to infer a building's function based on pattern-of-life analysis.

What China is doing: The government has been working closely with Huawei, the military and private companies in the same manner.

Logistics

Use in Aircrafts — Instead of making repairs when an aircraft breaks or in accordance with standardized fleet-wide maintenance schedules, the Air Force is testing an AI-enabled approach that tailors maintenance schedules to the needs of individual aircraft even as a means of midair repair. In addition, the Army's Logistics Support Activity will analyze shipping flows for repair parts distribution, attempting to determine the most time- and cost-efficient means to deliver supplies.

What China is doing: Same.

Cyberspace operations

Conventional cybersecurity tools look for historical matches to known malicious code, so hackers only have to modify small portions of that code to circumvent the defense. AI-enabled tools, on the other hand, can be trained to detect anomalies in broader patterns of network activity, thus presenting a more comprehensive and dynamic barrier to attack.

What China is doing: Same.

Information operations and "deep fakes"

Deep fake technology could be used against the United States and US allies to generate false news reports, influence public discourse, erode public trust, and attempt to blackmail diplomats. The Media Forensics

(MediFor) project, which seeks to "automatically detect manipulations, provide detailed information about how these manipulations were performed, and reason about the overall integrity of visual media". The Media Forensics Project brings together world class researchers to level the playing field to attack the manipulator. It will attempt to detect media manipulation and find out how, where, and who did it. Presumably, Russia will be the target of this technology. It has been extraordinarily successful in interfering in elections in many countries through false information and manipulation.

What China is doing: China is ahead in facial recognition technology.

Command and control

Multi-Domain Command and Control (MDC2) aims to centralize planning and execution of air, space, cyberspace, sea, and land-based operations. This is aimed at allowing any sensor to provide data to any shooter from any service, ally, or partner…to achieve effects against any target. It is the most advanced application of IoT to AI that the world knows.

What China is doing: Same.

Semi-autonomous and autonomous vehicles

AI may enable the "loyal wingman" to accomplish tasks for its inhabited flight lead, such as jamming electronic threats or carrying extra weapons.

What China is doing: China is currently ahead in autonomous vehicles.

Lethal autonomous weapon systems (LAWS)

A special class of weapon systems that use sensor suites and computer algorithms to independently identify a target and employ an onboard weapon system to engage and destroy the target without manual human control of the system.

What China is doing: Same.

In the greater scheme of things, we very clearly see sides being taken and lines being drawn. A great silicon curtain is descending from Vladivostok in the north to Singapore in the South. There is a degree to which AI is being weaponized by both sides.

Closing Thoughts: Declining Trust in America as China Tries to Earn New Trust

Governments in Beijing and Washington are corralling universities to do their bidding. Money for R&D will be very national in nature. Only Americans will get US Government money. Chinese need not apply — that goes for visa holders or perhaps even first generation. Only Chinese will get Chinese money. Americans need not apply.

The private sector in both countries is under a new set of instructions to see the common welfare in terms of national security. Jack Ma got caught in the pincers between shareholders of Alibaba and the State Council. In a similar vein, both the CSR and Schmidt Report are very clear that the narrative must change and that the private sector must bow to new national security initiatives. So, people like Mark Zuckerberg, Eric Schmidt, Tim Cook, and Peter Thiel will all need to accommodate a new understanding of the common welfare which includes maintaining global supremacy. At the very least, they will need to become part-time state actors and accommodate national policy to take on China. This means forging much closer cooperation with the Pentagon whether they like it or not.

Investors everywhere — in both public and private equity — will need to focus on government policy more now than at any time in the past 20 years. They will need access to experts in national policy. They will need to speak to people familiar with the evolution of the Cold War during 1959–1989. They will need to speak to lobbyists to see which major listed companies are likely or not to receive major contracts for government-led technology initiatives to challenge Russia or China. They will need to have a Cold War mentality, since both countries will slowly — and unfortunately — develop loyalty tests. The discomforting reality is that investors will need to pick sides. This is the new reality as millennials grab the baton from a fractionalized society and an America in search of itself. This America will employ tools from a generational go to try to maintain strategic alliances, adapt leading technologies, consolidate geographical reach, extend military presence in a world which no longer sees the US as the "Shining city on the hill".

Chinese millennials are going from strength to strength with great confidence to a precarious new chapter where its once closest ally — a frightened and insular US — now wishes ill on its society and economy. They, too, need to forge new alliances along the Silk Road with countries who see Chinese funded infrastructure programs as a means for China to turn un-financeable loans into physical assets like ports or plantations. They must convince their neighbors in SE Asia that the heavy naval presence in the South China Sea will result in a fair and just security umbrella, and they need to convince countries from Myanmar to Turkey along the Silk Road that their intentions are to spread wealth and not create an imperial presence.

Our closing thought is simple: may the best man win.

Bibliography

Analytics, FP. "5G Explained — The Competitive Landscape." *Foreign Policy*. Accessed on February 24, 2020. https://foreignpolicy.com/2020/02/24/5g-cellular-huawei-china-networks-supply-chain-competitive-landscape-power-map/.

Archibald, R. "Tuition Fees, Higher Education." *Encyclopedia of International Higher Education Systems and Institutions*, 2018, 1–6.

Axelrod, T. "House Democrats Call for Facebook to Halt Cryptocurrency Project." *TheHill*. Accessed on July 3, 2019. https://thehill.com/homenews/house/451459-house-democrats-call-for-facebook-to-halt-cryptocurrency-project.

Barkin, S. L., W. J. Heerman, M. D. Warren, and C. Rennhoff. "Millennials and the World of Work: The Impact of Obesity on Health and Productivity." *Journal of Business and Psychology* 25, no. 2 (July 2010): 239–45.

"Beijing's Grip on Internet Finance Is Tightening." Peterson Institute for International Economics. Accessed on August 31, 2018. https://www. piie. com/blogs/china-economic-watch/beijings-grip-internet-finance-tightening.

Bullard, N. "China Is Winning the Race to Dominate Electric Cars." *Bloomberg*. Accessed on September 20, 2019. https://www.bloomberg.com/opinion/articles/2019-09-20/electric-vehicle-market-so-far-belongs-to-china.

"China: A Digital Payments Revolution." CGAP. Accessed on September 2019. https://www.cgap.org/research/publication/china-digital-payments-revolution.

Cochrane, E., E. Wong, and K. Bradsher. "Trump Signs Hong Kong Democracy Legislation, Angering China." *The New York Times*. Accessed on November 27, 2019. https://www.nytimes.com/2019/11/27/us/politics/trump-hong-kong.html.

"Comparing United States and China by Economy." *Statistics Times*. Accessed on March 31, 2020. http://statisticstimes.com/economy/united-states-vs-china-economy.php.

"Deaths from Drug Overdoses." *OECD Economic Surveys: United States OECD Economic Surveys: United States 2018*, 2018.

Deitz, R. and J. R. Abel. "Despite Rising Costs, College Is Still a Good Investment." Liberty Street Economics. Federal Reserve Bank of New York. Accessed on June 5, 2019. https://libertystreeteconomics.newyorkfed.org/2019/06/despite-rising-costs-college-is-still-a-good-investment.html.

Easterly, W. *The Elusive Quest for Growth: Economists Adventures and Misadventures in the Tropics*. Cambridge, MA: MIT Press, 2001.

Eichenwald, K. "The Deafness Before the Storm." *The New York Times*. Accessed on September 11, 2012. https://www.nytimes.com/2012/09/11/opinion/the-bush-white-house-was-deaf-to-9-11-warnings.html.

Eisen, B. "Workers Are Fleeing Big Cities for Smaller Ones-and Taking Their Jobs With Them." *The Wall Street Journal*, Accessed on September 7, 2019. https://www.wsj.com/articles/workers-are-fleeing-big-cities-for-small-ones-and-taking-their-jobs-with-them-11567848600.

Feng, E. "American Graduates Of China's Yenching Academy Are Being Questioned by The FBI." NPR. Accessed on August 2, 2019. https://www.npr.org/2019/08/01/746355146/american-graduates-of-chinas-yenching-academy-are-being-questioned-by-the-fbi.

Fischer, D. *History of the International Atomic Energy Agency: The First Forty Years*. Vienna: IAEA, 1997.

Fortune Editors. "How Smart Cities and Homes Will Take China Into the Future." *Fortune*. Accessed November 8, 2019. https://fortune.com/2019/11/07/china-smart-cities/.

Gaines, P. "California's First Surgeon General: Screen Every Student for Childhood Trauma." *NBCNews*. Accessed on October 17, 2019. https://www.nbcnews.com/news/nbcblk/california-s-first-surgeon-general-screen-every-student-childhood-trauma-n1064286.

"GDP (Current US$) — European Union, United States, China." World Bank Data. Accessed on March 31, 2020. https://data.worldbank.org/indicator/NY.GDP.MKTP.CD?locations=EU-US-CN.

Goodnough, A. "A New Drug Scourge: Deaths Involving Meth Are Rising Fast." *The New York Times*. Accessed on December 17, 2019. https://www.nytimes.com/2019/12/17/health/meth-deaths-opioids.html.

Gordon, K. "Topic: Huawei." www.statista.com, Accessed on July 15, 2019. https://www.statista.com/topics/2305/huawei/.

Harvey, A. "I'm a Founder with OCD, Here's Why I Don't Hide It from My Employees." *Fast Company*. Accessed on March 11, 2019. https://www.fastcompany.com/90290428/founder-shares-importance-of-opening-up-about-mental-health.

Johnson, K. and E. Groll. "The Improbable Rise of Huawei." Foreign Policy. Accessed on April 3, 2019. https://foreignpolicy.com/2019/04/03/the-improbable-rise-of-huawei-5g-global-network-china/.

Kharpal, A. "With Xi's Backing, China Looks to Become a World Leader in Blockchain as US Policy Is Absent." *CNBC*. Accessed on December 16, 2019. https://www.cnbc.com/2019/12/16/china-looks-to-become-blockchain-world-leader-with-xi-jinping-backing.html.

Kounang, N. "What You Need to Know about Fentanyl." *CNN*. Accessed on November 5, 2018. https://www.cnn.com/2016/05/10/health/fentanyl-opioid-explainer/index.html.

"Latest Employment Numbers." U.S. Department of Labor, n.d. https://www.dol.gov/agencies/vets/latest-numbers.

Lipsman, A. "Ecommerce Sales - Reports, Statistics & Marketing Trends." eMarketer. Accessed on March 10, 2020. https://www.emarketer.com/topics/topic/ecommerce-sales.

Luo, S. and A. Murphy. "Understanding the Exposure at Default Risk of Commercial Real Estate Construction and Land Development Loans." *Federal Reserve Bank of Dallas, Working Papers* 2020, no. 2007 (2020).

MacLellan, L. "Millennials Experience Work-Disrupting Anxiety at Twice the US Average Rate." *Quartz* at Work. Accessed on December 5, 2018. https://qz.com/work/1483697/millennials-experience-work-disrupting-anxiety-at-twice-the-us-average-rate/.

Maizland, L. "Huawei: China's Controversial Tech Giant." Council on Foreign Relations, n.d. https://www.cfr.org/backgrounder/huawei-chinas-controversial-tech-giant.

Marte, S. "A Talent Pool That Many Companies Neglect: Employees with Disabilities." Center for Talent Innovation, n.d.

Minter, A. "China's War on Trash Is the World's, Too." *Bloomberg*. Accessed on June 29, 2019. https://www.bloomberg.com/opinion/articles/2019-06-30/china-s-new-recycling-campaign-is-critical-to-saving-environment.

Moody, J. "A Guide to the Changing Number of U.S. Universities." *U.S. News & World Report*. Accessed on February 15, 2019. https://www.usnews.com/education/best-colleges/articles/2019-02-15/how-many-universities-are-in-the-us-and-why-that-number-is-changing.

Na, C. "Over One Tenth of Chinese People Have Mental Health Problems: Report." Chinese Academy of Sciences. Accessed on February 26, 2019. http://english.cas.cn/newsroom/news/201902/t20190226_205676.shtml.

"National Veteran Suicide Prevention Annual Report," n.d.

Patel, V., S. Saxena, C. Lund, G. Thornicroft, F. Baingana, P. Bolton, D. Chisholm, *et al.* "The Lancet Commission on Global Mental Health and Sustainable Development." *Lancet* (London, England). U.S. National Library of Medicine. Accessed on October 27, 2018. https://www.ncbi.nlm.nih.gov/pubmed/30314863.

"Products - Data Briefs - Number 294 - December 2017." Centers for Disease Control and Prevention. Accessed on December 21, 2017. https://www.cdc.gov/nchs/products/databriefs/db294.htm.

Rainie, L. and A. Perrin. "Key Findings about Americans' Declining Trust in Government and Each Other." Pew Research Center. Accessed on July 22, 2019.https://www.pewresearch.org/fact-tank/2019/07/22/key-findings-about-americans-declining-trust-in-government-and-each-other/.

Richter, W. "US National Debt Spiked $363 Billion in Two Weeks, $1 Trillion in 12 Months. But Who Bought This Pile of Treasury Securities?" *Wolf Street*. Accessed on August 26, 2019. https://wolfstreet.com/2019/08/17/us-gross-national-debt-spiked-363-billion-in-two-weeks-1-trillion-in-12-months-who-bought-these-treasury-securities/.

Ritchie, H. and M. Roser. "Drug Use." Our World in Data. Accessed on December 5, 2019. https://ourworldindata.org/drug-use.

Schulte, P. "East vs West: AI and National Security." Schulte Research. Accessed on January 4, 2020. http://www.schulte-research.com/east-vs-west-ai-and-national-security/.

Schulte, P. and D. Lee. *AI & Quantum Computing for Finance & Insurance: Fortunes and Challenges for China and America*. Singapore: World Scientific Publishing Co. Pte. Ltd., 2019.

Segal, A. "Keeping Our Edge: Overview of the Innovation and National Security Task Force Report." Council on Foreign Relations. Accessed on September 18, 2019. https://www.cfr.org/blog/keeping-our-edge-overview-innovation-and-national-security-task-force-report.

Solly, M. "U.S. Life Expectancy Drops for Third Year in a Row, Reflecting Rising Drug Overdoses, Suicides." Smithsonian.com. Smithsonian Institution. Accessed on December 3, 2018. https://www.smithsonianmag.com/smart-news/us-life-expectancy-drops-third-year-row-reflecting-rising-drug-overdose-suicide-rates-180970942/.

"Students - Secondary Graduation Rate - OECD Data." The OECD, 2019. https://data.oecd.org/students/secondary-graduation-rate.htm.

Su, J. "Huawei Fortifies #2 Spot In Global Smartphone Market, Beating Apple Again." *Forbes*. Accessed on November 3, 2018. https://www.forbes.com/sites/jeanbaptiste/2018/11/02/huawei-fortifies-2-spot-in-global-smartphone-market-beating-apple-again/#8bc482613055.

"Suicide Rate By Country 2020." World Population Review, n.d. https://worldpopulationreview.com/countries/suicide-rate-by-country/.

"Suicide Statistics." AFSP. Accessed on April 16, 2019. https://afsp.org/about-suicide/suicide-statistics/.

Téral, S. "Global Mobile Infrastructure Market." IEEE Communications Society. Accessed on April 3, 2019. https://techblog.comsoc.org/category/global-mobile-infrastructure-market/.

"The Belt and Road Initiative in the Global Trade, Investment and Finance Landscape." *OECD Business and Finance Outlook OECD Business and Finance Outlook 2018*, March 2018, 61–101.

The President's Daily Brief. Accessed on March 31, 2020. https://nsarchive2.gwu.edu//NSAEBB/NSAEBB116/index.htm.

"The Ultimate Cost of Our Endless Wars." The American Scholar. Accessed on March 4, 2019. https://theamericanscholar.org/the-ultimate-cost-of-our-endless-wars/#.XoO4UNNKgfM.

"Tuition Fees for Master's Degrees in the USA - Average Costs for Popular Subjects." *MastersPortal*. Accessed on December 18, 2019. https://www.mastersportal.com/articles/1762/tuition-fees-for-masters-degrees-in-the-usa-average-costs-for-popular-subjects.html.

"Two Million Commercially Insured Americans Diagnosed with Major Depression Are Not Seeking Any Treatment." Blue Cross Blue Shield. Accessed on March 31, 2020. https://www.bcbs.com/the-health-of-america/articles/two-million-commercially-insured-americans-diagnosed-major-depression-not-seeking-treatment.

"Two Million Commercially Insured Americans Diagnosed with Major Depression Are Not Seeking Any Treatment." Blue Cross Blue Shield. Accessed on March 4, 2019. https://www.bcbs.com/the-health-of-america/articles/two-million-commercially-insured-americans-diagnosed-major-depression-not-seeking-treatment.

"Two Months Before 9/11, an Urgent Warning to Rice." *The Washington Post*. WP Company, Accessed on October 1, 2006. https://www.washingtonpost.com/wp-dyn/content/article/2006/09/30/AR2006093000282.html.

"VA.gov: Veterans Affairs." How Common is PTSD in Veterans? Accessed on July 24, 2018. https://www.ptsd.va.gov/understand/common/common_veterans.asp.

"200,000 Veterans Come Home Every Year." JPMorgan Chase & Co., 2019. https://www.jpmorganchase.com/corporate/news/stories/gen-odierno.htm.

Wagner, P. and B. Rabuy. "Following the Money of Mass Incarceration." Prison Policy Initiative. Accessed on January 25, 2017. https://www.prisonpolicy.org/reports/money.html.

"What Should We Understand about Urbanization in China?" Yale Insights. Accessed on February 14, 2020. https://insights.som.yale.edu/insights/what-should-we-understand-about-urbanization-in-china.

Yan, W., Li, Y., and Sui, N. "The Relationship between Recent Stressful Life Events, Personality Traits, Perceived Family Functioning and Internet Addiction among College Students." *Stress and Health*, 30, no. 1 (2013): 3–11.

Yuanyuan, L. "China Strives to Speed Up Development of EV Charging Stations." Renewable Energy World. Accessed on September 9, 2019. https://

www.renewableenergyworld.com/2018/06/01/china-strives-to-speed-up-development-of-ev-charging-stations/#gref.

Zegers, K. "By the Numbers: School Shootings Since Columbine." *NECN*. Accessed on April 19, 2019. https://www.necn.com/news/national-international/school-shootings-since-columbine/1908046/.

Index